MW01129616

ROCKS & MINERALS

Identification Book

- Companion Field Guide -

Hello Nature

Your Feedback is Appreciated!!!

Please consider leaving us "5 Stars" on your
Amazon review.

Thank you!

Copyright © 2022 Hello Nature

All rights reserved.

This book or any portion thereof may not be reproduced or used in any manner
whatsoever without the express written permission of the publisher except by
reviewers, who may use brief quotations in a book review.

This Rock Identification Book
Belongs To:

_____

General

Date: _____ GPS Location: _____

Location: ○ Public Land ○ Private Land ○ Pay-to-Dig Site ○ Quarry
○ Roadcut ○ Outcrop ○ Riverbed ○ Creek Bed ○ Beach
○ Mine Tailing ○ Fresh Overturned Soil ○ Other_____

Weather: ○ Sunny & Clear ○ Cloudy/Overcast ○ Windy ○ Rainy / Drizzle
○ Snow ○ Stormy ○ Fog ○ Drought ○ Other_____

Rock Type: ○ Igneous ○ Sedimentary ○ Metamorphic

Equipment Checklist:
(Rockhounding)
○ Eye Protection ○ Heavy-Duty Gloves ○ Boots / Waterproof
○ First-Aid Kit ○ Hard Hat ○ Rock Hammer / Pick ○ Sieve
○ Colander ○ Small Picks ○ Trowel ○ Small Knife ○ Chisel
○ Small Broom ○ Crack Hammer ○ Pry Bar ○ Sledgehammer
○ Mason's Hammer ○ Shovel ○ Backpack ○ Bucket ○ Map
○ Wrapping Material ○ Small Tubes ○ Boxes / Containers
○ Loupe ○ Magnifying Glass ○ Magnet ○ Compass / GPS

Notes: _____

Mineral Identification

Color: ○ Light ○ Dark Specific Colors: _____

Luster: ○ Metallic ○ Gold ○ Brass
○ Bronze ○ Iron
○ Steel ○ Lead
○ Silver ○ Alum.
○ Non-Metallic ○ Adamantine ○ Vitreous
○ Resinous ○ Pearly ○ Dull
○ Greasy ○ Earthy ○ Silky

Cleavage: ○ 1 Direction ○ 2 Directions at 90° ○ 2 Directions not at 90°
○ 3 Directions at 90° (cubic) ○ 3 Directions not at 90° (rhombohedral)
○ 4 Directions (octahedral) ○ 6 Directions (dodecahedral)

Fracture: ○ Conchoidal (smooth, shell-like, or glass-like breaks) ○ Uneven (irregular, but not conchoidal) ○ Hackly (jagged, as of a metal)
○ Splintery (occurs in aggregates of many slender, brittle crystals) ○ Fibrous (occurs in aggregates of many slender, threadlike crystals)

Crystal Habit: ○ Prismatic ○ Acicular ○ Striated ○ Botryoidal ○ Dendritic
○ Nodular ○ Banded ○ Other_____

Hardness: (Mohs Scale)
○ 1 Talc ○ 2 Gypsum ○ 2.5 Fingernail ○ 3 Calcite ○ 4 Fluorite
○ 5 Apatite ○ 5.5 Glass ○ 6 Feldspar ○ 6.5 Steel File
○ 7 Quartz ○ 8 Topaz ○ 9 Corundrum ○ 10 Diamond

Specific Gravity:
○ Average (like quartz = 2.6 - 2.8)
○ Heavy (like galeno = 7.5)
○ Light (lighter than quartz = <2.6)

$$\frac{\text{mass of mineral}}{\text{mass of same volume of water}} = \frac{\text{weight of mineral in air}}{\text{weight of equal volume of water}}$$

Tenacity: ○ Brittle ○ Ductile ○ Elastic ○ Flexible ○ Friable
○ Malleable ○ Sectile

Diaphaneity: ○ Transparent ○ Translucent ○ Opaque

Notes: _____

Notes

_____
_____
_____
_____
_____
_____
_____
_____
_____

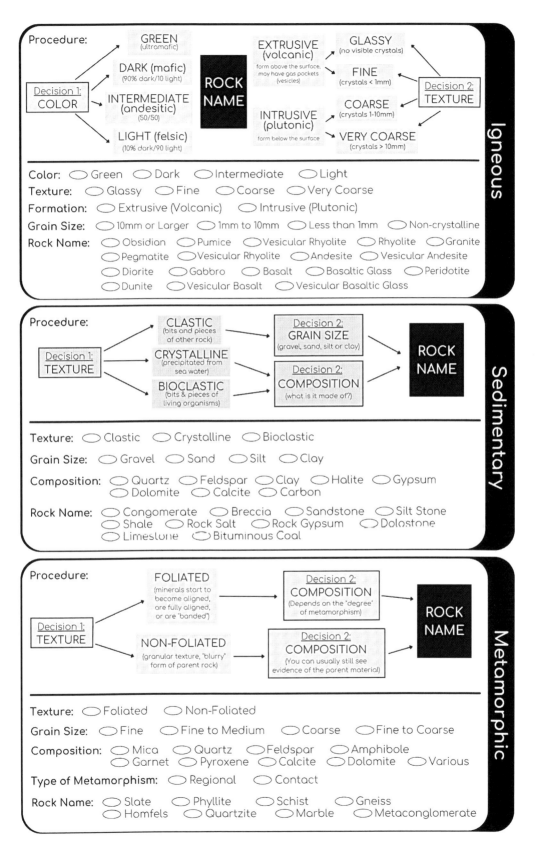

General

Date: _____   GPS Location: _____

Location: ○ Public Land   ○ Private Land   ○ Pay-to-Dig Site   ○ Quarry
○ Roadcut   ○ Outcrop   ○ Riverbed   ○ Creek Bed   ○ Beach
○ Mine Tailing   ○ Fresh Overturned Soil   ○ Other_____

Weather: ○ Sunny & Clear   ○ Cloudy/Overcast   ○ Windy   ○ Rainy / Drizzle
○ Snow   ○ Stormy   ○ Fog   ○ Drought   ○ Other_____

Rock Type: ○ Igneous   ○ Sedimentary   ○ Metamorphic

Equipment Checklist:
(Rockhounding)
○ Eye Protection   ○ Heavy-Duty Gloves   ○ Boots / Waterproof
○ First-Aid Kit   ○ Hard Hat   ○ Rock Hammer / Pick   ○ Sieve
○ Colander   ○ Small Picks   ○ Trowel   ○ Small Knife   ○ Chisel
○ Small Broom   ○ Crack Hammer   ○ Pry Bar   ○ Sledgehammer
○ Mason's Hammer   ○ Shovel   ○ Backpack   ○ Bucket   ○ Map
○ Wrapping Material   ○ Small Tubes   ○ Boxes / Containers
○ Loupe   ○ Magnifying Glass   ○ Magnet   ○ Compass / GPS

Notes: _____

Mineral Identification

Color: ○ Light   ○ Dark   Specific Colors: _____

Luster: ○ Metallic   ○ Gold   ○ Brass   ○ Non-Metallic   ○ Adamantine   ○ Vitreous
○ Bronze   ○ Iron   ○ Resinous   ○ Pearly   ○ Dull
○ Steel   ○ Lead   ○ Greasy   ○ Earthy   ○ Silky
○ Silver   ○ Alum.

Cleavage: ○ 1 Direction   ○ 2 Directions at 90°   ○ 2 Directions not at 90°
○ 3 Directions at 90° (cubic)   ○ 3 Directions not at 90° (rhombohedral)
○ 4 Directions (octahedral)   ○ 6 Directions (dodecahedral)

Fracture: ○ Conchoidal (smooth, shell-like, or glass-like breaks)   ○ Uneven (irregular, but not conchoidal)   ○ Hackly (jagged, as of a metal)
○ Splintery (occurs in aggregates of many slender, brittle crystals)   ○ Fibrous (occurs in aggregates of many slender, threadlike crystals)

Crystal Habit: ○ Prismatic   ○ Acicular   ○ Striated   ○ Botryoidal   ○ Dendritic
○ Nodular   ○ Banded   ○ Other_____

Hardness: (Mohs Scale)
○ 1 Talc   ○ 2 Gypsum   ○ 2.5 Fingernail   ○ 3 Calcite   ○ 4 Fluorite
○ 5 Apatite   ○ 5.5 Glass   ○ 6 Feldspar   ○ 6.5 Steel File
○ 7 Quartz   ○ 8 Topaz   ○ 9 Corundrum   ○ 10 Diamond

Specific Gravity:
○ Average (like quartz = 2.6 - 2.8)
○ Heavy (like galena = 7.5)
○ Light (lighter than quartz = <2.6)

$$\frac{\text{mass of mineral}}{\text{mass of same volume of water}} = \frac{\text{weight of mineral in air}}{\text{weight of equal volume of water}}$$

Tenacity: ○ Brittle   ○ Ductile   ○ Elastic   ○ Flexible   ○ Friable
○ Malleable   ○ Sectile

Diaphaneity: ○ Transparent   ○ Translucent   ○ Opaque

Notes: _____

Notes

_____
_____
_____
_____
_____
_____
_____
_____
_____

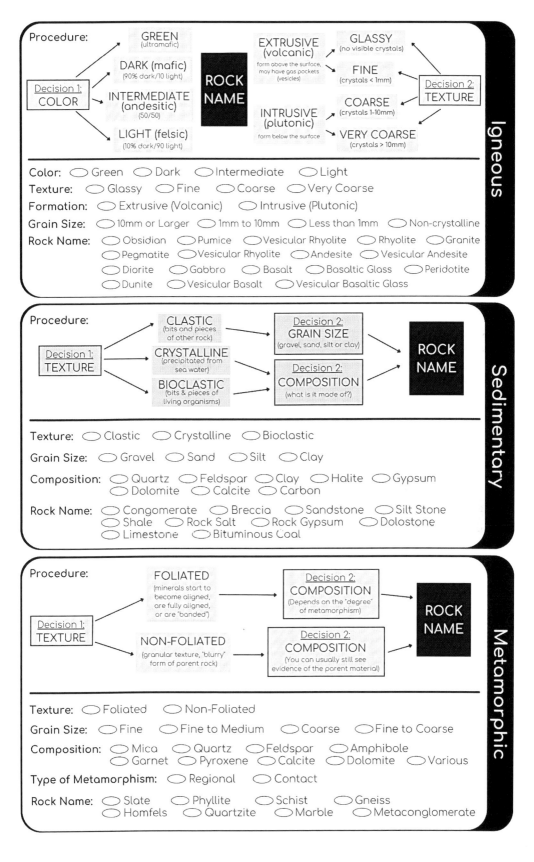

Igneous

Procedure:

Decision 1: COLOR
- GREEN (ultramafic)
- DARK (mafic) (90% dark/10 light)
- INTERMEDIATE (andesitic) (50/50)
- LIGHT (felsic) (10% dark/90 light)

ROCK NAME

- EXTRUSIVE (volcanic) — form above the surface, may have gas pockets (vesicles)
- INTRUSIVE (plutonic) — form below the surface

Decision 2: TEXTURE
- GLASSY (no visible crystals)
- FINE (crystals < 1mm)
- COARSE (crystals 1-10mm)
- VERY COARSE (crystals > 10mm)

Color: ◯ Green ◯ Dark ◯ Intermediate ◯ Light
Texture: ◯ Glassy ◯ Fine ◯ Coarse ◯ Very Coarse
Formation: ◯ Extrusive (Volcanic) ◯ Intrusive (Plutonic)
Grain Size: ◯ 10mm or Larger ◯ 1mm to 10mm ◯ Less than 1mm ◯ Non-crystalline
Rock Name: ◯ Obsidian ◯ Pumice ◯ Vesicular Rhyolite ◯ Rhyolite ◯ Granite ◯ Pegmatite ◯ Vesicular Rhyolite ◯ Andesite ◯ Vesicular Andesite ◯ Diorite ◯ Gabbro ◯ Basalt ◯ Basaltic Glass ◯ Peridotite ◯ Dunite ◯ Vesicular Basalt ◯ Vesicular Basaltic Glass

Sedimentary

Procedure:

Decision 1: TEXTURE
- CLASTIC (bits and pieces of other rock)
- CRYSTALLINE (precipitated from sea water)
- BIOCLASTIC (bits & pieces of living organisms)

Decision 2: GRAIN SIZE (gravel, sand, silt or clay)
Decision 2: COMPOSITION (what is it made of?)

ROCK NAME

Texture: ◯ Clastic ◯ Crystalline ◯ Bioclastic
Grain Size: ◯ Gravel ◯ Sand ◯ Silt ◯ Clay
Composition: ◯ Quartz ◯ Feldspar ◯ Clay ◯ Halite ◯ Gypsum ◯ Dolomite ◯ Calcite ◯ Carbon
Rock Name: ◯ Congomerate ◯ Breccia ◯ Sandstone ◯ Silt Stone ◯ Shale ◯ Rock Salt ◯ Rock Gypsum ◯ Dolostone ◯ Limestone ◯ Bituminous Coal

Metamorphic

Procedure:

Decision 1: TEXTURE
- FOLIATED (minerals start to become aligned, are fully aligned, or are "banded")
- NON-FOLIATED (granular texture, "blurry" form of parent rock)

Decision 2: COMPOSITION (Depends on the "degree" of metamorphism)
Decision 2: COMPOSITION (You can usually still see evidence of the parent material)

ROCK NAME

Texture: ◯ Foliated ◯ Non-Foliated
Grain Size: ◯ Fine ◯ Fine to Medium ◯ Coarse ◯ Fine to Coarse
Composition: ◯ Mica ◯ Quartz ◯ Feldspar ◯ Amphibole ◯ Garnet ◯ Pyroxene ◯ Calcite ◯ Dolomite ◯ Various
Type of Metamorphism: ◯ Regional ◯ Contact
Rock Name: ◯ Slate ◯ Phyllite ◯ Schist ◯ Gneiss ◯ Homfels ◯ Quartzite ◯ Marble ◯ Metaconglomerate

General

Date: _____ GPS Location: _____

Location: ◯ Public Land ◯ Private Land ◯ Pay-to-Dig Site ◯ Quarry
◯ Roadcut ◯ Outcrop ◯ Riverbed ◯ Creek Bed ◯ Beach
◯ Mine Tailing ◯ Fresh Overturned Soil ◯ Other_____

Weather: ◯ Sunny & Clear ◯ Cloudy/Overcast ◯ Windy ◯ Rainy / Drizzle
◯ Snow ◯ Stormy ◯ Fog ◯ Drought ◯ Other_____

Rock Type: ◯ Igneous ◯ Sedimentary ◯ Metamorphic

Equipment
Checklist:
(Rockhounding)
◯ Eye Protection ◯ Heavy-Duty Gloves ◯ Boots / Waterproof
◯ First-Aid Kit ◯ Hard Hat ◯ Rock Hammer / Pick ◯ Sieve
◯ Colander ◯ Small Picks ◯ Trowel ◯ Small Knife ◯ Chisel
◯ Small Broom ◯ Crack Hammer ◯ Pry Bar ◯ Sledgehammer
◯ Mason's Hammer ◯ Shovel ◯ Backpack ◯ Bucket ◯ Map
◯ Wrapping Material ◯ Small Tubes ◯ Boxes / Containers
◯ Loupe ◯ Magnifying Glass ◯ Magnet ◯ Compass / GPS

Notes: _____

Mineral Identification

Color: ◯ Light ◯ Dark Specific Colors: _____

Luster: ◯ Metallic ◯ Gold ◯ Brass ◯ Non-Metallic ◯ Adamantine ◯ Vitreous
◯ Bronze ◯ Iron ◯ Resinous ◯ Pearly ◯ Dull
◯ Steel ◯ Lead ◯ Greasy ◯ Earthy ◯ Silky
◯ Silver ◯ Alum.

Cleavage: ◯ 1 Direction ◯ 2 Directions at 90° ◯ 2 Directions not at 90°
◯ 3 Directions at 90° (cubic) ◯ 3 Directions not at 90° (rhombohedral)
◯ 4 Directions (octahedral) ◯ 6 Directions (dodecahedral)

Fracture: ◯ Conchoidal (smooth, shell-like, or glass-like breaks) ◯ Uneven (irregular, but not conchoidal) ◯ Hackly (jagged, as of a metal)
◯ Splintery (occurs in aggregates of many slender, brittle crystals) ◯ Fibrous (occurs in aggregates of many slender, threadlike crystals)

Crystal
Habit:
◯ Prismatic ◯ Acicular ◯ Striated ◯ Botryoidal ◯ Dendritic
◯ Nodular ◯ Banded ◯ Other_____

Hardness:
(Mohs Scale)
◯ 1 Talc ◯ 2 Gypsum ◯ 2.5 Fingernail ◯ 3 Calcite ◯ 4 Fluorite
◯ 5 Apatite ◯ 5.5 Glass ◯ 6 Feldspar ◯ 6.5 Steel File
◯ 7 Quartz ◯ 8 Topaz ◯ 9 Corundum ◯ 10 Diamond

Specific
Gravity:
◯ Average (like quartz = 2.6 - 2.8)
◯ Heavy (like galena = 7.5)
◯ Light (lighter than quartz = <2.6)

$$\frac{\text{mass of mineral}}{\text{mass of same volume of water}} = \frac{\text{weight of mineral in air}}{\text{weight of equal volume of water}}$$

Tenacity: ◯ Brittle ◯ Ductile ◯ Elastic ◯ Flexible ◯ Friable
◯ Malleable ◯ Sectile

Diaphaneity: ◯ Transparent ◯ Translucent ◯ Opaque

Notes: _____

Notes

_____
_____
_____
_____
_____
_____
_____
_____

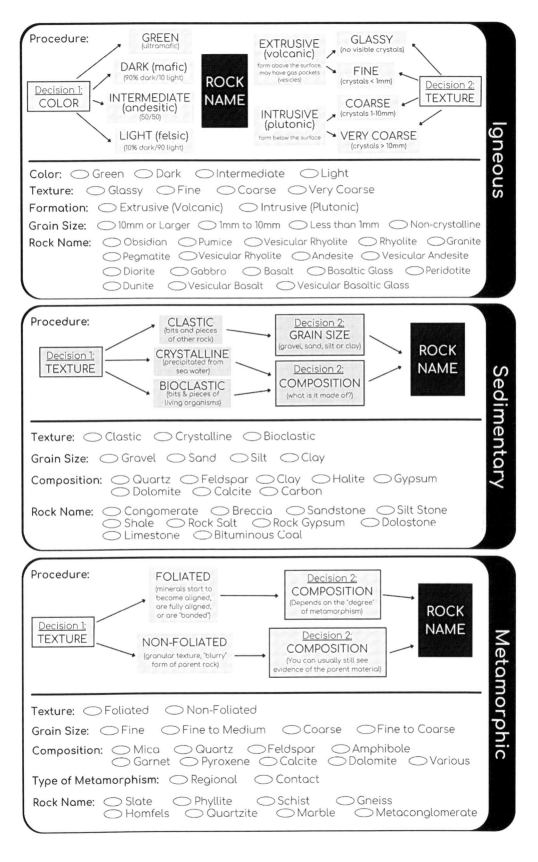

Igneous

Procedure:

Decision 1: COLOR
- GREEN (ultramafic)
- DARK (mafic) (90% dark/10 light)
- INTERMEDIATE (andesitic) (50/50)
- LIGHT (felsic) (10% dark/90 light)

ROCK NAME

EXTRUSIVE (volcanic) — form above the surface, may have gas pockets (vesicles)

INTRUSIVE (plutonic) — form below the surface

Decision 2: TEXTURE
- GLASSY (no visible crystals)
- FINE (crystals < 1mm)
- COARSE (crystals 1-10mm)
- VERY COARSE (crystals > 10mm)

Color: ◯ Green ◯ Dark ◯ Intermediate ◯ Light

Texture: ◯ Glassy ◯ Fine ◯ Coarse ◯ Very Coarse

Formation: ◯ Extrusive (Volcanic) ◯ Intrusive (Plutonic)

Grain Size: ◯ 10mm or Larger ◯ 1mm to 10mm ◯ Less than 1mm ◯ Non-crystalline

Rock Name: ◯ Obsidian ◯ Pumice ◯ Vesicular Rhyolite ◯ Rhyolite ◯ Granite
◯ Pegmatite ◯ Vesicular Rhyolite ◯ Andesite ◯ Vesicular Andesite
◯ Diorite ◯ Gabbro ◯ Basalt ◯ Basaltic Glass ◯ Peridotite
◯ Dunite ◯ Vesicular Basalt ◯ Vesicular Basaltic Glass

Sedimentary

Procedure:

Decision 1: TEXTURE
- CLASTIC (bits and pieces of other rock)
- CRYSTALLINE (precipitated from sea water)
- BIOCLASTIC (bits & pieces of living organisms)

Decision 2: GRAIN SIZE (gravel, sand, silt or clay)

Decision 2: COMPOSITION (what is it made of?)

ROCK NAME

Texture: ◯ Clastic ◯ Crystalline ◯ Bioclastic

Grain Size: ◯ Gravel ◯ Sand ◯ Silt ◯ Clay

Composition: ◯ Quartz ◯ Feldspar ◯ Clay ◯ Halite ◯ Gypsum
◯ Dolomite ◯ Calcite ◯ Carbon

Rock Name: ◯ Congomerate ◯ Breccia ◯ Sandstone ◯ Silt Stone
◯ Shale ◯ Rock Salt ◯ Rock Gypsum ◯ Dolostone
◯ Limestone ◯ Bituminous Coal

Metamorphic

Procedure:

Decision 1: TEXTURE
- FOLIATED (minerals start to become aligned, are fully aligned, or are "banded")
- NON-FOLIATED (granular texture, "blurry" form of parent rock)

Decision 2: COMPOSITION (Depends on the "degree" of metamorphism)

Decision 2: COMPOSITION (You can usually still see evidence of the parent material)

ROCK NAME

Texture: ◯ Foliated ◯ Non-Foliated

Grain Size: ◯ Fine ◯ Fine to Medium ◯ Coarse ◯ Fine to Coarse

Composition: ◯ Mica ◯ Quartz ◯ Feldspar ◯ Amphibole
◯ Garnet ◯ Pyroxene ◯ Calcite ◯ Dolomite ◯ Various

Type of Metamorphism: ◯ Regional ◯ Contact

Rock Name: ◯ Slate ◯ Phyllite ◯ Schist ◯ Gneiss
◯ Homfels ◯ Quartzite ◯ Marble ◯ Metaconglomerate

General

Date: _____   GPS Location: _____

Location: ⃝ Public Land   ⃝ Private Land   ⃝ Pay-to-Dig Site   ⃝ Quarry   ⃝ Roadcut   ⃝ Outcrop   ⃝ Riverbed   ⃝ Creek Bed   ⃝ Beach   ⃝ Mine Tailing   ⃝ Fresh Overturned Soil   ⃝ Other_____

Weather: ⃝ Sunny & Clear   ⃝ Cloudy/Overcast   ⃝ Windy   ⃝ Rainy / Drizzle   ⃝ Snow   ⃝ Stormy   ⃝ Fog   ⃝ Drought   ⃝ Other_____

Rock Type: ⃝ Igneous   ⃝ Sedimentary   ⃝ Metamorphic

Equipment Checklist:
(Rockhounding)
⃝ Eye Protection   ⃝ Heavy-Duty Gloves   ⃝ Boots / Waterproof
⃝ First-Aid Kit   ⃝ Hard Hat   ⃝ Rock Hammer / Pick   ⃝ Sieve
⃝ Colander   ⃝ Small Picks   ⃝ Trowel   ⃝ Small Knife   ⃝ Chisel
⃝ Small Broom   ⃝ Crack Hammer   ⃝ Pry Bar   ⃝ Sledgehammer
⃝ Mason's Hammer   ⃝ Shovel   ⃝ Backpack   ⃝ Bucket   ⃝ Map
⃝ Wrapping Material   ⃝ Small Tubes   ⃝ Boxes / Containers
⃝ Loupe   ⃝ Magnifying Glass   ⃝ Magnet   ⃝ Compass / GPS

Notes: _____

Mineral Identification

Color: ⃝ Light   ⃝ Dark   Specific Colors: _____

Luster: ⃝ <u>Metallic</u>   ⃝ Gold ⃝ Brass   ⃝ <u>Non-Metallic</u>   ⃝ Adamantine ⃝ Vitreous
⃝ Bronze ⃝ Iron   ⃝ Resinous ⃝ Pearly ⃝ Dull
⃝ Steel ⃝ Lead   ⃝ Greasy ⃝ Earthy ⃝ Silky
⃝ Silver ⃝ Alum.

Cleavage: ⃝ 1 Direction   ⃝ 2 Directions at 90°   ⃝ 2 Directions not at 90°
⃝ 3 Directions at 90° (cubic)   ⃝ 3 Directions not at 90° (rhombohedral)
⃝ 4 Directions (octahedral)   ⃝ 6 Directions (dodecahedral)

Fracture: ⃝ Conchoidal (smooth, shell-like, or glass-like breaks)   ⃝ Uneven (irregular, but not conchoidal)   ⃝ Hackly (jagged, as of a metal)
⃝ Splintery (occurs in aggregates of many slender, brittle crystals)   ⃝ Fibrous (occurs in aggregates of many slender, threadlike crystals)

Crystal Habit: ⃝ Prismatic   ⃝ Acicular   ⃝ Striated   ⃝ Botryoidal   ⃝ Dendritic
⃝ Nodular   ⃝ Banded   ⃝ Other_____

Hardness:
(Mohs Scale)
⃝ 1 Talc   ⃝ 2 Gypsum   ⃝ 2.5 Fingernail   ⃝ 3 Calcite   ⃝ 4 Fluorite
⃝ 5 Apatite   ⃝ 5.5 Glass   ⃝ 6 Feldspar   ⃝ 6.5 Steel File
⃝ 7 Quartz   ⃝ 8 Topaz   ⃝ 9 Corundrum   ⃝ 10 Diamond

Specific Gravity: ⃝ Average (like quartz = 2.6 - 2.8)   ⃝ Heavy (like galena = 7.5)   ⃝ Light (lighter than quartz = <2.6)

$$\frac{\text{mass of mineral}}{\text{mass of same volume of water}} = \frac{\text{weight of mineral in air}}{\text{weight of equal volume of water}}$$

Tenacity: ⃝ Brittle   ⃝ Ductile   ⃝ Elastic   ⃝ Flexible   ⃝ Friable
⃝ Malleable   ⃝ Sectile

Diaphaneity: ⃝ Transparent   ⃝ Translucent   ⃝ Opaque

Notes:_____

Notes

_____
_____
_____
_____
_____
_____
_____
_____
_____
_____

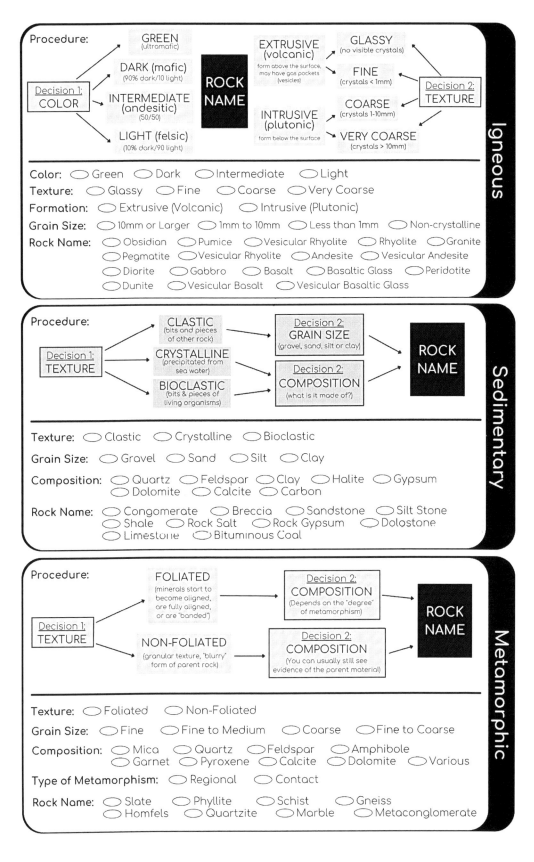

Igneous

Procedure:

Decision 1: COLOR
- GREEN (ultramafic)
- DARK (mafic) (90% dark/10 light)
- INTERMEDIATE (andesitic) (50/50)
- LIGHT (felsic) (10% dark/90 light)

ROCK NAME

EXTRUSIVE (volcanic) — form above the surface, may have gas pockets (vesicles)

INTRUSIVE (plutonic) — form below the surface

Decision 2: TEXTURE
- GLASSY (no visible crystals)
- FINE (crystals < 1mm)
- COARSE (crystals 1-10mm)
- VERY COARSE (crystals > 10mm)

Color: ◯ Green ◯ Dark ◯ Intermediate ◯ Light

Texture: ◯ Glassy ◯ Fine ◯ Coarse ◯ Very Coarse

Formation: ◯ Extrusive (Volcanic) ◯ Intrusive (Plutonic)

Grain Size: ◯ 10mm or Larger ◯ 1mm to 10mm ◯ Less than 1mm ◯ Non-crystalline

Rock Name: ◯ Obsidian ◯ Pumice ◯ Vesicular Rhyolite ◯ Rhyolite ◯ Granite
◯ Pegmatite ◯ Vesicular Rhyolite ◯ Andesite ◯ Vesicular Andesite
◯ Diorite ◯ Gabbro ◯ Basalt ◯ Basaltic Glass ◯ Peridotite
◯ Dunite ◯ Vesicular Basalt ◯ Vesicular Basaltic Glass

Sedimentary

Procedure:

Decision 1: TEXTURE
- CLASTIC (bits and pieces of other rock)
- CRYSTALLINE (precipitated from sea water)
- BIOCLASTIC (bits & pieces of living organisms)

Decision 2: GRAIN SIZE (gravel, sand, silt or clay)

Decision 2: COMPOSITION (what is it made of?)

ROCK NAME

Texture: ◯ Clastic ◯ Crystalline ◯ Bioclastic

Grain Size: ◯ Gravel ◯ Sand ◯ Silt ◯ Clay

Composition: ◯ Quartz ◯ Feldspar ◯ Clay ◯ Halite ◯ Gypsum
◯ Dolomite ◯ Calcite ◯ Carbon

Rock Name: ◯ Conglomerate ◯ Breccia ◯ Sandstone ◯ Silt Stone
◯ Shale ◯ Rock Salt ◯ Rock Gypsum ◯ Dolostone
◯ Limestone ◯ Bituminous Coal

Metamorphic

Procedure:

Decision 1: TEXTURE
- FOLIATED (minerals start to become aligned, are fully aligned, or are "banded")
- NON-FOLIATED (granular texture, "blurry" form of parent rock)

Decision 2: COMPOSITION (Depends on the "degree" of metamorphism)

Decision 2: COMPOSITION (You can usually still see evidence of the parent material)

ROCK NAME

Texture: ◯ Foliated ◯ Non-Foliated

Grain Size: ◯ Fine ◯ Fine to Medium ◯ Coarse ◯ Fine to Coarse

Composition: ◯ Mica ◯ Quartz ◯ Feldspar ◯ Amphibole
◯ Garnet ◯ Pyroxene ◯ Calcite ◯ Dolomite ◯ Various

Type of Metamorphism: ◯ Regional ◯ Contact

Rock Name: ◯ Slate ◯ Phyllite ◯ Schist ◯ Gneiss
◯ Hornfels ◯ Quartzite ◯ Marble ◯ Metaconglomerate

General

Date: _____ GPS Location: _____

Location: ○ Public Land ○ Private Land ○ Pay-to-Dig Site ○ Quarry
○ Roadcut ○ Outcrop ○ Riverbed ○ Creek Bed ○ Beach
○ Mine Tailing ○ Fresh Overturned Soil ○ Other_____

Weather: ○ Sunny & Clear ○ Cloudy/Overcast ○ Windy ○ Rainy / Drizzle
○ Snow ○ Stormy ○ Fog ○ Drought ○ Other_____

Rock Type: ○ Igneous ○ Sedimentary ○ Metamorphic

Equipment
Checklist:
(Rockhounding)
○ Eye Protection ○ Heavy-Duty Gloves ○ Boots / Waterproof
○ First-Aid Kit ○ Hard Hat ○ Rock Hammer / Pick ○ Sieve
○ Colander ○ Small Picks ○ Trowel ○ Small Knife ○ Chisel
○ Small Broom ○ Crack Hammer ○ Pry Bar ○ Sledgehammer
○ Mason's Hammer ○ Shovel ○ Backpack ○ Bucket ○ Map
○ Wrapping Material ○ Small Tubes ○ Boxes / Containers
○ Loupe ○ Magnifying Glass ○ Magnet ○ Compass / GPS

Notes: _____

Mineral Identification

Color: ○ Light ○ Dark Specific Colors: _____

Luster: ○ Metallic ○ Gold ○ Brass ○ Non-Metallic ○ Adamantine ○ Vitreous
○ Bronze ○ Iron ○ Resinous ○ Pearly ○ Dull
○ Steel ○ Lead ○ Greasy ○ Earthy ○ Silky
○ Silver ○ Alum.

Cleavage: ○ 1 Direction ○ 2 Directions at 90° ○ 2 Directions not at 90°
○ 3 Directions at 90° (cubic) ○ 3 Directions not at 90° (rhombohedral)
○ 4 Directions (octahedral) ○ 6 Directions (dodecahedral)

Fracture: ○ Conchoidal (smooth, shell-like, or glass-like breaks) ○ Uneven (irregular, but not conchoidal) ○ Hackly (jagged, as of a metal)
○ Splintery (occurs in aggregates of many slender, brittle crystals) ○ Fibrous (occurs in aggregates of many slender, threadlike crystals)

Crystal
Habit:
○ Prismatic ○ Acicular ○ Striated ○ Botryoidal ○ Dendritic
○ Nodular ○ Banded ○ Other_____

Hardness:
(Mohs Scale)
○ 1 Talc ○ 2 Gypsum ○ 2.5 Fingernail ○ 3 Calcite ○ 4 Fluorite
○ 5 Apatite ○ 5.5 Glass ○ 6 Feldspar ○ 6.5 Steel File
○ 7 Quartz ○ 8 Topaz ○ 9 Corundrum ○ 10 Diamond

Specific
Gravity:
○ Average (like quartz = 2.6 - 2.8) $\frac{\text{mass of mineral}}{\text{mass of same volume of water}} = \frac{\text{weight of mineral in air}}{\text{weight of equal volume of water}}$
○ Heavy (like galena = 7.5)
○ Light (lighter than quartz = <2.6)

Tenacity: ○ Brittle ○ Ductile ○ Elastic ○ Flexible ○ Friable
○ Malleable ○ Sectile

Diaphaneity: ○ Transparent ○ Translucent ○ Opaque

Notes:_____

Notes

_____
_____
_____
_____
_____
_____
_____
_____
_____
_____

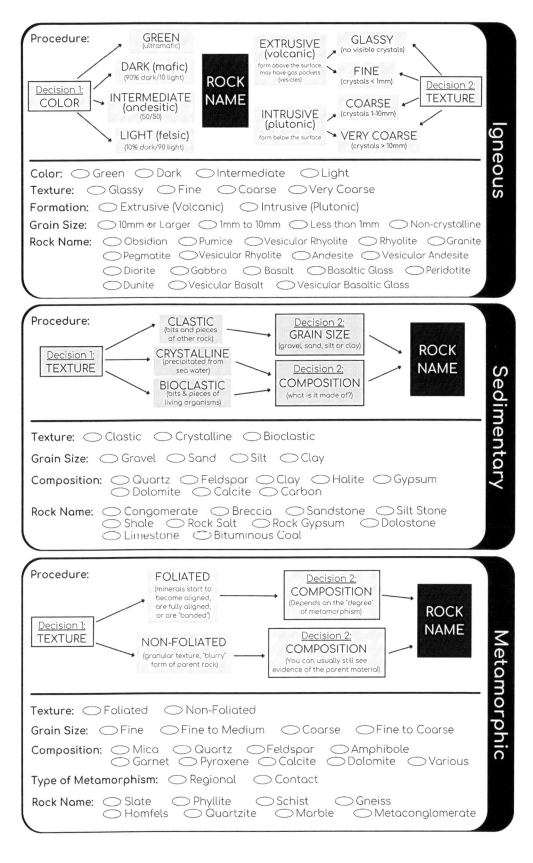

Igneous

Procedure:

Decision 1: COLOR
- GREEN (ultramafic)
- DARK (mafic) (90% dark/10 light)
- INTERMEDIATE (andesitic) (50/50)
- LIGHT (felsic) (10% dark/90 light)

ROCK NAME

- EXTRUSIVE (volcanic) form above the surface, may have gas pockets (vesicles)
- INTRUSIVE (plutonic) form below the surface

- GLASSY (no visible crystals)
- FINE (crystals < 1mm)
- COARSE (crystals 1-10mm)
- VERY COARSE (crystals > 10mm)

Decision 2: TEXTURE

Color: ○ Green ○ Dark ○ Intermediate ○ Light

Texture: ○ Glassy ○ Fine ○ Coarse ○ Very Coarse

Formation: ○ Extrusive (Volcanic) ○ Intrusive (Plutonic)

Grain Size: ○ 10mm or Larger ○ 1mm to 10mm ○ Less than 1mm ○ Non-crystalline

Rock Name: ○ Obsidian ○ Pumice ○ Vesicular Rhyolite ○ Rhyolite ○ Granite
○ Pegmatite ○ Vesicular Rhyolite ○ Andesite ○ Vesicular Andesite
○ Diorite ○ Gabbro ○ Basalt ○ Basaltic Glass ○ Peridotite
○ Dunite ○ Vesicular Basalt ○ Vesicular Basaltic Glass

Sedimentary

Procedure:

Decision 1: TEXTURE
- CLASTIC (bits and pieces of other rock)
- CRYSTALLINE (precipitated from sea water)
- BIOCLASTIC (bits & pieces of living organisms)

Decision 2: GRAIN SIZE (gravel, sand, silt or clay)

Decision 2: COMPOSITION (what is it made of?)

ROCK NAME

Texture: ○ Clastic ○ Crystalline ○ Bioclastic

Grain Size: ○ Gravel ○ Sand ○ Silt ○ Clay

Composition: ○ Quartz ○ Feldspar ○ Clay ○ Halite ○ Gypsum
○ Dolomite ○ Calcite ○ Carbon

Rock Name: ○ Congomerate ○ Breccia ○ Sandstone ○ Silt Stone
○ Shale ○ Rock Salt ○ Rock Gypsum ○ Dolostone
○ Limestone ○ Bituminous Coal

Metamorphic

Procedure:

Decision 1: TEXTURE
- FOLIATED (minerals start to become aligned, are fully aligned, or are "banded")
- NON-FOLIATED (granular texture, "blurry" form of parent rock)

Decision 2: COMPOSITION (Depends on the "degree" of metamorphism)

Decision 2: COMPOSITION (You can usually still see evidence of the parent material)

ROCK NAME

Texture: ○ Foliated ○ Non-Foliated

Grain Size: ○ Fine ○ Fine to Medium ○ Coarse ○ Fine to Coarse

Composition: ○ Mica ○ Quartz ○ Feldspar ○ Amphibole
○ Garnet ○ Pyroxene ○ Calcite ○ Dolomite ○ Various

Type of Metamorphism: ○ Regional ○ Contact

Rock Name: ○ Slate ○ Phyllite ○ Schist ○ Gneiss
○ Homfels ○ Quartzite ○ Marble ○ Metaconglomerate

General

Date: _____ GPS Location: _____

Location: ◯ Public Land ◯ Private Land ◯ Pay-to-Dig Site ◯ Quarry
◯ Roadcut ◯ Outcrop ◯ Riverbed ◯ Creek Bed ◯ Beach
◯ Mine Tailing ◯ Fresh Overturned Soil ◯ Other_____

Weather: ◯ Sunny & Clear ◯ Cloudy/Overcast ◯ Windy ◯ Rainy / Drizzle
◯ Snow ◯ Stormy ◯ Fog ◯ Drought ◯ Other_____

Rock Type: ◯ Igneous ◯ Sedimentary ◯ Metamorphic

Equipment Checklist:
(Rockhounding)
◯ Eye Protection ◯ Heavy-Duty Gloves ◯ Boots / Waterproof
◯ First-Aid Kit ◯ Hard Hat ◯ Rock Hammer / Pick ◯ Sieve
◯ Colander ◯ Small Picks ◯ Trowel ◯ Small Knife ◯ Chisel
◯ Small Broom ◯ Crack Hammer ◯ Pry Bar ◯ Sledgehammer
◯ Mason's Hammer ◯ Shovel ◯ Backpack ◯ Bucket ◯ Map
◯ Wrapping Material ◯ Small Tubes ◯ Boxes / Containers
◯ Loupe ◯ Magnifying Glass ◯ Magnet ◯ Compass / GPS

Notes: _____

Mineral Identification

Color: ◯ Light ◯ Dark Specific Colors: _____

Luster: ◯ Metallic ◯ Gold ◯ Brass ◯ Non-Metallic ◯ Adamantine ◯ Vitreous
◯ Bronze ◯ Iron ◯ Resinous ◯ Pearly ◯ Dull
◯ Steel ◯ Lead ◯ Greasy ◯ Earthy ◯ Silky
◯ Silver ◯ Alum.

Cleavage: ◯ 1 Direction ◯ 2 Directions at 90° ◯ 2 Directions not at 90°
◯ 3 Directions at 90° (cubic) ◯ 3 Directions not at 90° (rhombohedral)
◯ 4 Directions (octahedral) ◯ 6 Directions (dodecahedral)

Fracture: ◯ Conchoidal (smooth, shell-like, or glass-like breaks) ◯ Uneven (irregular, but not conchoidal) ◯ Hackly (jagged, as of a metal)
◯ Splintery (occurs in aggregates of many slender, brittle crystals) ◯ Fibrous (occurs in aggregates of many slender, threadlike crystals)

Crystal Habit: ◯ Prismatic ◯ Acicular ◯ Striated ◯ Botryoidal ◯ Dendritic
◯ Nodular ◯ Banded ◯ Other_____

Hardness: (Mohs Scale)
◯ 1 Talc ◯ 2 Gypsum ◯ 2.5 Fingernail ◯ 3 Calcite ◯ 4 Fluorite
◯ 5 Apatite ◯ 5.5 Glass ◯ 6 Feldspar ◯ 6.5 Steel File
◯ 7 Quartz ◯ 8 Topaz ◯ 9 Corundrum ◯ 10 Diamond

Specific Gravity:
◯ Average (like quartz = 2.6 - 2.8)
◯ Heavy (like galena = 7.5)
◯ Light (lighter than quartz = <2.6)

$$\frac{\text{mass of mineral}}{\text{mass of same volume of water}} = \frac{\text{weight of mineral in air}}{\text{weight of equal volume of water}}$$

Tenacity: ◯ Brittle ◯ Ductile ◯ Elastic ◯ Flexible ◯ Friable
◯ Malleable ◯ Sectile

Diaphaneity: ◯ Transparent ◯ Translucent ◯ Opaque

Notes: _____

Notes

_____
_____
_____
_____
_____
_____
_____
_____
_____

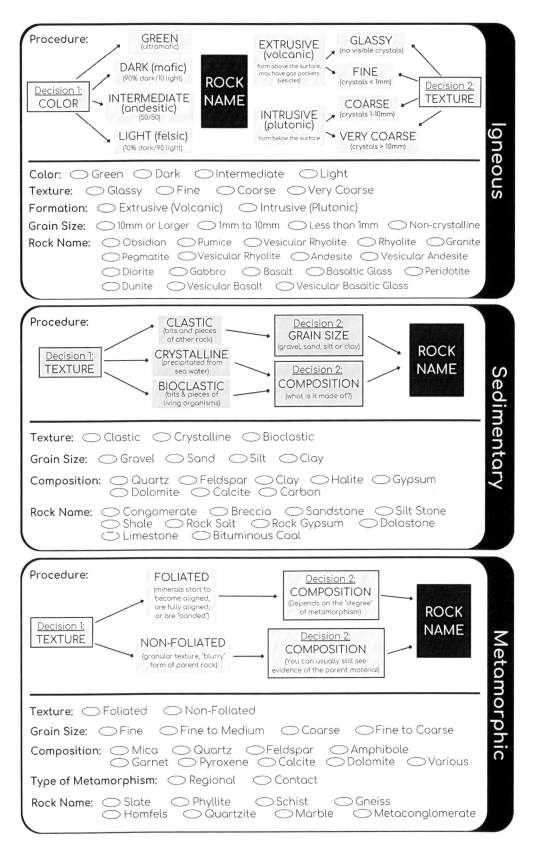

Igneous

Procedure:

Decision 1: COLOR →
- GREEN (ultramafic)
- DARK (mafic) (90% dark/10 light)
- INTERMEDIATE (andesitic) (50/50)
- LIGHT (felsic) (10% dark/90 light)

ROCK NAME

EXTRUSIVE (volcanic) — form above the surface, may have gas pockets (vesicles)

INTRUSIVE (plutonic) — form below the surface

- GLASSY (no visible crystals)
- FINE (crystals < 1mm)
- COARSE (crystals 1-10mm)
- VERY COARSE (crystals > 10mm)

Decision 2: TEXTURE

Color: ◯ Green ◯ Dark ◯ Intermediate ◯ Light

Texture: ◯ Glassy ◯ Fine ◯ Coarse ◯ Very Coarse

Formation: ◯ Extrusive (Volcanic) ◯ Intrusive (Plutonic)

Grain Size: ◯ 10mm or Larger ◯ 1mm to 10mm ◯ Less than 1mm ◯ Non-crystalline

Rock Name: ◯ Obsidian ◯ Pumice ◯ Vesicular Rhyolite ◯ Rhyolite ◯ Granite ◯ Pegmatite ◯ Vesicular Rhyolite ◯ Andesite ◯ Vesicular Andesite ◯ Diorite ◯ Gabbro ◯ Basalt ◯ Basaltic Glass ◯ Peridotite ◯ Dunite ◯ Vesicular Basalt ◯ Vesicular Basaltic Glass

Sedimentary

Procedure:

Decision 1: TEXTURE →
- CLASTIC (bits and pieces of other rock)
- CRYSTALLINE (precipitated from sea water)
- BIOCLASTIC (bits & pieces of living organisms)

Decision 2: GRAIN SIZE (gravel, sand, silt or clay)

Decision 2: COMPOSITION (what is it made of?)

ROCK NAME

Texture: ◯ Clastic ◯ Crystalline ◯ Bioclastic

Grain Size: ◯ Gravel ◯ Sand ◯ Silt ◯ Clay

Composition: ◯ Quartz ◯ Feldspar ◯ Clay ◯ Halite ◯ Gypsum ◯ Dolomite ◯ Calcite ◯ Carbon

Rock Name: ◯ Congomerate ◯ Breccia ◯ Sandstone ◯ Silt Stone ◯ Shale ◯ Rock Salt ◯ Rock Gypsum ◯ Dolostone ◯ Limestone ◯ Bituminous Coal

Metamorphic

Procedure:

Decision 1: TEXTURE →
- FOLIATED (minerals start to become aligned, are fully aligned, or are "banded")
- NON-FOLIATED (granular texture, "blurry" form of parent rock)

Decision 2: COMPOSITION (Depends on the "degree" of metamorphism)

Decision 2: COMPOSITION (You can usually still see evidence of the parent material)

ROCK NAME

Texture: ◯ Foliated ◯ Non-Foliated

Grain Size: ◯ Fine ◯ Fine to Medium ◯ Coarse ◯ Fine to Coarse

Composition: ◯ Mica ◯ Quartz ◯ Feldspar ◯ Amphibole ◯ Garnet ◯ Pyroxene ◯ Calcite ◯ Dolomite ◯ Various

Type of Metamorphism: ◯ Regional ◯ Contact

Rock Name: ◯ Slate ◯ Phyllite ◯ Schist ◯ Gneiss ◯ Homfels ◯ Quartzite ◯ Marble ◯ Metaconglomerate

General

Date: _____   GPS Location: _____

Location: ○ Public Land   ○ Private Land   ○ Pay-to-Dig Site   ○ Quarry
○ Roadcut   ○ Outcrop   ○ Riverbed   ○ Creek Bed   ○ Beach
○ Mine Tailing   ○ Fresh Overturned Soil   ○ Other_____

Weather: ○ Sunny & Clear   ○ Cloudy/Overcast   ○ Windy   ○ Rainy / Drizzle
○ Snow   ○ Stormy   ○ Fog   ○ Drought   ○ Other_____

Rock Type: ○ Igneous   ○ Sedimentary   ○ Metamorphic

Equipment Checklist:
(Rockhounding)
○ Eye Protection   ○ Heavy-Duty Gloves   ○ Boots / Waterproof
○ First-Aid Kit   ○ Hard Hat   ○ Rock Hammer / Pick   ○ Sieve
○ Colander   ○ Small Picks   ○ Trowel   ○ Small Knife   ○ Chisel
○ Small Broom   ○ Crack Hammer   ○ Pry Bar   ○ Sledgehammer
○ Mason's Hammer   ○ Shovel   ○ Backpack   ○ Bucket   ○ Map
○ Wrapping Material   ○ Small Tubes   ○ Boxes / Containers
○ Loupe   ○ Magnifying Glass   ○ Magnet   ○ Compass / GPS

Notes: _____

Mineral Identification

Color: ○ Light   ○ Dark   Specific Colors: _____

Luster: ○ Metallic   ○ Gold   ○ Brass   ○ Non-Metallic   ○ Adamantine   ○ Vitreous
○ Bronze   ○ Iron   ○ Resinous   ○ Pearly   ○ Dull
○ Steel   ○ Lead   ○ Greasy   ○ Earthy   ○ Silky
○ Silver   ○ Alum.

Cleavage: ○ 1 Direction   ○ 2 Directions at 90°   ○ 2 Directions not at 90°
○ 3 Directions at 90° (cubic)   ○ 3 Directions not at 90° (rhombohedral)
○ 4 Directions (octahedral)   ○ 6 Directions (dodecahedral)

Fracture: ○ Conchoidal (smooth, shell-like, or glass-like breaks)   ○ Uneven (irregular, but not conchoidal)   ○ Hackly (jagged, as of a metal)
○ Splintery (occurs in aggregates of many slender, brittle crystals)   ○ Fibrous (occurs in aggregates of many slender, threadlike crystals)

Crystal Habit: ○ Prismatic   ○ Acicular   ○ Striated   ○ Botryoidal   ○ Dendritic
○ Nodular   ○ Banded   ○ Other_____

Hardness: (Mohs Scale)
○ 1 Talc   ○ 2 Gypsum   ○ 2.5 Fingernail   ○ 3 Calcite   ○ 4 Fluorite
○ 5 Apatite   ○ 5.5 Glass   ○ 6 Feldspar   ○ 6.5 Steel File
○ 7 Quartz   ○ 8 Topaz   ○ 9 Corundrum   ○ 10 Diamond

Specific Gravity:
○ Average (like quartz = 2.6 - 2.8)
○ Heavy (like galena = 7.5)
○ Light (lighter than quartz = <2.6)

$$\frac{mass\ of\ mineral}{mass\ of\ same\ volume\ of\ water} = \frac{weight\ of\ mineral\ in\ air}{weight\ of\ equal\ volume\ of\ water}$$

Tenacity: ○ Brittle   ○ Ductile   ○ Elastic   ○ Flexible   ○ Friable
○ Malleable   ○ Sectile

Diaphaneity: ○ Transparent   ○ Translucent   ○ Opaque

Notes: _____

Notes

_____
_____
_____
_____
_____
_____
_____
_____
_____

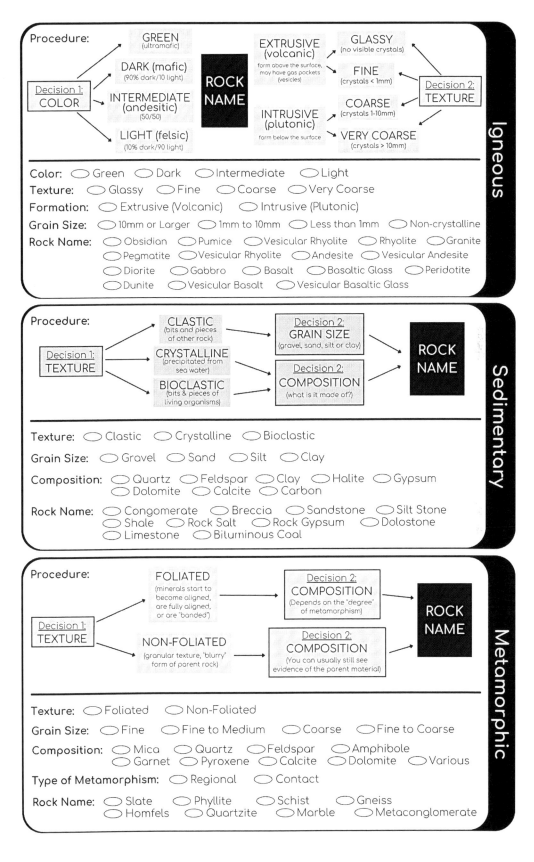

Igneous

Procedure:

Decision 1: COLOR
- GREEN (ultramafic)
- DARK (mafic) (90% dark/10 light)
- INTERMEDIATE (andesitic) (50/50)
- LIGHT (felsic) (10% dark/90 light)

ROCK NAME

EXTRUSIVE (volcanic) — form above the surface, may have gas pockets (vesicles)

INTRUSIVE (plutonic) — form below the surface

Decision 2: TEXTURE
- GLASSY (no visible crystals)
- FINE (crystals < 1mm)
- COARSE (crystals 1-10mm)
- VERY COARSE (crystals > 10mm)

Color: ⟨⟩ Green ⟨⟩ Dark ⟨⟩ Intermediate ⟨⟩ Light

Texture: ⟨⟩ Glassy ⟨⟩ Fine ⟨⟩ Coarse ⟨⟩ Very Coarse

Formation: ⟨⟩ Extrusive (Volcanic) ⟨⟩ Intrusive (Plutonic)

Grain Size: ⟨⟩ 10mm or Larger ⟨⟩ 1mm to 10mm ⟨⟩ Less than 1mm ⟨⟩ Non-crystalline

Rock Name: ⟨⟩ Obsidian ⟨⟩ Pumice ⟨⟩ Vesicular Rhyolite ⟨⟩ Rhyolite ⟨⟩ Granite
⟨⟩ Pegmatite ⟨⟩ Vesicular Rhyolite ⟨⟩ Andesite ⟨⟩ Vesicular Andesite
⟨⟩ Diorite ⟨⟩ Gabbro ⟨⟩ Basalt ⟨⟩ Basaltic Glass ⟨⟩ Peridotite
⟨⟩ Dunite ⟨⟩ Vesicular Basalt ⟨⟩ Vesicular Basaltic Glass

Sedimentary

Procedure:

Decision 1: TEXTURE
- CLASTIC (bits and pieces of other rock)
- CRYSTALLINE (precipitated from sea water)
- BIOCLASTIC (bits & pieces of living organisms)

Decision 2: GRAIN SIZE (gravel, sand, silt or clay)

Decision 2: COMPOSITION (what is it made of?)

ROCK NAME

Texture: ⟨⟩ Clastic ⟨⟩ Crystalline ⟨⟩ Bioclastic

Grain Size: ⟨⟩ Gravel ⟨⟩ Sand ⟨⟩ Silt ⟨⟩ Clay

Composition: ⟨⟩ Quartz ⟨⟩ Feldspar ⟨⟩ Clay ⟨⟩ Halite ⟨⟩ Gypsum
⟨⟩ Dolomite ⟨⟩ Calcite ⟨⟩ Carbon

Rock Name: ⟨⟩ Congomerate ⟨⟩ Breccia ⟨⟩ Sandstone ⟨⟩ Silt Stone
⟨⟩ Shale ⟨⟩ Rock Salt ⟨⟩ Rock Gypsum ⟨⟩ Dolostone
⟨⟩ Limestone ⟨⟩ Bituminous Coal

Metamorphic

Procedure:

Decision 1: TEXTURE
- FOLIATED (minerals start to become aligned, are fully aligned, or are "banded")
- NON-FOLIATED (granular texture, "blurry" form of parent rock)

Decision 2: COMPOSITION (Depends on the "degree" of metamorphism)

Decision 2: COMPOSITION (You can usually still see evidence of the parent material)

ROCK NAME

Texture: ⟨⟩ Foliated ⟨⟩ Non-Foliated

Grain Size: ⟨⟩ Fine ⟨⟩ Fine to Medium ⟨⟩ Coarse ⟨⟩ Fine to Coarse

Composition: ⟨⟩ Mica ⟨⟩ Quartz ⟨⟩ Feldspar ⟨⟩ Amphibole
⟨⟩ Garnet ⟨⟩ Pyroxene ⟨⟩ Calcite ⟨⟩ Dolomite ⟨⟩ Various

Type of Metamorphism: ⟨⟩ Regional ⟨⟩ Contact

Rock Name: ⟨⟩ Slate ⟨⟩ Phyllite ⟨⟩ Schist ⟨⟩ Gneiss
⟨⟩ Homfels ⟨⟩ Quartzite ⟨⟩ Marble ⟨⟩ Metaconglomerate

General

Date: _____ GPS Location: _____

Location: ○ Public Land ○ Private Land ○ Pay-to-Dig Site ○ Quarry
○ Roadcut ○ Outcrop ○ Riverbed ○ Creek Bed ○ Beach
○ Mine Tailing ○ Fresh Overturned Soil ○ Other_____

Weather: ○ Sunny & Clear ○ Cloudy/Overcast ○ Windy ○ Rainy / Drizzle
○ Snow ○ Stormy ○ Fog ○ Drought ○ Other_____

Rock Type: ○ Igneous ○ Sedimentary ○ Metamorphic

Equipment Checklist:
(Rockhounding)
○ Eye Protection ○ Heavy-Duty Gloves ○ Boots / Waterproof
○ First-Aid Kit ○ Hard Hat ○ Rock Hammer / Pick ○ Sieve
○ Colander ○ Small Picks ○ Trowel ○ Small Knife ○ Chisel
○ Small Broom ○ Crack Hammer ○ Pry Bar ○ Sledgehammer
○ Mason's Hammer ○ Shovel ○ Backpack ○ Bucket ○ Map
○ Wrapping Material ○ Small Tubes ○ Boxes / Containers
○ Loupe ○ Magnifying Glass ○ Magnet ○ Compass / GPS

Notes: _____

Mineral Identification

Color: ○ Light ○ Dark Specific Colors: _____

Luster: ○ Metallic ○ Gold ○ Brass ○ Non-Metallic ○ Adamantine ○ Vitreous
○ Bronze ○ Iron   ○ Resinous ○ Pearly ○ Dull
○ Steel ○ Lead   ○ Greasy ○ Earthy ○ Silky
○ Silver ○ Alum.

Cleavage: ○ 1 Direction ○ 2 Directions at 90° ○ 2 Directions not at 90°
○ 3 Directions at 90° (cubic) ○ 3 Directions not at 90° (rhombohedral)
○ 4 Directions (octahedral) ○ 6 Directions (dodecahedral)

Fracture: ○ Conchoidal (smooth, shell-like, or glass-like breaks) ○ Uneven (irregular, but not conchoidal) ○ Hackly (jagged, as of a metal)
○ Splintery (occurs in aggregates of many slender, brittle crystals) ○ Fibrous (occurs in aggregates of many slender, threadlike crystals)

Crystal Habit: ○ Prismatic ○ Acicular ○ Striated ○ Botryoidal ○ Dendritic
○ Nodular ○ Banded ○ Other_____

Hardness:
(Mohs Scale)
○ 1 Talc ○ 2 Gypsum ○ 2.5 Fingernail ○ 3 Calcite ○ 4 Fluorite
○ 5 Apatite ○ 5.5 Glass ○ 6 Feldspar ○ 6.5 Steel File
○ 7 Quartz ○ 8 Topaz ○ 9 Corundrum ○ 10 Diamond

Specific Gravity: ○ Average (like quartz = 2.6 - 2.8) $\frac{\text{mass of mineral}}{\text{mass of same volume of water}} = \frac{\text{weight of mineral in air}}{\text{weight of equal volume of water}}$
○ Heavy (like galena = 7.5)
○ Light (lighter than quartz = <2.6)

Tenacity: ○ Brittle ○ Ductile ○ Elastic ○ Flexible ○ Friable
○ Malleable ○ Sectile

Diaphaneity: ○ Transparent ○ Translucent ○ Opaque

Notes: _____

Notes

_____
_____
_____
_____
_____
_____
_____
_____
_____
_____

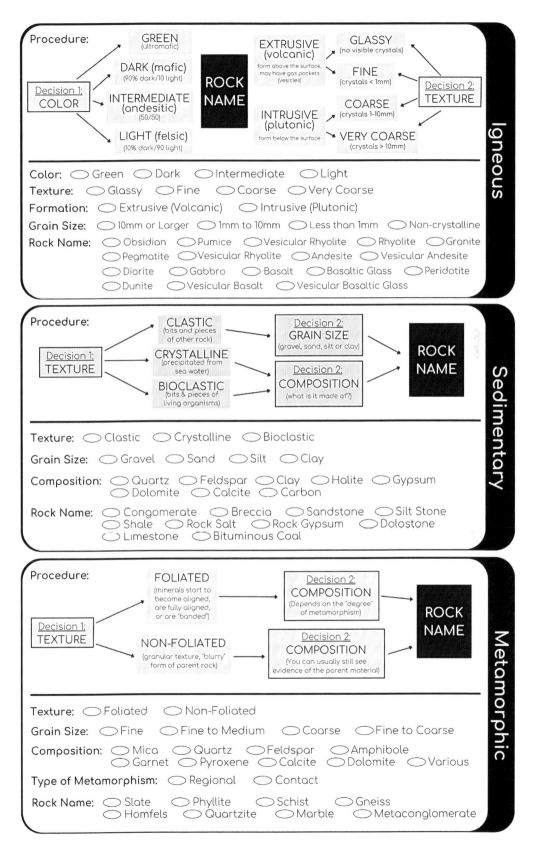

Igneous

Procedure:

Decision 1: COLOR
- GREEN (ultramafic)
- DARK (mafic) (90% dark/10 light)
- INTERMEDIATE (andesitic) (50/50)
- LIGHT (felsic) (10% dark/90 light)

ROCK NAME

- EXTRUSIVE (volcanic) — form above the surface, may have gas pockets (vesicles)
- INTRUSIVE (plutonic) — form below the surface

Decision 2: TEXTURE
- GLASSY (no visible crystals)
- FINE (crystals < 1mm)
- COARSE (crystals 1-10mm)
- VERY COARSE (crystals > 10mm)

Color: ◯ Green ◯ Dark ◯ Intermediate ◯ Light

Texture: ◯ Glassy ◯ Fine ◯ Coarse ◯ Very Coarse

Formation: ◯ Extrusive (Volcanic) ◯ Intrusive (Plutonic)

Grain Size: ◯ 10mm or Larger ◯ 1mm to 10mm ◯ Less than 1mm ◯ Non-crystalline

Rock Name: ◯ Obsidian ◯ Pumice ◯ Vesicular Rhyolite ◯ Rhyolite ◯ Granite
◯ Pegmatite ◯ Vesicular Rhyolite ◯ Andesite ◯ Vesicular Andesite
◯ Diorite ◯ Gabbro ◯ Basalt ◯ Basaltic Glass ◯ Peridotite
◯ Dunite ◯ Vesicular Basalt ◯ Vesicular Basaltic Glass

Sedimentary

Procedure:

Decision 1: TEXTURE
- CLASTIC (bits and pieces of other rock)
- CRYSTALLINE (precipitated from sea water)
- BIOCLASTIC (bits & pieces of living organisms)

Decision 2: GRAIN SIZE (gravel, sand, silt or clay)

Decision 2: COMPOSITION (what is it made of?)

ROCK NAME

Texture: ◯ Clastic ◯ Crystalline ◯ Bioclastic

Grain Size: ◯ Gravel ◯ Sand ◯ Silt ◯ Clay

Composition: ◯ Quartz ◯ Feldspar ◯ Clay ◯ Halite ◯ Gypsum
◯ Dolomite ◯ Calcite ◯ Carbon

Rock Name: ◯ Congomerate ◯ Breccia ◯ Sandstone ◯ Silt Stone
◯ Shale ◯ Rock Salt ◯ Rock Gypsum ◯ Dolostone
◯ Limestone ◯ Bituminous Coal

Metamorphic

Procedure:

Decision 1: TEXTURE
- FOLIATED (minerals start to become aligned, are fully aligned, or are "banded")
- NON-FOLIATED (granular texture, "blurry" form of parent rock)

Decision 2: COMPOSITION (Depends on the "degree" of metamorphism)

Decision 2: COMPOSITION (You can usually still see evidence of the parent material)

ROCK NAME

Texture: ◯ Foliated ◯ Non-Foliated

Grain Size: ◯ Fine ◯ Fine to Medium ◯ Coarse ◯ Fine to Coarse

Composition: ◯ Mica ◯ Quartz ◯ Feldspar ◯ Amphibole
◯ Garnet ◯ Pyroxene ◯ Calcite ◯ Dolomite ◯ Various

Type of Metamorphism: ◯ Regional ◯ Contact

Rock Name: ◯ Slate ◯ Phyllite ◯ Schist ◯ Gneiss
◯ Homfels ◯ Quartzite ◯ Marble ◯ Metaconglomerate

General

Date: _____ GPS Location: _____

Location: ◯ Public Land ◯ Private Land ◯ Pay-to-Dig Site ◯ Quarry
◯ Roadcut ◯ Outcrop ◯ Riverbed ◯ Creek Bed ◯ Beach
◯ Mine Tailing ◯ Fresh Overturned Soil ◯ Other_____

Weather: ◯ Sunny & Clear ◯ Cloudy/Overcast ◯ Windy ◯ Rainy / Drizzle
◯ Snow ◯ Stormy ◯ Fog ◯ Drought ◯ Other_____

Rock Type: ◯ Igneous ◯ Sedimentary ◯ Metamorphic

Equipment ◯ Eye Protection ◯ Heavy-Duty Gloves ◯ Boots / Waterproof
Checklist: ◯ First-Aid Kit ◯ Hard Hat ◯ Rock Hammer / Pick ◯ Sieve
(Rockhounding) ◯ Colander ◯ Small Picks ◯ Trowel ◯ Small Knife ◯ Chisel
◯ Small Broom ◯ Crack Hammer ◯ Pry Bar ◯ Sledgehammer
◯ Mason's Hammer ◯ Shovel ◯ Backpack ◯ Bucket ◯ Map
◯ Wrapping Material ◯ Small Tubes ◯ Boxes / Containers
◯ Loupe ◯ Magnifying Glass ◯ Magnet ◯ Compass / GPS

Notes: _____

Mineral Identification

Color: ◯ Light ◯ Dark Specific Colors: _____

Luster: ◯ Metallic ◯ Gold ◯ Brass   ◯ Non-Metallic ◯ Adamantine ◯ Vitreous
◯ Bronze ◯ Iron   ◯ Resinous ◯ Pearly ◯ Dull
◯ Steel ◯ Lead   ◯ Greasy ◯ Earthy ◯ Silky
◯ Silver ◯ Alum.

Cleavage: ◯ 1 Direction ◯ 2 Directions at 90° ◯ 2 Directions not at 90°
◯ 3 Directions at 90° (cubic) ◯ 3 Directions not at 90° (rhombohedral)
◯ 4 Directions (octahedral) ◯ 6 Directions (dodecahedral)

Fracture: ◯ Conchoidal (smooth, shell-like, or glass-like breaks) ◯ Uneven (irregular, but not conchoidal) ◯ Hackly (jagged, as of a metal)
◯ Splintery (occurs in aggregates of many slender, brittle crystals) ◯ Fibrous (occurs in aggregates of many slender, threadlike crystals)

Crystal ◯ Prismatic ◯ Acicular ◯ Striated ◯ Botryoidal ◯ Dendritic
Habit: ◯ Nodular ◯ Banded ◯ Other_____

Hardness: ◯ 1 Talc ◯ 2 Gypsum ◯ 2.5 Fingernail ◯ 3 Calcite ◯ 4 Fluorite
(Mohs Scale) ◯ 5 Apatite ◯ 5.5 Glass ◯ 6 Feldspar ◯ 6.5 Steel File
◯ 7 Quartz ◯ 8 Topaz ◯ 9 Corundum ◯ 10 Diamond

Specific ◯ Average (like quartz = 2.6 - 2.8)
Gravity: ◯ Heavy (like galena = 7.5) $\dfrac{\text{mass of mineral}}{\text{mass of same volume of water}} = \dfrac{\text{weight of mineral in air}}{\text{weight of equal volume of water}}$
◯ Light (lighter than quartz = <2.6)

Tenacity: ◯ Brittle ◯ Ductile ◯ Elastic ◯ Flexible ◯ Friable
◯ Malleable ◯ Sectile

Diaphaneity: ◯ Transparent ◯ Translucent ◯ Opaque

Notes: _____

Notes

_____
_____
_____
_____
_____
_____
_____
_____
_____

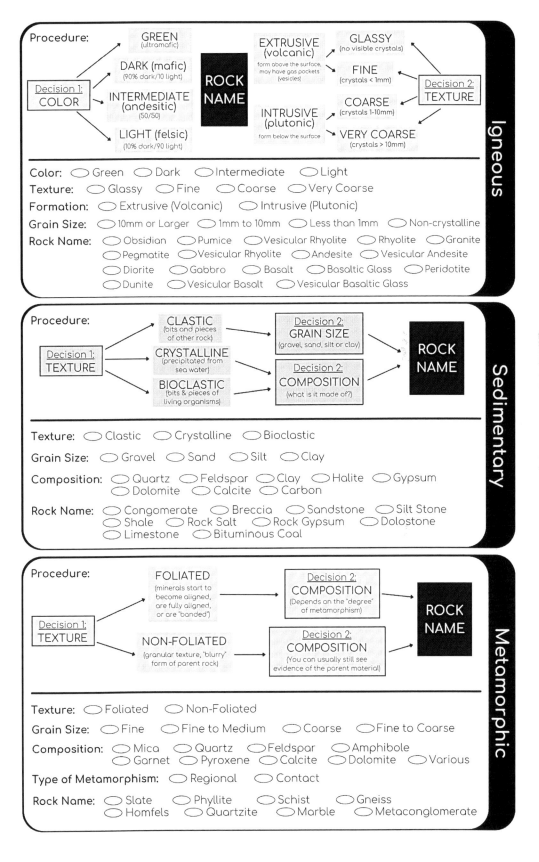

Igneous

Procedure:

Decision 1: COLOR
- GREEN (ultramafic)
- DARK (mafic) (90% dark/10 light)
- INTERMEDIATE (andesitic) (50/50)
- LIGHT (felsic) (10% dark/90 light)

ROCK NAME

EXTRUSIVE (volcanic) — form above the surface, may have gas pockets (vesicles)

INTRUSIVE (plutonic) — form below the surface

Decision 2: TEXTURE
- GLASSY (no visible crystals)
- FINE (crystals < 1mm)
- COARSE (crystals 1-10mm)
- VERY COARSE (crystals > 10mm)

Color: ◯ Green ◯ Dark ◯ Intermediate ◯ Light

Texture: ◯ Glassy ◯ Fine ◯ Coarse ◯ Very Coarse

Formation: ◯ Extrusive (Volcanic) ◯ Intrusive (Plutonic)

Grain Size: ◯ 10mm or Larger ◯ 1mm to 10mm ◯ Less than 1mm ◯ Non-crystalline

Rock Name: ◯ Obsidian ◯ Pumice ◯ Vesicular Rhyolite ◯ Rhyolite ◯ Granite ◯ Pegmatite ◯ Vesicular Rhyolite ◯ Andesite ◯ Vesicular Andesite ◯ Diorite ◯ Gabbro ◯ Basalt ◯ Basaltic Glass ◯ Peridotite ◯ Dunite ◯ Vesicular Basalt ◯ Vesicular Basaltic Glass

Sedimentary

Procedure:

Decision 1: TEXTURE
- CLASTIC (bits and pieces of other rock)
- CRYSTALLINE (precipitated from sea water)
- BIOCLASTIC (bits & pieces of living organisms)

Decision 2: GRAIN SIZE (gravel, sand, silt or clay)

Decision 2: COMPOSITION (what is it made of?)

ROCK NAME

Texture: ◯ Clastic ◯ Crystalline ◯ Bioclastic

Grain Size: ◯ Gravel ◯ Sand ◯ Silt ◯ Clay

Composition: ◯ Quartz ◯ Feldspar ◯ Clay ◯ Halite ◯ Gypsum ◯ Dolomite ◯ Calcite ◯ Carbon

Rock Name: ◯ Congomerate ◯ Breccia ◯ Sandstone ◯ Silt Stone ◯ Shale ◯ Rock Salt ◯ Rock Gypsum ◯ Dolostone ◯ Limestone ◯ Bituminous Coal

Metamorphic

Procedure:

Decision 1: TEXTURE
- FOLIATED (minerals start to become aligned, are fully aligned, or are "banded")
- NON-FOLIATED (granular texture, "blurry" form of parent rock)

Decision 2: COMPOSITION (Depends on the "degree" of metamorphism)

Decision 2: COMPOSITION (You can usually still see evidence of the parent material)

ROCK NAME

Texture: ◯ Foliated ◯ Non-Foliated

Grain Size: ◯ Fine ◯ Fine to Medium ◯ Coarse ◯ Fine to Coarse

Composition: ◯ Mica ◯ Quartz ◯ Feldspar ◯ Amphibole ◯ Garnet ◯ Pyroxene ◯ Calcite ◯ Dolomite ◯ Various

Type of Metamorphism: ◯ Regional ◯ Contact

Rock Name: ◯ Slate ◯ Phyllite ◯ Schist ◯ Gneiss ◯ Homfels ◯ Quartzite ◯ Marble ◯ Metaconglomerate

General

Date: _____   GPS Location: _____

Location: ⬭ Public Land   ⬭ Private Land   ⬭ Pay-to-Dig Site   ⬭ Quarry
⬭ Roadcut   ⬭ Outcrop   ⬭ Riverbed   ⬭ Creek Bed   ⬭ Beach
⬭ Mine Tailing   ⬭ Fresh Overturned Soil   ⬭ Other_____

Weather: ⬭ Sunny & Clear   ⬭ Cloudy/Overcast   ⬭ Windy   ⬭ Rainy / Drizzle
⬭ Snow   ⬭ Stormy   ⬭ Fog   ⬭ Drought   ⬭ Other_____

Rock Type: ⬭ Igneous   ⬭ Sedimentary   ⬭ Metamorphic

Equipment Checklist:
(Rockhounding)
⬭ Eye Protection   ⬭ Heavy-Duty Gloves   ⬭ Boots / Waterproof
⬭ First-Aid Kit   ⬭ Hard Hat   ⬭ Rock Hammer / Pick   ⬭ Sieve
⬭ Colander   ⬭ Small Picks   ⬭ Trowel   ⬭ Small Knife   ⬭ Chisel
⬭ Small Broom   ⬭ Crack Hammer   ⬭ Pry Bar   ⬭ Sledgehammer
⬭ Mason's Hammer   ⬭ Shovel   ⬭ Backpack   ⬭ Bucket   ⬭ Map
⬭ Wrapping Material   ⬭ Small Tubes   ⬭ Boxes / Containers
⬭ Loupe   ⬭ Magnifying Glass   ⬭ Magnet   ⬭ Compass / GPS

Notes: _____

Mineral Identification

Color: ⬭ Light   ⬭ Dark   Specific Colors: _____

Luster: ⬭ Metallic   ⬭ Gold   ⬭ Brass   ⬭ Bronze   ⬭ Iron   ⬭ Steel   ⬭ Lead   ⬭ Silver   ⬭ Alum.
⬭ Non-Metallic   ⬭ Adamantine   ⬭ Vitreous   ⬭ Resinous   ⬭ Pearly   ⬭ Dull   ⬭ Greasy   ⬭ Earthy   ⬭ Silky

Cleavage: ⬭ 1 Direction   ⬭ 2 Directions at 90°   ⬭ 2 Directions not at 90°
⬭ 3 Directions at 90° (cubic)   ⬭ 3 Directions not at 90° (rhombohedral)
⬭ 4 Directions (octahedral)   ⬭ 6 Directions (dodecahedral)

Fracture: ⬭ Conchoidal (smooth, shell-like, or glass-like breaks)   ⬭ Uneven (irregular, but not conchoidal)   ⬭ Hackly (jagged, as of a metal)
⬭ Splintery (occurs in aggregates of many slender, brittle crystals)   ⬭ Fibrous (occurs in aggregates of many slender, threadlike crystals)

Crystal Habit: ⬭ Prismatic   ⬭ Acicular   ⬭ Striated   ⬭ Botryoidal   ⬭ Dendritic
⬭ Nodular   ⬭ Banded   ⬭ Other_____

Hardness: (Mohs Scale)
⬭ 1 Talc   ⬭ 2 Gypsum   ⬭ 2.5 Fingernail   ⬭ 3 Calcite   ⬭ 4 Fluorite
⬭ 5 Apatite   ⬭ 5.5 Glass   ⬭ 6 Feldspar   ⬭ 6.5 Steel File
⬭ 7 Quartz   ⬭ 8 Topaz   ⬭ 9 Corundrum   ⬭ 10 Diamond

Specific Gravity:
⬭ Average (like quartz = 2.6 - 2.8)
⬭ Heavy (like galena = 7.5)
⬭ Light (lighter than quartz = <2.6)

$$\frac{\text{mass of mineral}}{\text{mass of same volume of water}} = \frac{\text{weight of mineral in air}}{\text{weight of equal volume of water}}$$

Tenacity: ⬭ Brittle   ⬭ Ductile   ⬭ Elastic   ⬭ Flexible   ⬭ Friable
⬭ Malleable   ⬭ Sectile

Diaphaneity: ⬭ Transparent   ⬭ Translucent   ⬭ Opaque

Notes:_____

Notes

_____
_____
_____
_____
_____
_____
_____
_____
_____
_____

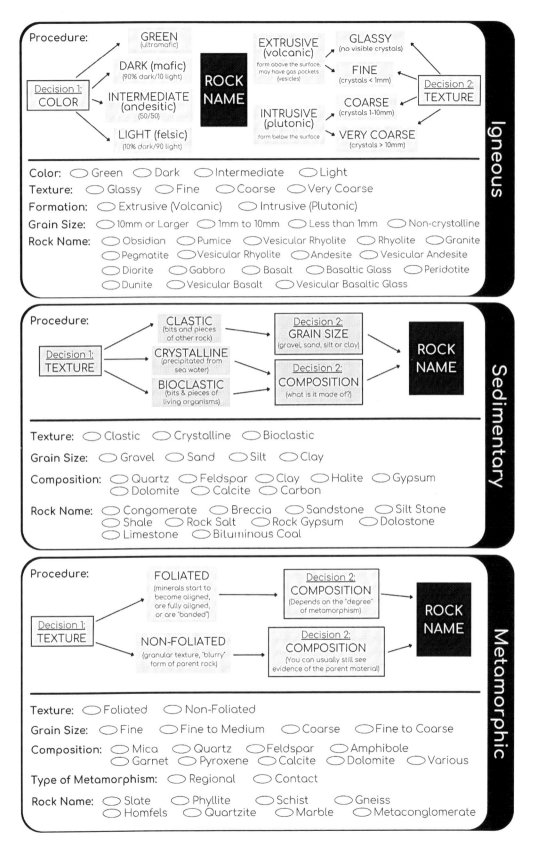

Igneous

Procedure:

Decision 1: COLOR
- GREEN (ultramafic)
- DARK (mafic) (90% dark/10 light)
- INTERMEDIATE (andesitic) (50/50)
- LIGHT (felsic) (10% dark/90 light)

ROCK NAME

- EXTRUSIVE (volcanic) form above the surface, may have gas pockets (vesicles)
  - GLASSY (no visible crystals)
  - FINE (crystals < 1mm)
- INTRUSIVE (plutonic) form below the surface
  - COARSE (crystals 1-10mm)
  - VERY COARSE (crystals > 10mm)

Decision 2: TEXTURE

Color: ◯ Green ◯ Dark ◯ Intermediate ◯ Light

Texture: ◯ Glassy ◯ Fine ◯ Coarse ◯ Very Coarse

Formation: ◯ Extrusive (Volcanic) ◯ Intrusive (Plutonic)

Grain Size: ◯ 10mm or Larger ◯ 1mm to 10mm ◯ Less than 1mm ◯ Non-crystalline

Rock Name: ◯ Obsidian ◯ Pumice ◯ Vesicular Rhyolite ◯ Rhyolite ◯ Granite ◯ Pegmatite ◯ Vesicular Rhyolite ◯ Andesite ◯ Vesicular Andesite ◯ Diorite ◯ Gabbro ◯ Basalt ◯ Basaltic Glass ◯ Peridotite ◯ Dunite ◯ Vesicular Basalt ◯ Vesicular Basaltic Glass

Sedimentary

Procedure:

Decision 1: TEXTURE
- CLASTIC (bits and pieces of other rock)
- CRYSTALLINE (precipitated from sea water)
- BIOCLASTIC (bits & pieces of living organisms)

Decision 2: GRAIN SIZE (gravel, sand, silt or clay)

Decision 2: COMPOSITION (what is it made of?)

ROCK NAME

Texture: ◯ Clastic ◯ Crystalline ◯ Bioclastic

Grain Size: ◯ Gravel ◯ Sand ◯ Silt ◯ Clay

Composition: ◯ Quartz ◯ Feldspar ◯ Clay ◯ Halite ◯ Gypsum ◯ Dolomite ◯ Calcite ◯ Carbon

Rock Name: ◯ Congomerate ◯ Breccia ◯ Sandstone ◯ Silt Stone ◯ Shale ◯ Rock Salt ◯ Rock Gypsum ◯ Dolostone ◯ Limestone ◯ Bituminous Coal

Metamorphic

Procedure:

Decision 1: TEXTURE
- FOLIATED (minerals start to become aligned, are fully aligned, or are "banded")
- NON-FOLIATED (granular texture, "blurry" form of parent rock)

Decision 2: COMPOSITION (Depends on the "degree" of metamorphism)

Decision 2: COMPOSITION (You can usually still see evidence of the parent material)

ROCK NAME

Texture: ◯ Foliated ◯ Non-Foliated

Grain Size: ◯ Fine ◯ Fine to Medium ◯ Coarse ◯ Fine to Coarse

Composition: ◯ Mica ◯ Quartz ◯ Feldspar ◯ Amphibole ◯ Garnet ◯ Pyroxene ◯ Calcite ◯ Dolomite ◯ Various

Type of Metamorphism: ◯ Regional ◯ Contact

Rock Name: ◯ Slate ◯ Phyllite ◯ Schist ◯ Gneiss ◯ Homfels ◯ Quartzite ◯ Marble ◯ Metaconglomerate

General

Date: _____ GPS Location: _____

Location: ○ Public Land ○ Private Land ○ Pay-to-Dig Site ○ Quarry
○ Roadcut ○ Outcrop ○ Riverbed ○ Creek Bed ○ Beach
○ Mine Tailing ○ Fresh Overturned Soil ○ Other_____

Weather: ○ Sunny & Clear ○ Cloudy/Overcast ○ Windy ○ Rainy / Drizzle
○ Snow ○ Stormy ○ Fog ○ Drought ○ Other_____

Rock Type: ○ Igneous ○ Sedimentary ○ Metamorphic

Equipment ○ Eye Protection ○ Heavy-Duty Gloves ○ Boots / Waterproof
Checklist: ○ First-Aid Kit ○ Hard Hat ○ Rock Hammer / Pick ○ Sieve
(Rockhounding) ○ Colander ○ Small Picks ○ Trowel ○ Small Knife ○ Chisel
○ Small Broom ○ Crack Hammer ○ Pry Bar ○ Sledgehammer
○ Mason's Hammer ○ Shovel ○ Backpack ○ Bucket ○ Map
○ Wrapping Material ○ Small Tubes ○ Boxes / Containers
○ Loupe ○ Magnifying Glass ○ Magnet ○ Compass / GPS

Notes: _____

Mineral Identification

Color: ○ Light ○ Dark   Specific Colors: _____

Luster: ○ Metallic ○ Gold ○ Brass   ○ Non-Metallic ○ Adamantine ○ Vitreous
                  ○ Bronze ○ Iron   ○ Resinous ○ Pearly ○ Dull
                  ○ Steel ○ Lead   ○ Greasy ○ Earthy ○ Silky
                  ○ Silver ○ Alum.

Cleavage: ○ 1 Direction   ○ 2 Directions at 90°   ○ 2 Directions not at 90°
○ 3 Directions at 90° (cubic)   ○ 3 Directions not at 90° (rhombohedral)
○ 4 Directions (octahedral)   ○ 6 Directions (dodecahedral)

Fracture: ○ Conchoidal (smooth, shell-like, or glass-like breaks) ○ Uneven (irregular, but not conchoidal) ○ Hackly (jagged, as of a metal)
○ Splintery (occurs in aggregates of many slender, brittle crystals) ○ Fibrous (occurs in aggregates of many slender, threadlike crystals)

Crystal ○ Prismatic ○ Acicular ○ Striated ○ Botryoidal ○ Dendritic
Habit: ○ Nodular ○ Banded ○ Other_____

Hardness: ○ 1 Talc ○ 2 Gypsum ○ 2.5 Fingernail ○ 3 Calcite ○ 4 Fluorite
(Mohs Scale) ○ 5 Apatite ○ 5.5 Glass ○ 6 Feldspar ○ 6.5 Steel File
○ 7 Quartz ○ 8 Topaz ○ 9 Corundrum ○ 10 Diamond

Specific ○ Average (like quartz = 2.6 - 2.8)   mass of mineral _____ = weight of mineral in air
Gravity: ○ Heavy (like galena = 7.5)   mass of same volume of water   weight of equal volume of water
○ Light (lighter than quartz = <2.6)

Tenacity: ○ Brittle ○ Ductile ○ Elastic ○ Flexible ○ Friable
○ Malleable ○ Sectile

Diaphaneity: ○ Transparent ○ Translucent ○ Opaque

Notes: _____

Notes

_____
_____
_____
_____
_____
_____
_____
_____
_____
_____

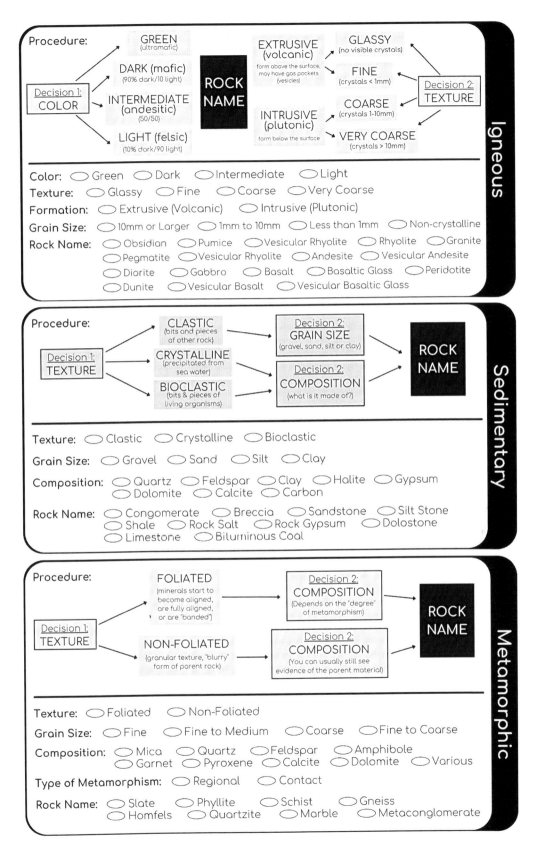

Igneous

Procedure:

Decision 1: COLOR →
- GREEN (ultramafic)
- DARK (mafic) (90% dark/10 light)
- INTERMEDIATE (andesitic) (50/50)
- LIGHT (felsic) (10% dark/90 light)

ROCK NAME

EXTRUSIVE (volcanic) — form above the surface, may have gas pockets (vesicles) →
- GLASSY (no visible crystals)
- FINE (crystals < 1mm)

INTRUSIVE (plutonic) — form below the surface →
- COARSE (crystals 1-10mm)
- VERY COARSE (crystals > 10mm)

Decision 2: TEXTURE

Color: ◯ Green ◯ Dark ◯ Intermediate ◯ Light
Texture: ◯ Glassy ◯ Fine ◯ Coarse ◯ Very Coarse
Formation: ◯ Extrusive (Volcanic) ◯ Intrusive (Plutonic)
Grain Size: ◯ 10mm or Larger ◯ 1mm to 10mm ◯ Less than 1mm ◯ Non-crystalline
Rock Name: ◯ Obsidian ◯ Pumice ◯ Vesicular Rhyolite ◯ Rhyolite ◯ Granite ◯ Pegmatite ◯ Vesicular Rhyolite ◯ Andesite ◯ Vesicular Andesite ◯ Diorite ◯ Gabbro ◯ Basalt ◯ Basaltic Glass ◯ Peridotite ◯ Dunite ◯ Vesicular Basalt ◯ Vesicular Basaltic Glass

Sedimentary

Procedure:

Decision 1: TEXTURE →
- CLASTIC (bits and pieces of other rock)
- CRYSTALLINE (precipitated from sea water)
- BIOCLASTIC (bits & pieces of living organisms)

Decision 2: GRAIN SIZE (gravel, sand, silt or clay)
Decision 2: COMPOSITION (what is it made of?)

ROCK NAME

Texture: ◯ Clastic ◯ Crystalline ◯ Bioclastic
Grain Size: ◯ Gravel ◯ Sand ◯ Silt ◯ Clay
Composition: ◯ Quartz ◯ Feldspar ◯ Clay ◯ Halite ◯ Gypsum ◯ Dolomite ◯ Calcite ◯ Carbon
Rock Name: ◯ Conglomerate ◯ Breccia ◯ Sandstone ◯ Silt Stone ◯ Shale ◯ Rock Salt ◯ Rock Gypsum ◯ Dolostone ◯ Limestone ◯ Bituminous Coal

Metamorphic

Procedure:

Decision 1: TEXTURE →
- FOLIATED (minerals start to become aligned, are fully aligned, or are "banded")
- NON-FOLIATED (granular texture, "blurry" form of parent rock)

Decision 2: COMPOSITION (Depends on the 'degree' of metamorphism)
Decision 2: COMPOSITION (You can usually still see evidence of the parent material!)

ROCK NAME

Texture: ◯ Foliated ◯ Non-Foliated
Grain Size: ◯ Fine ◯ Fine to Medium ◯ Coarse ◯ Fine to Coarse
Composition: ◯ Mica ◯ Quartz ◯ Feldspar ◯ Amphibole ◯ Garnet ◯ Pyroxene ◯ Calcite ◯ Dolomite ◯ Various
Type of Metamorphism: ◯ Regional ◯ Contact
Rock Name: ◯ Slate ◯ Phyllite ◯ Schist ◯ Gneiss ◯ Hornfels ◯ Quartzite ◯ Marble ◯ Metaconglomerate

General

Date: _____ GPS Location: _____

Location: ○ Public Land ○ Private Land ○ Pay-to-Dig Site ○ Quarry
○ Roadcut ○ Outcrop ○ Riverbed ○ Creek Bed ○ Beach
○ Mine Tailing ○ Fresh Overturned Soil ○ Other_____

Weather: ○ Sunny & Clear ○ Cloudy/Overcast ○ Windy ○ Rainy / Drizzle
○ Snow ○ Stormy ○ Fog ○ Drought ○ Other_____

Rock Type: ○ Igneous ○ Sedimentary ○ Metamorphic

Equipment
Checklist:
(Rockhounding)
○ Eye Protection ○ Heavy-Duty Gloves ○ Boots / Waterproof
○ First-Aid Kit ○ Hard Hat ○ Rock Hammer / Pick ○ Sieve
○ Colander ○ Small Picks ○ Trowel ○ Small Knife ○ Chisel
○ Small Broom ○ Crack Hammer ○ Pry Bar ○ Sledgehammer
○ Mason's Hammer ○ Shovel ○ Backpack ○ Bucket ○ Map
○ Wrapping Material ○ Small Tubes ○ Boxes / Containers
○ Loupe ○ Magnifying Glass ○ Magnet ○ Compass / GPS

Notes: _____

Mineral Identification

Color: ○ Light ○ Dark Specific Colors: _____

Luster: ○ Metallic ○ Gold ○ Brass   ○ Non-Metallic ○ Adamantine ○ Vitreous
○ Bronze ○ Iron   ○ Resinous ○ Pearly ○ Dull
○ Steel ○ Lead   ○ Greasy ○ Earthy ○ Silky
○ Silver ○ Alum.

Cleavage: ○ 1 Direction   ○ 2 Directions at 90°   ○ 2 Directions not at 90°
○ 3 Directions at 90° (cubic)   ○ 3 Directions not at 90° (rhombohedral)
○ 4 Directions (octahedral)   ○ 6 Directions (dodecahedral)

Fracture: ○ Conchoidal (smooth, shell-like, or glass-like breaks) ○ Uneven (irregular, but not conchoidal) ○ Hackly (jagged, as of a metal)
○ Splintery (occurs in aggregates of many slender, brittle crystals) ○ Fibrous (occurs in aggregates of many slender, threadlike crystals)

Crystal
Habit:
○ Prismatic ○ Acicular ○ Striated ○ Botryoidal ○ Dendritic
○ Nodular ○ Banded ○ Other_____

Hardness:
(Mohs Scale)
○ 1 Talc ○ 2 Gypsum ○ 2.5 Fingernail ○ 3 Calcite ○ 4 Fluorite
○ 5 Apatite ○ 5.5 Glass ○ 6 Feldspar ○ 6.5 Steel File
○ 7 Quartz ○ 8 Topaz ○ 9 Corundrum ○ 10 Diamond

Specific
Gravity:
○ Average (like quartz = 2.6 - 2.8)
○ Heavy (like galeno = 7.5)
○ Light (lighter than quartz = <2.6)

$$\frac{mass\ of\ mineral}{mass\ of\ same\ volume\ of\ water} = \frac{weight\ of\ mineral\ in\ air}{weight\ of\ equal\ volume\ of\ water}$$

Tenacity: ○ Brittle ○ Ductile ○ Elastic ○ Flexible ○ Friable
○ Malleable ○ Sectile

Diaphaneity: ○ Transparent ○ Translucent ○ Opaque

Notes:_____

Notes

_____
_____
_____
_____
_____
_____
_____
_____
_____

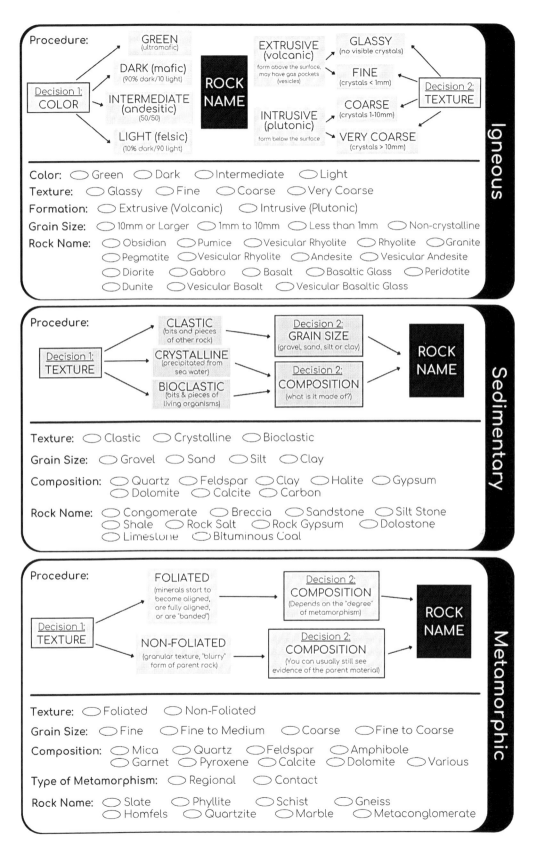

Igneous

Procedure:

Decision 1: COLOR →
- GREEN (ultramafic)
- DARK (mafic) (90% dark/10 light)
- INTERMEDIATE (andesitic) (50/50)
- LIGHT (felsic) (10% dark/90 light)

ROCK NAME

EXTRUSIVE (volcanic) — form above the surface, may have gas pockets (vesicles)

INTRUSIVE (plutonic) — form below the surface

Decision 2: TEXTURE →
- GLASSY (no visible crystals)
- FINE (crystals < 1mm)
- COARSE (crystals 1-10mm)
- VERY COARSE (crystals > 10mm)

Color: ◯ Green ◯ Dark ◯ Intermediate ◯ Light
Texture: ◯ Glassy ◯ Fine ◯ Coarse ◯ Very Coarse
Formation: ◯ Extrusive (Volcanic) ◯ Intrusive (Plutonic)
Grain Size: ◯ 10mm or Larger ◯ 1mm to 10mm ◯ Less than 1mm ◯ Non-crystalline
Rock Name: ◯ Obsidian ◯ Pumice ◯ Vesicular Rhyolite ◯ Rhyolite ◯ Granite
◯ Pegmatite ◯ Vesicular Rhyolite ◯ Andesite ◯ Vesicular Andesite
◯ Diorite ◯ Gabbro ◯ Basalt ◯ Basaltic Glass ◯ Peridotite
◯ Dunite ◯ Vesicular Basalt ◯ Vesicular Basaltic Glass

Sedimentary

Procedure:

Decision 1: TEXTURE →
- CLASTIC (bits and pieces of other rock)
- CRYSTALLINE (precipitated from sea water)
- BIOCLASTIC (bits & pieces of living organisms)

Decision 2: GRAIN SIZE (gravel, sand, silt or clay)

Decision 2: COMPOSITION (what is it made of?)

ROCK NAME

Texture: ◯ Clastic ◯ Crystalline ◯ Bioclastic
Grain Size: ◯ Gravel ◯ Sand ◯ Silt ◯ Clay
Composition: ◯ Quartz ◯ Feldspar ◯ Clay ◯ Halite ◯ Gypsum
◯ Dolomite ◯ Calcite ◯ Carbon
Rock Name: ◯ Congomerate ◯ Breccia ◯ Sandstone ◯ Silt Stone
◯ Shale ◯ Rock Salt ◯ Rock Gypsum ◯ Dolostone
◯ Limestone ◯ Bituminous Coal

Metamorphic

Procedure:

Decision 1: TEXTURE →
- FOLIATED (minerals start to become aligned, are fully aligned, or are "banded")
- NON-FOLIATED (granular texture, "blurry" form of parent rock)

Decision 2: COMPOSITION (Depends on the "degree" of metamorphism)

Decision 2: COMPOSITION (You can usually still see evidence of the parent material)

ROCK NAME

Texture: ◯ Foliated ◯ Non-Foliated
Grain Size: ◯ Fine ◯ Fine to Medium ◯ Coarse ◯ Fine to Coarse
Composition: ◯ Mica ◯ Quartz ◯ Feldspar ◯ Amphibole
◯ Garnet ◯ Pyroxene ◯ Calcite ◯ Dolomite ◯ Various
Type of Metamorphism: ◯ Regional ◯ Contact
Rock Name: ◯ Slate ◯ Phyllite ◯ Schist ◯ Gneiss
◯ Homfels ◯ Quartzite ◯ Marble ◯ Metaconglomerate

General

Date: _____ GPS Location: _____

Location: ◯ Public Land ◯ Private Land ◯ Pay-to-Dig Site ◯ Quarry
◯ Roadcut ◯ Outcrop ◯ Riverbed ◯ Creek Bed ◯ Beach
◯ Mine Tailing ◯ Fresh Overturned Soil ◯ Other_____

Weather: ◯ Sunny & Clear ◯ Cloudy/Overcast ◯ Windy ◯ Rainy / Drizzle
◯ Snow ◯ Stormy ◯ Fog ◯ Drought ◯ Other_____

Rock Type: ◯ Igneous ◯ Sedimentary ◯ Metamorphic

Equipment Checklist:
(Rockhounding)
◯ Eye Protection ◯ Heavy-Duty Gloves ◯ Boots / Waterproof
◯ First-Aid Kit ◯ Hard Hat ◯ Rock Hammer / Pick ◯ Sieve
◯ Colander ◯ Small Picks ◯ Trowel ◯ Small Knife ◯ Chisel
◯ Small Broom ◯ Crack Hammer ◯ Pry Bar ◯ Sledgehammer
◯ Mason's Hammer ◯ Shovel ◯ Backpack ◯ Bucket ◯ Map
◯ Wrapping Material ◯ Small Tubes ◯ Boxes / Containers
◯ Loupe ◯ Magnifying Glass ◯ Magnet ◯ Compass / GPS

Notes: _____

Mineral Identification

Color: ◯ Light ◯ Dark Specific Colors: _____

Luster: ◯ Metallic ◯ Gold ◯ Brass ◯ Bronze ◯ Iron ◯ Steel ◯ Lead ◯ Silver ◯ Alum. ◯ Non-Metallic ◯ Adamantine ◯ Vitreous ◯ Resinous ◯ Pearly ◯ Dull ◯ Greasy ◯ Earthy ◯ Silky

Cleavage: ◯ 1 Direction ◯ 2 Directions at 90° ◯ 2 Directions not at 90°
◯ 3 Directions at 90° (cubic) ◯ 3 Directions not at 90° (rhombohedral)
◯ 4 Directions (octahedral) ◯ 6 Directions (dodecahedral)

Fracture: ◯ Conchoidal (smooth, shell-like, or glass-like breaks) ◯ Uneven (irregular, but not conchoidal) ◯ Hackly (jagged, as of a metal)
◯ Splintery (occurs in aggregates of many slender, brittle crystals) ◯ Fibrous (occurs in aggregates of many slender, threadlike crystals)

Crystal Habit: ◯ Prismatic ◯ Acicular ◯ Striated ◯ Botryoidal ◯ Dendritic
◯ Nodular ◯ Banded ◯ Other_____

Hardness:
(Mohs Scale)
◯ 1 Talc ◯ 2 Gypsum ◯ 2.5 Fingernail ◯ 3 Calcite ◯ 4 Fluorite
◯ 5 Apatite ◯ 5.5 Glass ◯ 6 Feldspar ◯ 6.5 Steel File
◯ 7 Quartz ◯ 8 Topaz ◯ 9 Corundum ◯ 10 Diamond

Specific Gravity: ◯ Average (like quartz = 2.6 - 2.8) ◯ Heavy (like galena = 7.5) ◯ Light (lighter than quartz = <2.6)

$$\frac{\text{mass of mineral}}{\text{mass of same volume of water}} = \frac{\text{weight of mineral in air}}{\text{weight of equal volume of water}}$$

Tenacity: ◯ Brittle ◯ Ductile ◯ Elastic ◯ Flexible ◯ Friable
◯ Malleable ◯ Sectile

Diaphaneity: ◯ Transparent ◯ Translucent ◯ Opaque

Notes: _____

Notes

_____
_____
_____
_____
_____
_____
_____
_____
_____
_____

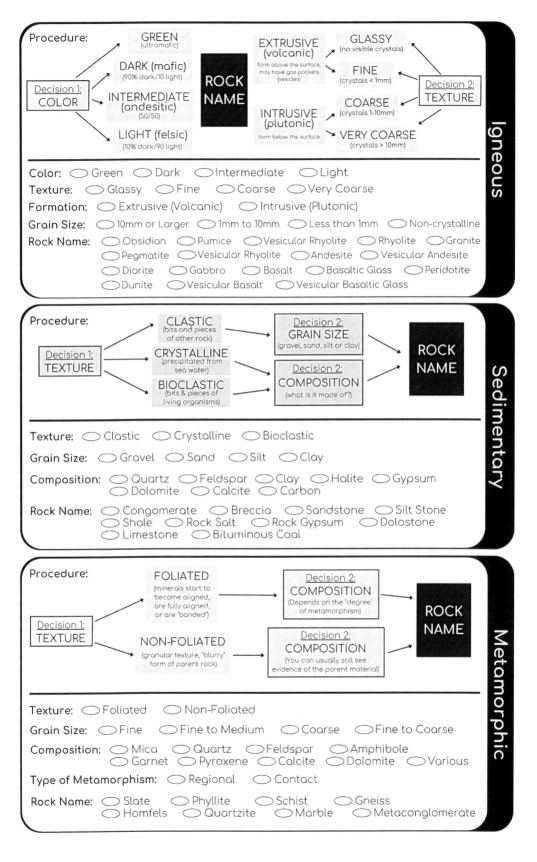

General

Date: _____ GPS Location: _____

Location: ◯ Public Land ◯ Private Land ◯ Pay-to-Dig Site ◯ Quarry
◯ Roadcut ◯ Outcrop ◯ Riverbed ◯ Creek Bed ◯ Beach
◯ Mine Tailing ◯ Fresh Overturned Soil ◯ Other_____

Weather: ◯ Sunny & Clear ◯ Cloudy/Overcast ◯ Windy ◯ Rainy / Drizzle
◯ Snow ◯ Stormy ◯ Fog ◯ Drought ◯ Other_____

Rock Type: ◯ Igneous ◯ Sedimentary ◯ Metamorphic

Equipment Checklist: (Rockhounding)
◯ Eye Protection ◯ Heavy-Duty Gloves ◯ Boots / Waterproof
◯ First-Aid Kit ◯ Hard Hat ◯ Rock Hammer / Pick ◯ Sieve
◯ Colander ◯ Small Picks ◯ Trowel ◯ Small Knife ◯ Chisel
◯ Small Broom ◯ Crack Hammer ◯ Pry Bar ◯ Sledgehammer
◯ Mason's Hammer ◯ Shovel ◯ Backpack ◯ Bucket ◯ Map
◯ Wrapping Material ◯ Small Tubes ◯ Boxes / Containers
◯ Loupe ◯ Magnifying Glass ◯ Magnet ◯ Compass / GPS

Notes: _____

Mineral Identification

Color: ◯ Light ◯ Dark (Specific Colors: _____)

Luster: ◯ <u>Metallic</u> ◯ Gold ◯ Brass ◯ Bronze ◯ Iron ◯ Steel ◯ Lead ◯ Silver ◯ Alum.
◯ <u>Non-Metallic</u> ◯ Adamantine ◯ Vitreous ◯ Resinous ◯ Pearly ◯ Dull ◯ Greasy ◯ Earthy ◯ Silky

Cleavage: ◯ 1 Direction ◯ 2 Directions at 90° ◯ 2 Directions not at 90°
◯ 3 Directions at 90° (cubic) ◯ 3 Directions not at 90° (rhombohedral)
◯ 4 Directions (octahedral) ◯ 6 Directions (dodecahedral)

Fracture: ◯ Conchoidal (smooth, shell-like, or glass-like breaks) ◯ Uneven (irregular, but not conchoidal) ◯ Hackly (jagged, as of a metal)
◯ Splintery (occurs in aggregates of many slender, brittle crystals) ◯ Fibrous (occurs in aggregates of many slender, threadlike crystals)

Crystal Habit: ◯ Prismatic ◯ Acicular ◯ Striated ◯ Botryoidal ◯ Dendritic
◯ Nodular ◯ Banded ◯ Other_____

Hardness: (Mohs Scale)
◯ 1 Talc ◯ 2 Gypsum ◯ 2.5 Fingernail ◯ 3 Calcite ◯ 4 Fluorite
◯ 5 Apatite ◯ 5.5 Glass ◯ 6 Feldspar ◯ 6.5 Steel File
◯ 7 Quartz ◯ 8 Topaz ◯ 9 Corundrum ◯ 10 Diamond

Specific Gravity:
◯ Average (like quartz = 2.6 - 2.8)
◯ Heavy (like galena = 7.5)
◯ Light (lighter than quartz = <2.6)

$$\frac{\text{mass of mineral}}{\text{mass of same volume of water}} = \frac{\text{weight of mineral in air}}{\text{weight of equal volume of water}}$$

Tenacity: ◯ Brittle ◯ Ductile ◯ Elastic ◯ Flexible ◯ Friable
◯ Malleable ◯ Sectile

Diaphaneity: ◯ Transparent ◯ Translucent ◯ Opaque

Notes:_____

Notes

_____
_____
_____
_____
_____
_____
_____
_____
_____

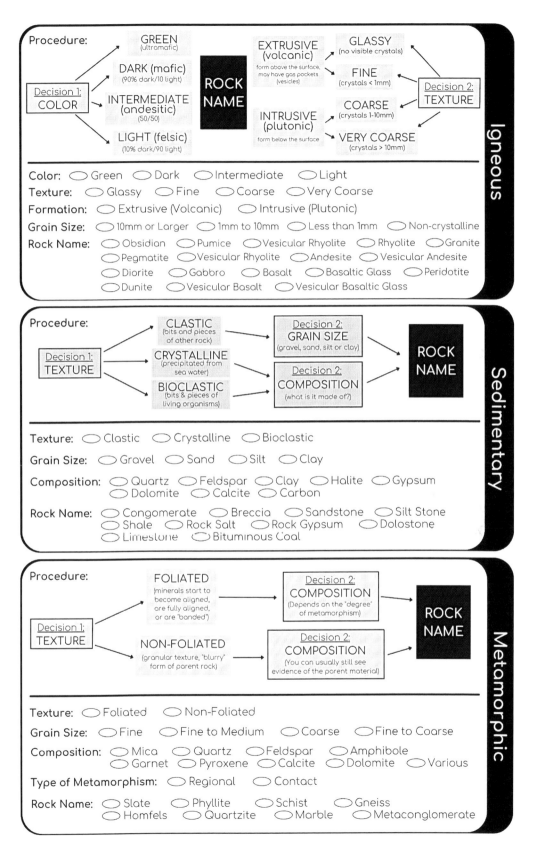

Igneous

Procedure:

Decision 1: COLOR →
- GREEN (ultramafic)
- DARK (mafic) (90% dark/10 light)
- INTERMEDIATE (andesitic) (50/50)
- LIGHT (felsic) (10% dark/90 light)

ROCK NAME

EXTRUSIVE (volcanic) — form above the surface, may have gas pockets (vesicles)

INTRUSIVE (plutonic) — form below the surface

Decision 2: TEXTURE →
- GLASSY (no visible crystals)
- FINE (crystals < 1mm)
- COARSE (crystals 1-10mm)
- VERY COARSE (crystals > 10mm)

Color: ◯ Green ◯ Dark ◯ Intermediate ◯ Light

Texture: ◯ Glassy ◯ Fine ◯ Coarse ◯ Very Coarse

Formation: ◯ Extrusive (Volcanic) ◯ Intrusive (Plutonic)

Grain Size: ◯ 10mm or Larger ◯ 1mm to 10mm ◯ Less than 1mm ◯ Non-crystalline

Rock Name: ◯ Obsidian ◯ Pumice ◯ Vesicular Rhyolite ◯ Rhyolite ◯ Granite ◯ Pegmatite ◯ Vesicular Rhyolite ◯ Andesite ◯ Vesicular Andesite ◯ Diorite ◯ Gabbro ◯ Basalt ◯ Basaltic Glass ◯ Peridotite ◯ Dunite ◯ Vesicular Basalt ◯ Vesicular Basaltic Glass

Sedimentary

Procedure:

Decision 1: TEXTURE →
- CLASTIC (bits and pieces of other rock)
- CRYSTALLINE (precipitated from sea water)
- BIOCLASTIC (bits & pieces of living organisms)

Decision 2: GRAIN SIZE (gravel, sand, silt or clay) → ROCK NAME

Decision 2: COMPOSITION (what is it made of?) → ROCK NAME

Texture: ◯ Clastic ◯ Crystalline ◯ Bioclastic

Grain Size: ◯ Gravel ◯ Sand ◯ Silt ◯ Clay

Composition: ◯ Quartz ◯ Feldspar ◯ Clay ◯ Halite ◯ Gypsum ◯ Dolomite ◯ Calcite ◯ Carbon

Rock Name: ◯ Congomerate ◯ Breccia ◯ Sandstone ◯ Silt Stone ◯ Shale ◯ Rock Salt ◯ Rock Gypsum ◯ Dolostone ◯ Limestone ◯ Bituminous Coal

Metamorphic

Procedure:

Decision 1: TEXTURE →
- FOLIATED (minerals start to become aligned, are fully aligned, or are "banded")
- NON-FOLIATED (granular texture, "blurry" form of parent rock)

Decision 2: COMPOSITION (Depends on the "degree" of metamorphism) → ROCK NAME

Decision 2: COMPOSITION (You can usually still see evidence of the parent material) → ROCK NAME

Texture: ◯ Foliated ◯ Non-Foliated

Grain Size: ◯ Fine ◯ Fine to Medium ◯ Coarse ◯ Fine to Coarse

Composition: ◯ Mica ◯ Quartz ◯ Feldspar ◯ Amphibole ◯ Garnet ◯ Pyroxene ◯ Calcite ◯ Dolomite ◯ Various

Type of Metamorphism: ◯ Regional ◯ Contact

Rock Name: ◯ Slate ◯ Phyllite ◯ Schist ◯ Gneiss ◯ Hornfels ◯ Quartzite ◯ Marble ◯ Metaconglomerate

General

Date: _____ GPS Location: _____

Location: ◯ Public Land ◯ Private Land ◯ Pay-to-Dig Site ◯ Quarry
◯ Roadcut ◯ Outcrop ◯ Riverbed ◯ Creek Bed ◯ Beach
◯ Mine Tailing ◯ Fresh Overturned Soil ◯ Other_____

Weather: ◯ Sunny & Clear ◯ Cloudy/Overcast ◯ Windy ◯ Rainy / Drizzle
◯ Snow ◯ Stormy ◯ Fog ◯ Drought ◯ Other_____

Rock Type: ◯ Igneous ◯ Sedimentary ◯ Metamorphic

Equipment Checklist:
(Rockhounding)
◯ Eye Protection ◯ Heavy-Duty Gloves ◯ Boots / Waterproof
◯ First-Aid Kit ◯ Hard Hat ◯ Rock Hammer / Pick ◯ Sieve
◯ Colander ◯ Small Picks ◯ Trowel ◯ Small Knife ◯ Chisel
◯ Small Broom ◯ Crack Hammer ◯ Pry Bar ◯ Sledgehammer
◯ Mason's Hammer ◯ Shovel ◯ Backpack ◯ Bucket ◯ Map
◯ Wrapping Material ◯ Small Tubes ◯ Boxes / Containers
◯ Loupe ◯ Magnifying Glass ◯ Magnet ◯ Compass / GPS

Notes: _____

Mineral Identification

Color: ◯ Light ◯ Dark Specific Colors: _____

Luster: ◯ Metallic ◯ Gold ◯ Brass   ◯ Non-Metallic ◯ Adamantine ◯ Vitreous
◯ Bronze ◯ Iron   ◯ Resinous ◯ Pearly ◯ Dull
◯ Steel ◯ Lead   ◯ Greasy ◯ Earthy ◯ Silky
◯ Silver ◯ Alum.

Cleavage: ◯ 1 Direction ◯ 2 Directions at 90° ◯ 2 Directions not at 90°
◯ 3 Directions at 90° (cubic) ◯ 3 Directions not at 90° (rhombohedral)
◯ 4 Directions (octahedral) ◯ 6 Directions (dodecahedral)

Fracture: ◯ Conchoidal (smooth, shell-like, or glass-like breaks) ◯ Uneven (irregular, but not conchoidal) ◯ Hackly (jagged, as of a metal)
◯ Splintery (occurs in aggregates of many slender, brittle crystals) ◯ Fibrous (occurs in aggregates of many slender, threadlike crystals)

Crystal Habit: ◯ Prismatic ◯ Acicular ◯ Striated ◯ Botryoidal ◯ Dendritic
◯ Nodular ◯ Banded ◯ Other_____

Hardness: (Mohs Scale) ◯ 1 Talc ◯ 2 Gypsum ◯ 2.5 Fingernail ◯ 3 Calcite ◯ 4 Fluorite
◯ 5 Apatite ◯ 5.5 Glass ◯ 6 Feldspar ◯ 6.5 Steel File
◯ 7 Quartz ◯ 8 Topaz ◯ 9 Corundrum ◯ 10 Diamond

Specific Gravity: ◯ Average (like quartz = 2.6 - 2.8) ◯ Heavy (like galena = 7.5) ◯ Light (lighter than quartz = <2.6)

$$\frac{\text{mass of mineral}}{\text{mass of same volume of water}} = \frac{\text{weight of mineral in air}}{\text{weight of equal volume of water}}$$

Tenacity: ◯ Brittle ◯ Ductile ◯ Elastic ◯ Flexible ◯ Friable
◯ Malleable ◯ Sectile

Diaphaneity: ◯ Transparent ◯ Translucent ◯ Opaque

Notes: _____

Notes

_____
_____
_____
_____
_____
_____
_____
_____
_____

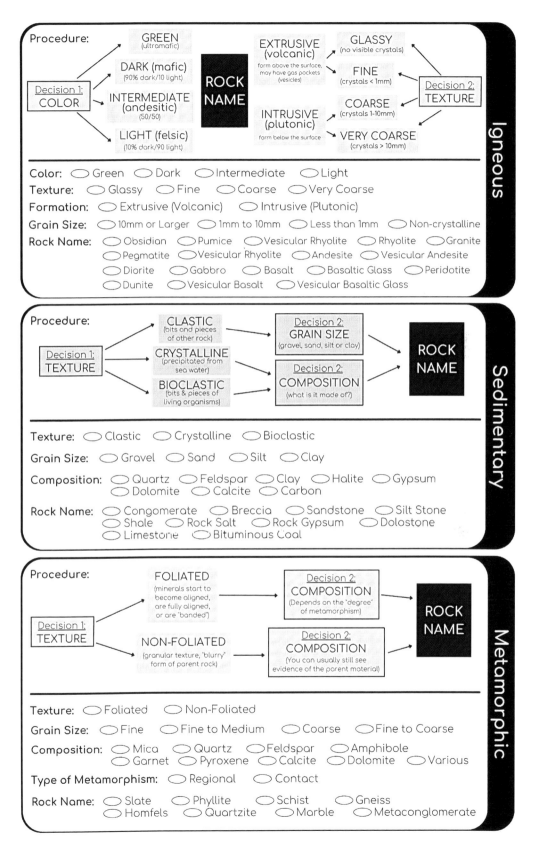

Igneous

Procedure:

Decision 1: COLOR
- GREEN (ultramafic)
- DARK (mafic) (90% dark/10 light)
- INTERMEDIATE (andesitic) (50/50)
- LIGHT (felsic) (10% dark/90 light)

ROCK NAME

EXTRUSIVE (volcanic) — form above the surface, may have gas pockets (vesicles)

INTRUSIVE (plutonic) — form below the surface

Decision 2: TEXTURE
- GLASSY (no visible crystals)
- FINE (crystals < 1mm)
- COARSE (crystals 1-10mm)
- VERY COARSE (crystals > 10mm)

Color: ◯ Green ◯ Dark ◯ Intermediate ◯ Light

Texture: ◯ Glassy ◯ Fine ◯ Coarse ◯ Very Coarse

Formation: ◯ Extrusive (Volcanic) ◯ Intrusive (Plutonic)

Grain Size: ◯ 10mm or Larger ◯ 1mm to 10mm ◯ Less than 1mm ◯ Non-crystalline

Rock Name: ◯ Obsidian ◯ Pumice ◯ Vesicular Rhyolite ◯ Rhyolite ◯ Granite
◯ Pegmatite ◯ Vesicular Rhyolite ◯ Andesite ◯ Vesicular Andesite
◯ Diorite ◯ Gabbro ◯ Basalt ◯ Basaltic Glass ◯ Peridotite
◯ Dunite ◯ Vesicular Basalt ◯ Vesicular Basaltic Glass

Sedimentary

Procedure:

Decision 1: TEXTURE
- CLASTIC (bits and pieces of other rock)
- CRYSTALLINE (precipitated from sea water)
- BIOCLASTIC (bits & pieces of living organisms)

Decision 2: GRAIN SIZE (gravel, sand, silt or clay)

Decision 2: COMPOSITION (what is it made of?)

ROCK NAME

Texture: ◯ Clastic ◯ Crystalline ◯ Bioclastic

Grain Size: ◯ Gravel ◯ Sand ◯ Silt ◯ Clay

Composition: ◯ Quartz ◯ Feldspar ◯ Clay ◯ Halite ◯ Gypsum
◯ Dolomite ◯ Calcite ◯ Carbon

Rock Name: ◯ Congomerate ◯ Breccia ◯ Sandstone ◯ Silt Stone
◯ Shale ◯ Rock Salt ◯ Rock Gypsum ◯ Dolostone
◯ Limestone ◯ Bituminous Coal

Metamorphic

Procedure:

Decision 1: TEXTURE
- FOLIATED (minerals start to become aligned, are fully aligned, or are "banded")
- NON-FOLIATED (granular texture, "blurry" form of parent rock)

Decision 2: COMPOSITION (Depends on the "degree" of metamorphism)

Decision 2: COMPOSITION (You can usually still see evidence of the parent material)

ROCK NAME

Texture: ◯ Foliated ◯ Non-Foliated

Grain Size: ◯ Fine ◯ Fine to Medium ◯ Coarse ◯ Fine to Coarse

Composition: ◯ Mica ◯ Quartz ◯ Feldspar ◯ Amphibole
◯ Garnet ◯ Pyroxene ◯ Calcite ◯ Dolomite ◯ Various

Type of Metamorphism: ◯ Regional ◯ Contact

Rock Name: ◯ Slate ◯ Phyllite ◯ Schist ◯ Gneiss
◯ Homfels ◯ Quartzite ◯ Marble ◯ Metaconglomerate

General

Date: _____ GPS Location: _____

Location: ○ Public Land ○ Private Land ○ Pay-to-Dig Site ○ Quarry
○ Roadcut ○ Outcrop ○ Riverbed ○ Creek Bed ○ Beach
○ Mine Tailing ○ Fresh Overturned Soil ○ Other_____

Weather: ○ Sunny & Clear ○ Cloudy/Overcast ○ Windy ○ Rainy / Drizzle
○ Snow ○ Stormy ○ Fog ○ Drought ○ Other_____

Rock Type: ○ Igneous ○ Sedimentary ○ Metamorphic

Equipment Checklist:
(Rockhounding)
○ Eye Protection ○ Heavy-Duty Gloves ○ Boots / Waterproof
○ First-Aid Kit ○ Hard Hat ○ Rock Hammer / Pick ○ Sieve
○ Colander ○ Small Picks ○ Trowel ○ Small Knife ○ Chisel
○ Small Broom ○ Crack Hammer ○ Pry Bar ○ Sledgehammer
○ Mason's Hammer ○ Shovel ○ Backpack ○ Bucket ○ Map
○ Wrapping Material ○ Small Tubes ○ Boxes / Containers
○ Loupe ○ Magnifying Glass ○ Magnet ○ Compass / GPS

Notes: _____

Mineral Identification

Color: ○ Light ○ Dark Specific Colors: _____

Luster: ○ Metallic ○ Gold ○ Brass ○ Bronze ○ Iron ○ Steel ○ Lead ○ Silver ○ Alum.
○ Non-Metallic ○ Adamantine ○ Vitreous ○ Resinous ○ Pearly ○ Dull ○ Greasy ○ Earthy ○ Silky

Cleavage: ○ 1 Direction ○ 2 Directions at 90° ○ 2 Directions not at 90°
○ 3 Directions at 90° (cubic) ○ 3 Directions not at 90° (rhombohedral)
○ 4 Directions (octahedral) ○ 6 Directions (dodecahedral)

Fracture: ○ Conchoidal (smooth, shell-like, or glass-like breaks) ○ Uneven (irregular, but not conchoidal) ○ Hackly (jagged, as of a metal)
○ Splintery (occurs in aggregates of many slender, brittle crystals) ○ Fibrous (occurs in aggregates of many slender, threadlike crystals)

Crystal Habit: ○ Prismatic ○ Acicular ○ Striated ○ Botryoidal ○ Dendritic
○ Nodular ○ Banded ○ Other_____

Hardness: (Mohs Scale)
○ 1 Talc ○ 2 Gypsum ○ 2.5 Fingernail ○ 3 Calcite ○ 4 Fluorite
○ 5 Apatite ○ 5.5 Glass ○ 6 Feldspar ○ 6.5 Steel File
○ 7 Quartz ○ 8 Topaz ○ 9 Corundrum ○ 10 Diamond

Specific Gravity: ○ Average (like quartz = 2.6 - 2.8) ○ Heavy (like galena = 7.5) ○ Light (lighter than quartz = <2.6)

$$\frac{\text{mass of mineral}}{\text{mass of same volume of water}} = \frac{\text{weight of mineral in air}}{\text{weight of equal volume of water}}$$

Tenacity: ○ Brittle ○ Ductile ○ Elastic ○ Flexible ○ Friable
○ Malleable ○ Sectile

Diaphaneity: ○ Transparent ○ Translucent ○ Opaque

Notes: _____

Notes

_____
_____
_____
_____
_____
_____
_____
_____
_____
_____

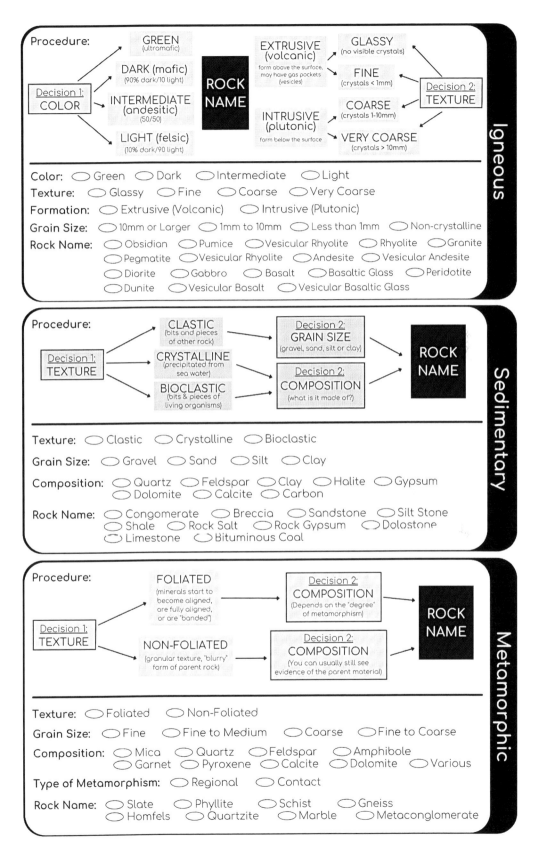

Igneous

Procedure:

Decision 1: COLOR
- GREEN (ultramafic)
- DARK (mafic) (90% dark/10 light)
- INTERMEDIATE (andesitic) (50/50)
- LIGHT (felsic) (10% dark/90 light)

ROCK NAME

EXTRUSIVE (volcanic) form above the surface, may have gas pockets (vesicles)

INTRUSIVE (plutonic) form below the surface

- GLASSY (no visible crystals)
- FINE (crystals < 1mm)
- COARSE (crystals 1-10mm)
- VERY COARSE (crystals > 10mm)

Decision 2: TEXTURE

Color: ◯ Green ◯ Dark ◯ Intermediate ◯ Light

Texture: ◯ Glassy ◯ Fine ◯ Coarse ◯ Very Coarse

Formation: ◯ Extrusive (Volcanic) ◯ Intrusive (Plutonic)

Grain Size: ◯ 10mm or Larger ◯ 1mm to 10mm ◯ Less than 1mm ◯ Non-crystalline

Rock Name: ◯ Obsidian ◯ Pumice ◯ Vesicular Rhyolite ◯ Rhyolite ◯ Granite ◯ Pegmatite ◯ Vesicular Rhyolite ◯ Andesite ◯ Vesicular Andesite ◯ Diorite ◯ Gabbro ◯ Basalt ◯ Basaltic Glass ◯ Peridotite ◯ Dunite ◯ Vesicular Basalt ◯ Vesicular Basaltic Glass

Sedimentary

Procedure:

Decision 1: TEXTURE
- CLASTIC (bits and pieces of other rock)
- CRYSTALLINE (precipitated from sea water)
- BIOCLASTIC (bits & pieces of living organisms)

Decision 2: GRAIN SIZE (gravel, sand, silt or clay)

Decision 2: COMPOSITION (what is it made of?)

ROCK NAME

Texture: ◯ Clastic ◯ Crystalline ◯ Bioclastic

Grain Size: ◯ Gravel ◯ Sand ◯ Silt ◯ Clay

Composition: ◯ Quartz ◯ Feldspar ◯ Clay ◯ Halite ◯ Gypsum ◯ Dolomite ◯ Calcite ◯ Carbon

Rock Name: ◯ Congomerate ◯ Breccia ◯ Sandstone ◯ Silt Stone ◯ Shale ◯ Rock Salt ◯ Rock Gypsum ◯ Dolastone ◯ Limestone ◯ Bituminous Coal

Metamorphic

Procedure:

Decision 1: TEXTURE
- FOLIATED (minerals start to become aligned, are fully aligned, or are "banded")
- NON-FOLIATED (granular texture, "blurry" form of parent rock)

Decision 2: COMPOSITION (Depends on the "degree" of metamorphism)

Decision 2: COMPOSITION (You can usually still see evidence of the parent material)

ROCK NAME

Texture: ◯ Foliated ◯ Non-Foliated

Grain Size: ◯ Fine ◯ Fine to Medium ◯ Coarse ◯ Fine to Coarse

Composition: ◯ Mica ◯ Quartz ◯ Feldspar ◯ Amphibole ◯ Garnet ◯ Pyroxene ◯ Calcite ◯ Dolomite ◯ Various

Type of Metamorphism: ◯ Regional ◯ Contact

Rock Name: ◯ Slate ◯ Phyllite ◯ Schist ◯ Gneiss ◯ Homfels ◯ Quartzite ◯ Marble ◯ Metaconglomerate

General

Date: _____   GPS Location: _____

Location: ○ Public Land ○ Private Land ○ Pay-to-Dig Site ○ Quarry
○ Roadcut ○ Outcrop ○ Riverbed ○ Creek Bed ○ Beach
○ Mine Tailing ○ Fresh Overturned Soil ○ Other_____

Weather: ○ Sunny & Clear ○ Cloudy/Overcast ○ Windy ○ Rainy / Drizzle
○ Snow ○ Stormy ○ Fog ○ Drought ○ Other_____

Rock Type: ○ Igneous ○ Sedimentary ○ Metamorphic

Equipment Checklist:
(Rockhounding)
○ Eye Protection ○ Heavy-Duty Gloves ○ Boots / Waterproof
○ First-Aid Kit ○ Hard Hat ○ Rock Hammer / Pick ○ Sieve
○ Colander ○ Small Picks ○ Trowel ○ Small Knife ○ Chisel
○ Small Broom ○ Crack Hammer ○ Pry Bar ○ Sledgehammer
○ Mason's Hammer ○ Shovel ○ Backpack ○ Bucket ○ Map
○ Wrapping Material ○ Small Tubes ○ Boxes / Containers
○ Loupe ○ Magnifying Glass ○ Magnet ○ Compass / GPS

Notes: _____

Mineral Identification

Color: ○ Light ○ Dark Specific Colors: _____

Luster: ○ Metallic ○ Gold ○ Brass ○ Bronze ○ Iron ○ Steel ○ Lead ○ Silver ○ Alum.
○ Non-Metallic ○ Adamantine ○ Vitreous ○ Resinous ○ Pearly ○ Dull ○ Greasy ○ Earthy ○ Silky

Cleavage: ○ 1 Direction ○ 2 Directions at 90° ○ 2 Directions not at 90°
○ 3 Directions at 90° (cubic) ○ 3 Directions not at 90° (rhombohedral)
○ 4 Directions (octahedral) ○ 6 Directions (dodecahedral)

Fracture: ○ Conchoidal (smooth, shell-like, or glass-like breaks) ○ Uneven (irregular, but not conchoidal) ○ Hackly (jagged, as of a metal)
○ Splintery (occurs in aggregates of many slender, brittle crystals) ○ Fibrous (occurs in aggregates of many slender, threadlike crystals)

Crystal Habit: ○ Prismatic ○ Acicular ○ Striated ○ Botryoidal ○ Dendritic
○ Nodular ○ Banded ○ Other_____

Hardness: (Mohs Scale)
○ 1 Talc ○ 2 Gypsum ○ 2.5 Fingernail ○ 3 Calcite ○ 4 Fluorite
○ 5 Apatite ○ 5.5 Glass ○ 6 Feldspar ○ 6.5 Steel File
○ 7 Quartz ○ 8 Topaz ○ 9 Corundrum ○ 10 Diamond

Specific Gravity:
○ Average (like quartz = 2.6 - 2.8) ○ Heavy (like galena = 7.5) ○ Light (lighter than quartz = <2.6)

$$\frac{\text{mass of mineral}}{\text{mass of same volume of water}} = \frac{\text{weight of mineral in air}}{\text{weight of equal volume of water}}$$

Tenacity: ○ Brittle ○ Ductile ○ Elastic ○ Flexible ○ Friable
○ Malleable ○ Sectile

Diaphaneity: ○ Transparent ○ Translucent ○ Opaque

Notes: _____

Notes

_____
_____
_____
_____
_____
_____
_____
_____
_____
_____

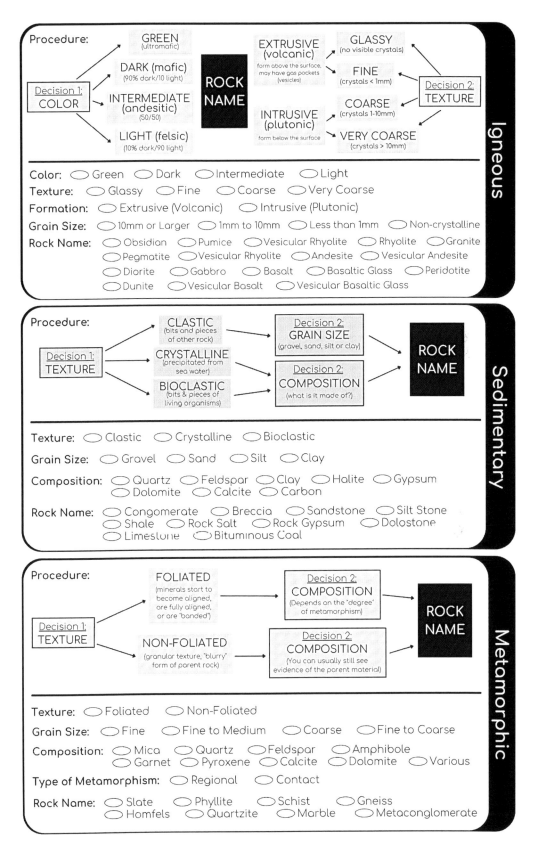

Igneous

Procedure:

Decision 1: COLOR
- GREEN (ultramafic)
- DARK (mafic) (90% dark/10 light)
- INTERMEDIATE (andesitic) (50/50)
- LIGHT (felsic) (10% dark/90 light)

ROCK NAME

EXTRUSIVE (volcanic) form above the surface, may have gas pockets (vesicles)

INTRUSIVE (plutonic) form below the surface

Decision 2: TEXTURE
- GLASSY (no visible crystals)
- FINE (crystals < 1mm)
- COARSE (crystals 1-10mm)
- VERY COARSE (crystals > 10mm)

Color: ◯ Green ◯ Dark ◯ Intermediate ◯ Light

Texture: ◯ Glassy ◯ Fine ◯ Coarse ◯ Very Coarse

Formation: ◯ Extrusive (Volcanic) ◯ Intrusive (Plutonic)

Grain Size: ◯ 10mm or Larger ◯ 1mm to 10mm ◯ Less than 1mm ◯ Non-crystalline

Rock Name: ◯ Obsidian ◯ Pumice ◯ Vesicular Rhyolite ◯ Rhyolite ◯ Granite
◯ Pegmatite ◯ Vesicular Rhyolite ◯ Andesite ◯ Vesicular Andesite
◯ Diorite ◯ Gabbro ◯ Basalt ◯ Basaltic Glass ◯ Peridotite
◯ Dunite ◯ Vesicular Basalt ◯ Vesicular Basaltic Glass

Sedimentary

Procedure:

Decision 1: TEXTURE
- CLASTIC (bits and pieces of other rock)
- CRYSTALLINE (precipitated from sea water)
- BIOCLASTIC (bits & pieces of living organisms)

Decision 2: GRAIN SIZE (gravel, sand, silt or clay)

Decision 2: COMPOSITION (what is it made of?)

ROCK NAME

Texture: ◯ Clastic ◯ Crystalline ◯ Bioclastic

Grain Size: ◯ Gravel ◯ Sand ◯ Silt ◯ Clay

Composition: ◯ Quartz ◯ Feldspar ◯ Clay ◯ Halite ◯ Gypsum
◯ Dolomite ◯ Calcite ◯ Carbon

Rock Name: ◯ Congomerate ◯ Breccia ◯ Sandstone ◯ Silt Stone
◯ Shale ◯ Rock Salt ◯ Rock Gypsum ◯ Dolostone
◯ Limestone ◯ Bituminous Coal

Metamorphic

Procedure:

Decision 1: TEXTURE
- FOLIATED (minerals start to become aligned, are fully aligned, or are "banded")
- NON-FOLIATED (granular texture, "blurry" form of parent rock)

Decision 2: COMPOSITION (Depends on the "degree" of metamorphism)

Decision 2: COMPOSITION (You can usually still see evidence of the parent material)

ROCK NAME

Texture: ◯ Foliated ◯ Non-Foliated

Grain Size: ◯ Fine ◯ Fine to Medium ◯ Coarse ◯ Fine to Coarse

Composition: ◯ Mica ◯ Quartz ◯ Feldspar ◯ Amphibole
◯ Garnet ◯ Pyroxene ◯ Calcite ◯ Dolomite ◯ Various

Type of Metamorphism: ◯ Regional ◯ Contact

Rock Name: ◯ Slate ◯ Phyllite ◯ Schist ◯ Gneiss
◯ Homfels ◯ Quartzite ◯ Marble ◯ Metaconglomerate

General

Date: _____ GPS Location: _____

Location: ○ Public Land ○ Private Land ○ Pay-to-Dig Site ○ Quarry
○ Roadcut ○ Outcrop ○ Riverbed ○ Creek Bed ○ Beach
○ Mine Tailing ○ Fresh Overturned Soil ○ Other_____

Weather: ○ Sunny & Clear ○ Cloudy/Overcast ○ Windy ○ Rainy / Drizzle
○ Snow ○ Stormy ○ Fog ○ Drought ○ Other_____

Rock Type: ○ Igneous ○ Sedimentary ○ Metamorphic

Equipment Checklist:
(Rockhounding)
○ Eye Protection ○ Heavy-Duty Gloves ○ Boots / Waterproof
○ First-Aid Kit ○ Hard Hat ○ Rock Hammer / Pick ○ Sieve
○ Colander ○ Small Picks ○ Trowel ○ Small Knife ○ Chisel
○ Small Broom ○ Crack Hammer ○ Pry Bar ○ Sledgehammer
○ Mason's Hammer ○ Shovel ○ Backpack ○ Bucket ○ Map
○ Wrapping Material ○ Small Tubes ○ Boxes / Containers
○ Loupe ○ Magnifying Glass ○ Magnet ○ Compass / GPS

Notes: _____

Mineral Identification

Color: ○ Light ○ Dark Specific Colors: _____

Luster: ○ Metallic ○ Gold ○ Brass   ○ Non-Metallic ○ Adamantine ○ Vitreous
○ Bronze ○ Iron   ○ Resinous ○ Pearly ○ Dull
○ Steel ○ Lead   ○ Greasy ○ Earthy ○ Silky
○ Silver ○ Alum.

Cleavage: ○ 1 Direction ○ 2 Directions at 90° ○ 2 Directions not at 90°
○ 3 Directions at 90° (cubic) ○ 3 Directions not at 90° (rhombohedral)
○ 4 Directions (octahedral) ○ 6 Directions (dodecahedral)

Fracture: ○ Conchoidal (smooth, shell-like, or glass-like breaks) ○ Uneven (irregular, but not conchoidal) ○ Hackly (jagged, as of a metal)
○ Splintery (occurs in aggregates of many slender, brittle crystals) ○ Fibrous (occurs in aggregates of many slender, threadlike crystals)

Crystal Habit: ○ Prismatic ○ Acicular ○ Striated ○ Botryoidal ○ Dendritic
○ Nodular ○ Banded ○ Other_____

Hardness:
(Mohs Scale)
○ 1 Talc ○ 2 Gypsum ○ 2.5 Fingernail ○ 3 Calcite ○ 4 Fluorite
○ 5 Apatite ○ 5.5 Glass ○ 6 Feldspar ○ 6.5 Steel File
○ 7 Quartz ○ 8 Topaz ○ 9 Corundrum ○ 10 Diamond

Specific Gravity: ○ Average (like quartz = 2.6 - 2.8) ○ Heavy (like galena = 7.5) ○ Light (lighter than quartz = <2.6)

$$\frac{\text{mass of mineral}}{\text{mass of same volume of water}} = \frac{\text{weight of mineral in air}}{\text{weight of equal volume of water}}$$

Tenacity: ○ Brittle ○ Ductile ○ Elastic ○ Flexible ○ Friable
○ Malleable ○ Sectile

Diaphaneity: ○ Transparent ○ Translucent ○ Opaque

Notes:_____

Notes

_____
_____
_____
_____
_____
_____
_____
_____
_____
_____

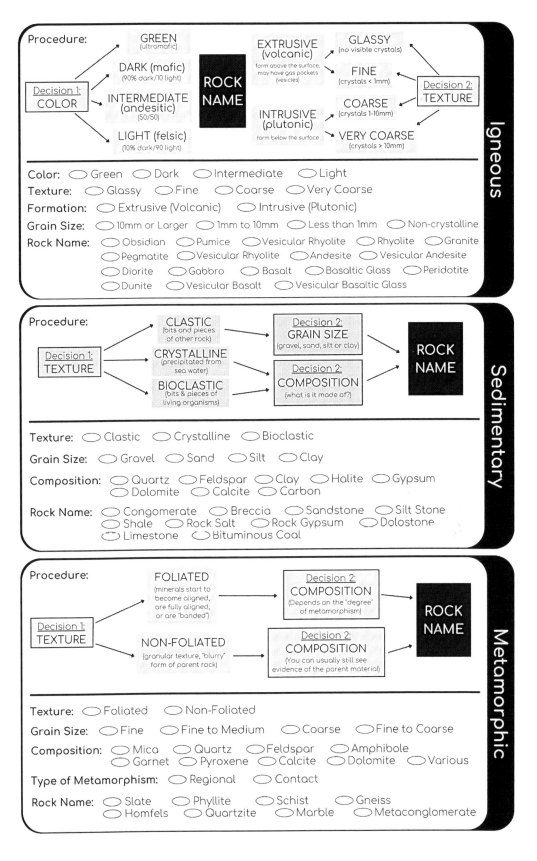

Igneous

Procedure:

Decision 1: COLOR
- GREEN (ultramafic)
- DARK (mafic) (90% dark/10 light)
- INTERMEDIATE (andesitic) (50/50)
- LIGHT (felsic) (10% dark/90 light)

ROCK NAME

- EXTRUSIVE (volcanic) — form above the surface, may have gas pockets (vesicles)
- INTRUSIVE (plutonic) — form below the surface

Decision 2: TEXTURE
- GLASSY (no visible crystals)
- FINE (crystals < 1mm)
- COARSE (crystals 1-10mm)
- VERY COARSE (crystals > 10mm)

Color: ◯ Green ◯ Dark ◯ Intermediate ◯ Light

Texture: ◯ Glassy ◯ Fine ◯ Coarse ◯ Very Coarse

Formation: ◯ Extrusive (Volcanic) ◯ Intrusive (Plutonic)

Grain Size: ◯ 10mm or Larger ◯ 1mm to 10mm ◯ Less than 1mm ◯ Non-crystalline

Rock Name: ◯ Obsidian ◯ Pumice ◯ Vesicular Rhyolite ◯ Rhyolite ◯ Granite ◯ Pegmatite ◯ Vesicular Rhyolite ◯ Andesite ◯ Vesicular Andesite ◯ Diorite ◯ Gabbro ◯ Basalt ◯ Basaltic Glass ◯ Peridotite ◯ Dunite ◯ Vesicular Basalt ◯ Vesicular Basaltic Glass

Sedimentary

Procedure:

Decision 1: TEXTURE
- CLASTIC (bits and pieces of other rock)
- CRYSTALLINE (precipitated from sea water)
- BIOCLASTIC (bits & pieces of living organisms)

Decision 2: GRAIN SIZE (gravel, sand, silt or clay)

Decision 2: COMPOSITION (what is it made of?)

ROCK NAME

Texture: ◯ Clastic ◯ Crystalline ◯ Bioclastic

Grain Size: ◯ Gravel ◯ Sand ◯ Silt ◯ Clay

Composition: ◯ Quartz ◯ Feldspar ◯ Clay ◯ Halite ◯ Gypsum ◯ Dolomite ◯ Calcite ◯ Carbon

Rock Name: ◯ Congomerate ◯ Breccia ◯ Sandstone ◯ Silt Stone ◯ Shale ◯ Rock Salt ◯ Rock Gypsum ◯ Dolostone ◯ Limestone ◯ Bituminous Coal

Metamorphic

Procedure:

Decision 1: TEXTURE
- FOLIATED (minerals start to become aligned, are fully aligned, or are "banded")
- NON-FOLIATED (granular texture, "blurry" form of parent rock)

Decision 2: COMPOSITION (Depends on the "degree" of metamorphism)

Decision 2: COMPOSITION (You can usually still see evidence of the parent material)

ROCK NAME

Texture: ◯ Foliated ◯ Non-Foliated

Grain Size: ◯ Fine ◯ Fine to Medium ◯ Coarse ◯ Fine to Coarse

Composition: ◯ Mica ◯ Quartz ◯ Feldspar ◯ Amphibole ◯ Garnet ◯ Pyroxene ◯ Calcite ◯ Dolomite ◯ Various

Type of Metamorphism: ◯ Regional ◯ Contact

Rock Name: ◯ Slate ◯ Phyllite ◯ Schist ◯ Gneiss ◯ Homfels ◯ Quartzite ◯ Marble ◯ Metaconglomerate

General

Date: _____   GPS Location: _____

Location: ○ Public Land ○ Private Land ○ Pay-to-Dig Site ○ Quarry
○ Roadcut ○ Outcrop ○ Riverbed ○ Creek Bed ○ Beach
○ Mine Tailing ○ Fresh Overturned Soil ○ Other_____

Weather: ○ Sunny & Clear ○ Cloudy/Overcast ○ Windy ○ Rainy / Drizzle
○ Snow ○ Stormy ○ Fog ○ Drought ○ Other_____

Rock Type: ○ Igneous ○ Sedimentary ○ Metamorphic

Equipment Checklist:
(Rockhounding)
○ Eye Protection ○ Heavy-Duty Gloves ○ Boots / Waterproof
○ First-Aid Kit ○ Hard Hat ○ Rock Hammer / Pick ○ Sieve
○ Colander ○ Small Picks ○ Trowel ○ Small Knife ○ Chisel
○ Small Broom ○ Crack Hammer ○ Pry Bar ○ Sledgehammer
○ Mason's Hammer ○ Shovel ○ Backpack ○ Bucket ○ Map
○ Wrapping Material ○ Small Tubes ○ Boxes / Containers
○ Loupe ○ Magnifying Glass ○ Magnet ○ Compass / GPS

Notes: _____

Mineral Identification

Color: ○ Light ○ Dark   Specific Colors: _____

Luster: ○ Metallic ○ Gold ○ Brass   ○ Non-Metallic ○ Adamantine ○ Vitreous
○ Bronze ○ Iron   ○ Resinous ○ Pearly ○ Dull
○ Steel ○ Lead   ○ Greasy ○ Earthy ○ Silky
○ Silver ○ Alum.

Cleavage: ○ 1 Direction ○ 2 Directions at 90° ○ 2 Directions not at 90°
○ 3 Directions at 90° (cubic) ○ 3 Directions not at 90° (rhombohedral)
○ 4 Directions (octahedral) ○ 6 Directions (dodecahedral)

Fracture: ○ Conchoidal (smooth, shell-like, or glass-like breaks) ○ Uneven (irregular, but not conchoidal) ○ Hackly (jagged, as of a metal)
○ Splintery (occurs in aggregates of many slender, brittle crystals) ○ Fibrous (occurs in aggregates of many slender, threadlike crystals)

Crystal Habit: ○ Prismatic ○ Acicular ○ Striated ○ Botryoidal ○ Dendritic
○ Nodular ○ Banded ○ Other_____

Hardness:
(Mohs Scale)
○ 1 Talc ○ 2 Gypsum ○ 2.5 Fingernail ○ 3 Calcite ○ 4 Fluorite
○ 5 Apatite ○ 5.5 Glass ○ 6 Feldspar ○ 6.5 Steel File
○ 7 Quartz ○ 8 Topaz ○ 9 Corundrum ○ 10 Diamond

Specific Gravity: ○ Average (like quartz = 2.6 - 2.8) $\frac{\text{mass of mineral}}{\text{mass of same volume of water}}$ = $\frac{\text{weight of mineral in air}}{\text{weight of equal volume of water}}$
○ Heavy (like galena = 7.5)
○ Light (lighter than quartz = <2.6)

Tenacity: ○ Brittle ○ Ductile ○ Elastic ○ Flexible ○ Friable
○ Malleable ○ Sectile

Diaphaneity: ○ Transparent ○ Translucent ○ Opaque

Notes: _____

Notes

_____
_____
_____
_____
_____
_____
_____
_____
_____
_____

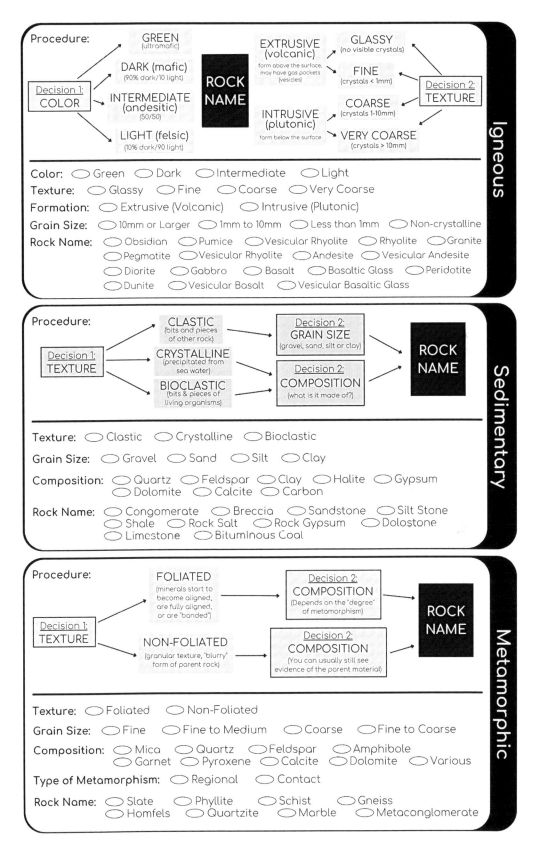

Igneous

Procedure:

Decision 1: COLOR
- GREEN (ultramafic)
- DARK (mafic) (90% dark/10 light)
- INTERMEDIATE (andesitic) (50/50)
- LIGHT (felsic) (10% dark/90 light)

ROCK NAME

- EXTRUSIVE (volcanic) — form above the surface, may have gas pockets (vesicles)
- INTRUSIVE (plutonic) — form below the surface

Decision 2: TEXTURE
- GLASSY (no visible crystals)
- FINE (crystals < 1mm)
- COARSE (crystals 1-10mm)
- VERY COARSE (crystals > 10mm)

Color: ◯ Green ◯ Dark ◯ Intermediate ◯ Light

Texture: ◯ Glassy ◯ Fine ◯ Coarse ◯ Very Coarse

Formation: ◯ Extrusive (Volcanic) ◯ Intrusive (Plutonic)

Grain Size: ◯ 10mm or Larger ◯ 1mm to 10mm ◯ Less than 1mm ◯ Non-crystalline

Rock Name: ◯ Obsidian ◯ Pumice ◯ Vesicular Rhyolite ◯ Rhyolite ◯ Granite
◯ Pegmatite ◯ Vesicular Rhyolite ◯ Andesite ◯ Vesicular Andesite
◯ Diorite ◯ Gabbro ◯ Basalt ◯ Basaltic Glass ◯ Peridotite
◯ Dunite ◯ Vesicular Basalt ◯ Vesicular Basaltic Glass

Sedimentary

Procedure:

Decision 1: TEXTURE
- CLASTIC (bits and pieces of other rock)
- CRYSTALLINE (precipitated from sea water)
- BIOCLASTIC (bits & pieces of living organisms)

Decision 2: GRAIN SIZE (gravel, sand, silt or clay)

Decision 2: COMPOSITION (what is it made of?)

ROCK NAME

Texture: ◯ Clastic ◯ Crystalline ◯ Bioclastic

Grain Size: ◯ Gravel ◯ Sand ◯ Silt ◯ Clay

Composition: ◯ Quartz ◯ Feldspar ◯ Clay ◯ Halite ◯ Gypsum
◯ Dolomite ◯ Calcite ◯ Carbon

Rock Name: ◯ Conglomerate ◯ Breccia ◯ Sandstone ◯ Silt Stone
◯ Shale ◯ Rock Salt ◯ Rock Gypsum ◯ Dolostone
◯ Limestone ◯ Bituminous Coal

Metamorphic

Procedure:

Decision 1: TEXTURE
- FOLIATED (minerals start to become aligned, are fully aligned, or are "banded")
- NON-FOLIATED (granular texture, "blurry" form of parent rock)

Decision 2: COMPOSITION (Depends on the "degree" of metamorphism)

Decision 2: COMPOSITION (You can usually still see evidence of the parent material)

ROCK NAME

Texture: ◯ Foliated ◯ Non-Foliated

Grain Size: ◯ Fine ◯ Fine to Medium ◯ Coarse ◯ Fine to Coarse

Composition: ◯ Mica ◯ Quartz ◯ Feldspar ◯ Amphibole
◯ Garnet ◯ Pyroxene ◯ Calcite ◯ Dolomite ◯ Various

Type of Metamorphism: ◯ Regional ◯ Contact

Rock Name: ◯ Slate ◯ Phyllite ◯ Schist ◯ Gneiss
◯ Homfels ◯ Quartzite ◯ Marble ◯ Metaconglomerate

General

Date: _____ GPS Location: _____

Location: ○ Public Land ○ Private Land ○ Pay-to-Dig Site ○ Quarry
○ Roadcut ○ Outcrop ○ Riverbed ○ Creek Bed ○ Beach
○ Mine Tailing ○ Fresh Overturned Soil ○ Other_____

Weather: ○ Sunny & Clear ○ Cloudy/Overcast ○ Windy ○ Rainy / Drizzle
○ Snow ○ Stormy ○ Fog ○ Drought ○ Other_____

Rock Type: ○ Igneous ○ Sedimentary ○ Metamorphic

Equipment Checklist:
(Rockhounding)
○ Eye Protection ○ Heavy-Duty Gloves ○ Boots / Waterproof
○ First-Aid Kit ○ Hard Hat ○ Rock Hammer / Pick ○ Sieve
○ Colander ○ Small Picks ○ Trowel ○ Small Knife ○ Chisel
○ Small Broom ○ Crack Hammer ○ Pry Bar ○ Sledgehammer
○ Mason's Hammer ○ Shovel ○ Backpack ○ Bucket ○ Map
○ Wrapping Material ○ Small Tubes ○ Boxes / Containers
○ Loupe ○ Magnifying Glass ○ Magnet ○ Compass / GPS

Notes: _____

Mineral Identification

Color: ○ Light ○ Dark Specific Colors: _____

Luster: ○ Metallic ○ Gold ○ Brass ○ Bronze ○ Iron ○ Steel ○ Lead ○ Silver ○ Alum.
○ Non-Metallic ○ Adamantine ○ Vitreous ○ Resinous ○ Pearly ○ Dull ○ Greasy ○ Earthy ○ Silky

Cleavage: ○ 1 Direction ○ 2 Directions at 90° ○ 2 Directions not at 90°
○ 3 Directions at 90° (cubic) ○ 3 Directions not at 90° (rhombohedral)
○ 4 Directions (octahedral) ○ 6 Directions (dodecahedral)

Fracture: ○ Conchoidal (smooth, shell-like, or glass-like breaks) ○ Uneven (irregular, but not conchoidal) ○ Hackly (jagged, as of a metal)
○ Splintery (occurs in aggregates of many slender, brittle crystals) ○ Fibrous (occurs in aggregates of many slender, threadlike crystals)

Crystal Habit: ○ Prismatic ○ Acicular ○ Striated ○ Botryoidal ○ Dendritic
○ Nodular ○ Banded ○ Other_____

Hardness:
(Mohs Scale)
○ 1 Talc ○ 2 Gypsum ○ 2.5 Fingernail ○ 3 Calcite ○ 4 Fluorite
○ 5 Apatite ○ 5.5 Glass ○ 6 Feldspar ○ 6.5 Steel File
○ 7 Quartz ○ 8 Topaz ○ 9 Corundrum ○ 10 Diamond

Specific Gravity: ○ Average (like quartz = 2.6 - 2.8) ○ Heavy (like galena = 7.5) ○ Light (lighter than quartz = <2.6)

$$\frac{\text{mass of mineral}}{\text{mass of same volume of water}} = \frac{\text{weight of mineral in air}}{\text{weight of equal volume of water}}$$

Tenacity: ○ Brittle ○ Ductile ○ Elastic ○ Flexible ○ Friable
○ Malleable ○ Sectile

Diaphaneity: ○ Transparent ○ Translucent ○ Opaque

Notes: _____

Notes

_____
_____
_____
_____
_____
_____
_____
_____
_____

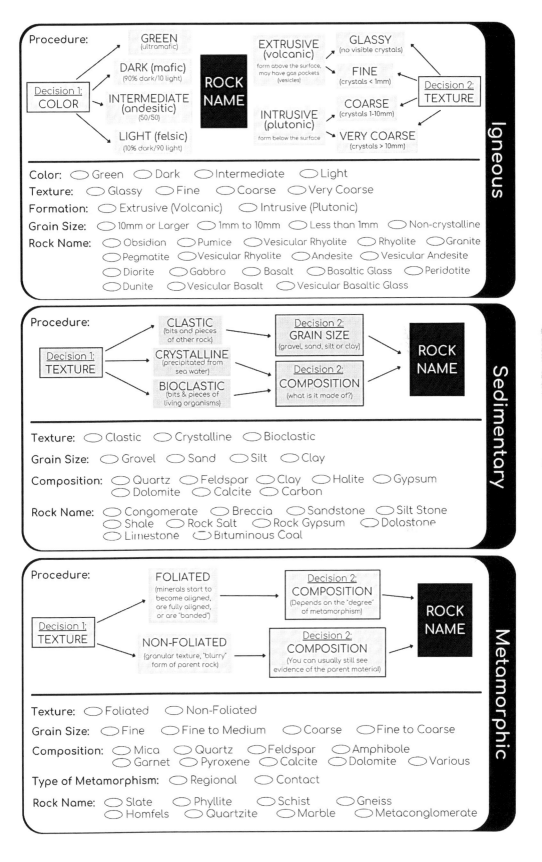

Igneous

Procedure:

Decision 1: COLOR →
- GREEN (ultramafic)
- DARK (mafic) (90% dark/10 light)
- INTERMEDIATE (andesitic) (50/50)
- LIGHT (felsic) (10% dark/90 light)

ROCK NAME

EXTRUSIVE (volcanic) form above the surface, may have gas pockets (vesicles)

INTRUSIVE (plutonic) form below the surface

Decision 2: TEXTURE →
- GLASSY (no visible crystals)
- FINE (crystals < 1mm)
- COARSE (crystals 1-10mm)
- VERY COARSE (crystals > 10mm)

Color: ◯ Green ◯ Dark ◯ Intermediate ◯ Light

Texture: ◯ Glassy ◯ Fine ◯ Coarse ◯ Very Coarse

Formation: ◯ Extrusive (Volcanic) ◯ Intrusive (Plutonic)

Grain Size: ◯ 10mm or Larger ◯ 1mm to 10mm ◯ Less than 1mm ◯ Non-crystalline

Rock Name: ◯ Obsidian ◯ Pumice ◯ Vesicular Rhyolite ◯ Rhyolite ◯ Granite ◯ Pegmatite ◯ Vesicular Rhyolite ◯ Andesite ◯ Vesicular Andesite ◯ Diorite ◯ Gabbro ◯ Basalt ◯ Basaltic Glass ◯ Peridotite ◯ Dunite ◯ Vesicular Basalt ◯ Vesicular Basaltic Glass

Sedimentary

Procedure:

Decision 1: TEXTURE →
- CLASTIC (bits and pieces of other rock)
- CRYSTALLINE (precipitated from sea water)
- BIOCLASTIC (bits & pieces of living organisms)

Decision 2: GRAIN SIZE (gravel, sand, silt or clay)

Decision 2: COMPOSITION (what is it made of?)

→ ROCK NAME

Texture: ◯ Clastic ◯ Crystalline ◯ Bioclastic

Grain Size: ◯ Gravel ◯ Sand ◯ Silt ◯ Clay

Composition: ◯ Quartz ◯ Feldspar ◯ Clay ◯ Halite ◯ Gypsum ◯ Dolomite ◯ Calcite ◯ Carbon

Rock Name: ◯ Congomerate ◯ Breccia ◯ Sandstone ◯ Silt Stone ◯ Shale ◯ Rock Salt ◯ Rock Gypsum ◯ Dolostone ◯ Limestone ◯ Bituminous Coal

Metamorphic

Procedure:

Decision 1: TEXTURE →
- FOLIATED (minerals start to become aligned, are fully aligned, or are "banded")
- NON-FOLIATED (granular texture, "blurry" form of parent rock)

Decision 2: COMPOSITION (Depends on the "degree" of metamorphism)

Decision 2: COMPOSITION (You can usually still see evidence of the parent material)

→ ROCK NAME

Texture: ◯ Foliated ◯ Non-Foliated

Grain Size: ◯ Fine ◯ Fine to Medium ◯ Coarse ◯ Fine to Coarse

Composition: ◯ Mica ◯ Quartz ◯ Feldspar ◯ Amphibole ◯ Garnet ◯ Pyroxene ◯ Calcite ◯ Dolomite ◯ Various

Type of Metamorphism: ◯ Regional ◯ Contact

Rock Name: ◯ Slate ◯ Phyllite ◯ Schist ◯ Gneiss ◯ Homfels ◯ Quartzite ◯ Marble ◯ Metaconglomerate

General

Date: _____ GPS Location: _____

Location: ⊙ Public Land ⊙ Private Land ⊙ Pay-to-Dig Site ⊙ Quarry
⊙ Roadcut ⊙ Outcrop ⊙ Riverbed ⊙ Creek Bed ⊙ Beach
⊙ Mine Tailing ⊙ Fresh Overturned Soil ⊙ Other_____

Weather: ⊙ Sunny & Clear ⊙ Cloudy/Overcast ⊙ Windy ⊙ Rainy / Drizzle
⊙ Snow ⊙ Stormy ⊙ Fog ⊙ Drought ⊙ Other_____

Rock Type: ⊙ Igneous ⊙ Sedimentary ⊙ Metamorphic

Equipment Checklist: (Rockhounding)
⊙ Eye Protection ⊙ Heavy-Duty Gloves ⊙ Boots / Waterproof
⊙ First-Aid Kit ⊙ Hard Hat ⊙ Rock Hammer / Pick ⊙ Sieve
⊙ Colander ⊙ Small Picks ⊙ Trowel ⊙ Small Knife ⊙ Chisel
⊙ Small Broom ⊙ Crack Hammer ⊙ Pry Bar ⊙ Sledgehammer
⊙ Mason's Hammer ⊙ Shovel ⊙ Backpack ⊙ Bucket ⊙ Map
⊙ Wrapping Material ⊙ Small Tubes ⊙ Boxes / Containers
⊙ Loupe ⊙ Magnifying Glass ⊙ Magnet ⊙ Compass / GPS

Notes: _____

Mineral Identification

Color: ⊙ Light ⊙ Dark Specific Colors: _____

Luster: ⊙ Metallic ⊙ Gold ⊙ Brass ⊙ Bronze ⊙ Iron ⊙ Steel ⊙ Lead ⊙ Silver ⊙ Alum.
⊙ Non-Metallic ⊙ Adamantine ⊙ Vitreous ⊙ Resinous ⊙ Pearly ⊙ Dull ⊙ Greasy ⊙ Earthy ⊙ Silky

Cleavage: ⊙ 1 Direction ⊙ 2 Directions at 90° ⊙ 2 Directions not at 90°
⊙ 3 Directions at 90° (cubic) ⊙ 3 Directions not at 90° (rhombohedral)
⊙ 4 Directions (octahedral) ⊙ 6 Directions (dodecahedral)

Fracture: ⊙ Conchoidal (smooth, shell-like, or glass-like breaks) ⊙ Uneven (irregular, but not conchoidal) ⊙ Hackly (jagged, as of a metal)
⊙ Splintery (occurs in aggregates of many slender, brittle crystals) ⊙ Fibrous (occurs in aggregates of many slender, threadlike crystals)

Crystal Habit: ⊙ Prismatic ⊙ Acicular ⊙ Striated ⊙ Botryoidal ⊙ Dendritic
⊙ Nodular ⊙ Banded ⊙ Other_____

Hardness: (Mohs Scale)
⊙ 1 Talc ⊙ 2 Gypsum ⊙ 2.5 Fingernail ⊙ 3 Calcite ⊙ 4 Fluorite
⊙ 5 Apatite ⊙ 5.5 Glass ⊙ 6 Feldspar ⊙ 6.5 Steel File
⊙ 7 Quartz ⊙ 8 Topaz ⊙ 9 Corundrum ⊙ 10 Diamond

Specific Gravity: ⊙ Average (like quartz = 2.6 - 2.8) ⊙ Heavy (like galena = 7.5) ⊙ Light (lighter than quartz = <2.6)

$$\frac{\text{mass of mineral}}{\text{mass of same volume of water}} = \frac{\text{weight of mineral in air}}{\text{weight of equal volume of water}}$$

Tenacity: ⊙ Brittle ⊙ Ductile ⊙ Elastic ⊙ Flexible ⊙ Friable
⊙ Malleable ⊙ Sectile

Diaphaneity: ⊙ Transparent ⊙ Translucent ⊙ Opaque

Notes: _____

Notes

_____
_____
_____
_____
_____
_____
_____
_____
_____

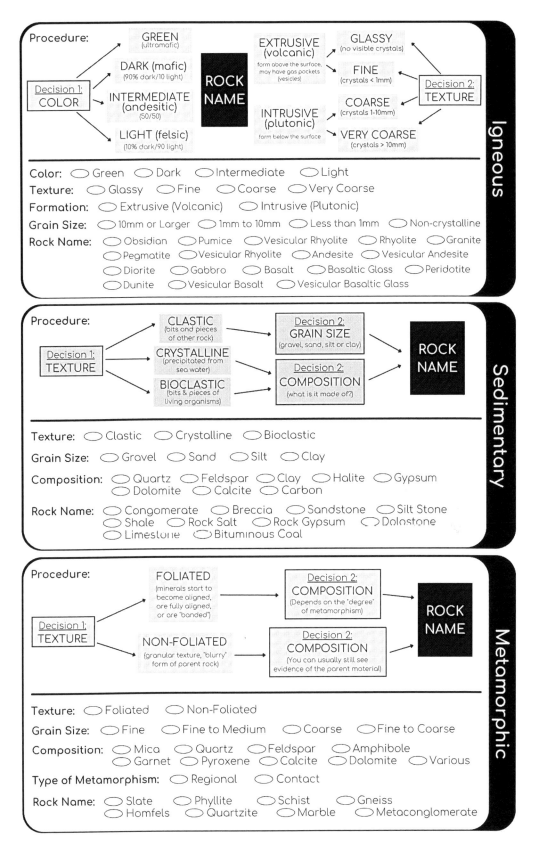

Igneous

Procedure:

Decision 1: COLOR
- GREEN (ultramafic)
- DARK (mafic) (90% dark/10 light)
- INTERMEDIATE (andesitic) (50/50)
- LIGHT (felsic) (10% dark/90 light)

ROCK NAME

EXTRUSIVE (volcanic) — form above the surface, may have gas pockets (vesicles)
INTRUSIVE (plutonic) — form below the surface

Decision 2: TEXTURE
- GLASSY (no visible crystals)
- FINE (crystals < 1mm)
- COARSE (crystals 1-10mm)
- VERY COARSE (crystals > 10mm)

Color: ◯ Green ◯ Dark ◯ Intermediate ◯ Light

Texture: ◯ Glassy ◯ Fine ◯ Coarse ◯ Very Coarse

Formation: ◯ Extrusive (Volcanic) ◯ Intrusive (Plutonic)

Grain Size: ◯ 10mm or Larger ◯ 1mm to 10mm ◯ Less than 1mm ◯ Non-crystalline

Rock Name: ◯ Obsidian ◯ Pumice ◯ Vesicular Rhyolite ◯ Rhyolite ◯ Granite
◯ Pegmatite ◯ Vesicular Rhyolite ◯ Andesite ◯ Vesicular Andesite
◯ Diorite ◯ Gabbro ◯ Basalt ◯ Basaltic Glass ◯ Peridotite
◯ Dunite ◯ Vesicular Basalt ◯ Vesicular Basaltic Glass

Sedimentary

Procedure:

Decision 1: TEXTURE
- CLASTIC (bits and pieces of other rock)
- CRYSTALLINE (precipitated from sea water)
- BIOCLASTIC (bits & pieces of living organisms)

Decision 2: GRAIN SIZE (gravel, sand, silt or clay)
Decision 2: COMPOSITION (what is it made of?)

ROCK NAME

Texture: ◯ Clastic ◯ Crystalline ◯ Bioclastic

Grain Size: ◯ Gravel ◯ Sand ◯ Silt ◯ Clay

Composition: ◯ Quartz ◯ Feldspar ◯ Clay ◯ Halite ◯ Gypsum
◯ Dolomite ◯ Calcite ◯ Carbon

Rock Name: ◯ Congomerate ◯ Breccia ◯ Sandstone ◯ Silt Stone
◯ Shale ◯ Rock Salt ◯ Rock Gypsum ◯ Dolostone
◯ Limestone ◯ Bituminous Coal

Metamorphic

Procedure:

Decision 1: TEXTURE
- FOLIATED (minerals start to become aligned, are fully aligned, or are "banded")
- NON-FOLIATED (granular texture, "blurry" form of parent rock)

Decision 2: COMPOSITION (Depends on the "degree" of metamorphism)
Decision 2: COMPOSITION (You can usually still see evidence of the parent material)

ROCK NAME

Texture: ◯ Foliated ◯ Non-Foliated

Grain Size: ◯ Fine ◯ Fine to Medium ◯ Coarse ◯ Fine to Coarse

Composition: ◯ Mica ◯ Quartz ◯ Feldspar ◯ Amphibole
◯ Garnet ◯ Pyroxene ◯ Calcite ◯ Dolomite ◯ Various

Type of Metamorphism: ◯ Regional ◯ Contact

Rock Name: ◯ Slate ◯ Phyllite ◯ Schist ◯ Gneiss
◯ Homfels ◯ Quartzite ◯ Marble ◯ Metaconglomerate

General

Date: _____ GPS Location: _____

Location: ○ Public Land   ○ Private Land   ○ Pay-to-Dig Site   ○ Quarry
○ Roadcut   ○ Outcrop   ○ Riverbed   ○ Creek Bed   ○ Beach
○ Mine Tailing   ○ Fresh Overturned Soil   ○ Other_____

Weather: ○ Sunny & Clear   ○ Cloudy/Overcast   ○ Windy   ○ Rainy / Drizzle
○ Snow   ○ Stormy   ○ Fog   ○ Drought   ○ Other_____

Rock Type: ○ Igneous   ○ Sedimentary   ○ Metamorphic

Equipment Checklist:
(Rockhounding)
○ Eye Protection   ○ Heavy-Duty Gloves   ○ Boots / Waterproof
○ First-Aid Kit   ○ Hard Hat   ○ Rock Hammer / Pick   ○ Sieve
○ Colander   ○ Small Picks   ○ Trowel   ○ Small Knife   ○ Chisel
○ Small Broom   ○ Crack Hammer   ○ Pry Bar   ○ Sledgehammer
○ Mason's Hammer   ○ Shovel   ○ Backpack   ○ Bucket   ○ Map
○ Wrapping Material   ○ Small Tubes   ○ Boxes / Containers
○ Loupe   ○ Magnifying Glass   ○ Magnet   ○ Compass / GPS

Notes: _____

Mineral Identification

Color: ○ Light   ○ Dark   Specific Colors: _____

Luster: ○ Metallic ○ Gold ○ Brass   ○ Non-Metallic ○ Adamantine ○ Vitreous
○ Bronze ○ Iron   ○ Resinous ○ Pearly ○ Dull
○ Steel ○ Lead   ○ Greasy ○ Earthy ○ Silky
○ Silver ○ Alum.

Cleavage: ○ 1 Direction   ○ 2 Directions at 90°   ○ 2 Directions not at 90°
○ 3 Directions at 90° (cubic)   ○ 3 Directions not at 90° (rhombohedral)
○ 4 Directions (octahedral)   ○ 6 Directions (dodecahedral)

Fracture: ○ Conchoidal (smooth, shell-like, or glass-like breaks)   ○ Uneven (irregular, but not conchoidal)   ○ Hackly (jagged, as of a metal)
○ Splintery (occurs in aggregates of many slender, brittle crystals)   ○ Fibrous (occurs in aggregates of many slender, threadlike crystals)

Crystal Habit: ○ Prismatic   ○ Acicular   ○ Striated   ○ Botryoidal   ○ Dendritic
○ Nodular   ○ Banded   ○ Other_____

Hardness: (Mohs Scale)
○ 1 Talc   ○ 2 Gypsum   ○ 2.5 Fingernail   ○ 3 Calcite   ○ 4 Fluorite
○ 5 Apatite   ○ 5.5 Glass   ○ 6 Feldspar   ○ 6.5 Steel File
○ 7 Quartz   ○ 8 Topaz   ○ 9 Corundrum   ○ 10 Diamond

Specific Gravity:
○ Average (like quartz = 2.6 - 2.8)
○ Heavy (like galena = 7.5)
○ Light (lighter than quartz = <2.6)

$$\frac{\text{mass of mineral}}{\text{mass of same volume of water}} = \frac{\text{weight of mineral in air}}{\text{weight of equal volume of water}}$$

Tenacity: ○ Brittle   ○ Ductile   ○ Elastic   ○ Flexible   ○ Friable
○ Malleable   ○ Sectile

Diaphaneity: ○ Transparent   ○ Translucent   ○ Opaque

Notes: _____

Notes

_____
_____
_____
_____
_____
_____
_____
_____
_____
_____

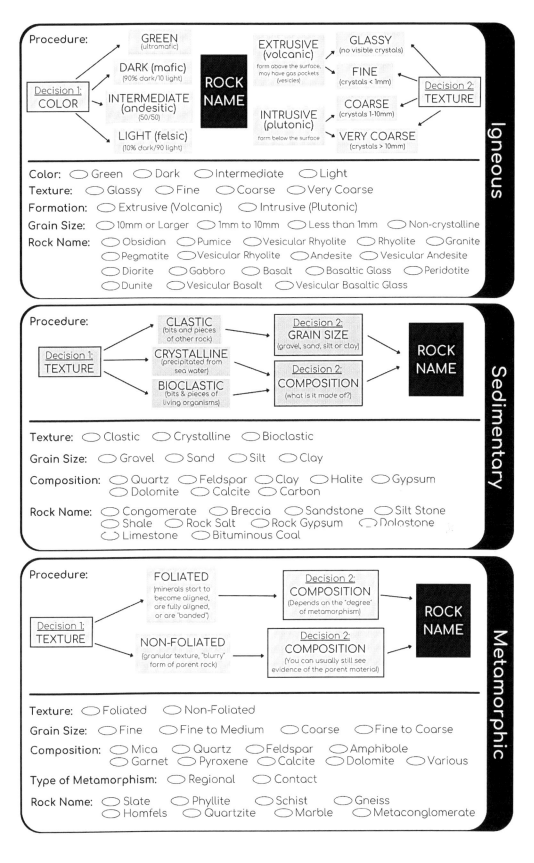

Igneous

Procedure:

Decision 1: COLOR →
- GREEN (ultramafic)
- DARK (mafic) (90% dark/10 light)
- INTERMEDIATE (andesitic) (50/50)
- LIGHT (felsic) (10% dark/90 light)

ROCK NAME

EXTRUSIVE (volcanic) — form above the surface, may have gas pockets (vesicles) →
- GLASSY (no visible crystals)
- FINE (crystals < 1mm)

INTRUSIVE (plutonic) — form below the surface →
- COARSE (crystals 1-10mm)
- VERY COARSE (crystals > 10mm)

Decision 2: TEXTURE

Color: ○ Green ○ Dark ○ Intermediate ○ Light

Texture: ○ Glassy ○ Fine ○ Coarse ○ Very Coarse

Formation: ○ Extrusive (Volcanic) ○ Intrusive (Plutonic)

Grain Size: ○ 10mm or Larger ○ 1mm to 10mm ○ Less than 1mm ○ Non-crystalline

Rock Name: ○ Obsidian ○ Pumice ○ Vesicular Rhyolite ○ Rhyolite ○ Granite
○ Pegmatite ○ Vesicular Rhyolite ○ Andesite ○ Vesicular Andesite
○ Diorite ○ Gabbro ○ Basalt ○ Basaltic Glass ○ Peridotite
○ Dunite ○ Vesicular Basalt ○ Vesicular Basaltic Glass

Sedimentary

Procedure:

Decision 1: TEXTURE →
- CLASTIC (bits and pieces of other rock)
- CRYSTALLINE (precipitated from sea water)
- BIOCLASTIC (bits & pieces of living organisms)

Decision 2: GRAIN SIZE (gravel, sand, silt or clay)

Decision 2: COMPOSITION (what is it made of?)

→ ROCK NAME

Texture: ○ Clastic ○ Crystalline ○ Bioclastic

Grain Size: ○ Gravel ○ Sand ○ Silt ○ Clay

Composition: ○ Quartz ○ Feldspar ○ Clay ○ Halite ○ Gypsum
○ Dolomite ○ Calcite ○ Carbon

Rock Name: ○ Conglomerate ○ Breccia ○ Sandstone ○ Silt Stone
○ Shale ○ Rock Salt ○ Rock Gypsum ○ Dolostone
○ Limestone ○ Bituminous Coal

Metamorphic

Procedure:

Decision 1: TEXTURE →
- FOLIATED (minerals start to become aligned, are fully aligned, or are "banded")
- NON-FOLIATED (granular texture, "blurry" form of parent rock)

Decision 2: COMPOSITION (Depends on the "degree" of metamorphism)

Decision 2: COMPOSITION (You can usually still see evidence of the parent material)

→ ROCK NAME

Texture: ○ Foliated ○ Non-Foliated

Grain Size: ○ Fine ○ Fine to Medium ○ Coarse ○ Fine to Coarse

Composition: ○ Mica ○ Quartz ○ Feldspar ○ Amphibole
○ Garnet ○ Pyroxene ○ Calcite ○ Dolomite ○ Various

Type of Metamorphism: ○ Regional ○ Contact

Rock Name: ○ Slate ○ Phyllite ○ Schist ○ Gneiss
○ Homfels ○ Quartzite ○ Marble ○ Metaconglomerate

General

Date: _____ GPS Location: _____

Location: ◯ Public Land ◯ Private Land ◯ Pay-to-Dig Site ◯ Quarry
◯ Roadcut ◯ Outcrop ◯ Riverbed ◯ Creek Bed ◯ Beach
◯ Mine Tailing ◯ Fresh Overturned Soil ◯ Other_____

Weather: ◯ Sunny & Clear ◯ Cloudy/Overcast ◯ Windy ◯ Rainy / Drizzle
◯ Snow ◯ Stormy ◯ Fog ◯ Drought ◯ Other_____

Rock Type: ◯ Igneous ◯ Sedimentary ◯ Metamorphic

Equipment Checklist:
(Rockhounding)
◯ Eye Protection ◯ Heavy-Duty Gloves ◯ Boots / Waterproof
◯ First-Aid Kit ◯ Hard Hat ◯ Rock Hammer / Pick ◯ Sieve
◯ Colander ◯ Small Picks ◯ Trowel ◯ Small Knife ◯ Chisel
◯ Small Broom ◯ Crack Hammer ◯ Pry Bar ◯ Sledgehammer
◯ Mason's Hammer ◯ Shovel ◯ Backpack ◯ Bucket ◯ Map
◯ Wrapping Material ◯ Small Tubes ◯ Boxes / Containers
◯ Loupe ◯ Magnifying Glass ◯ Magnet ◯ Compass / GPS

Notes: _____

Mineral Identification

Color: ◯ Light ◯ Dark Specific Colors: _____

Luster: ◯ Metallic ◯ Gold ◯ Brass ◯ Non-Metallic ◯ Adamantine ◯ Vitreous
◯ Bronze ◯ Iron ◯ Resinous ◯ Pearly ◯ Dull
◯ Steel ◯ Lead ◯ Greasy ◯ Earthy ◯ Silky
◯ Silver ◯ Alum.

Cleavage: ◯ 1 Direction ◯ 2 Directions at 90° ◯ 2 Directions not at 90°
◯ 3 Directions at 90° (cubic) ◯ 3 Directions not at 90° (rhombohedral)
◯ 4 Directions (octahedral) ◯ 6 Directions (dodecahedral)

Fracture: ◯ Conchoidal (smooth, shell-like, or glass-like breaks) ◯ Uneven (irregular, but not conchoidal) ◯ Hackly (jagged, as of a metal)
◯ Splintery (occurs in aggregates of many slender, brittle crystals) ◯ Fibrous (occurs in aggregates of many slender, threadlike crystals)

Crystal Habit: ◯ Prismatic ◯ Acicular ◯ Striated ◯ Botryoidal ◯ Dendritic
◯ Nodular ◯ Banded ◯ Other_____

Hardness: (Mohs Scale)
◯ 1 Talc ◯ 2 Gypsum ◯ 2.5 Fingernail ◯ 3 Calcite ◯ 4 Fluorite
◯ 5 Apatite ◯ 5.5 Glass ◯ 6 Feldspar ◯ 6.5 Steel File
◯ 7 Quartz ◯ 8 Topaz ◯ 9 Corundrum ◯ 10 Diamond

Specific Gravity:
◯ Average (like quartz = 2.6 - 2.8) $\frac{\text{mass of mineral}}{\text{mass of same volume of water}} = \frac{\text{weight of mineral in air}}{\text{weight of equal volume of water}}$
◯ Heavy (like galena = 7.5)
◯ Light (lighter than quartz = <2.6)

Tenacity: ◯ Brittle ◯ Ductile ◯ Elastic ◯ Flexible ◯ Friable
◯ Malleable ◯ Sectile

Diaphaneity: ◯ Transparent ◯ Translucent ◯ Opaque

Notes: _____

Notes

_____
_____
_____
_____
_____
_____
_____
_____
_____

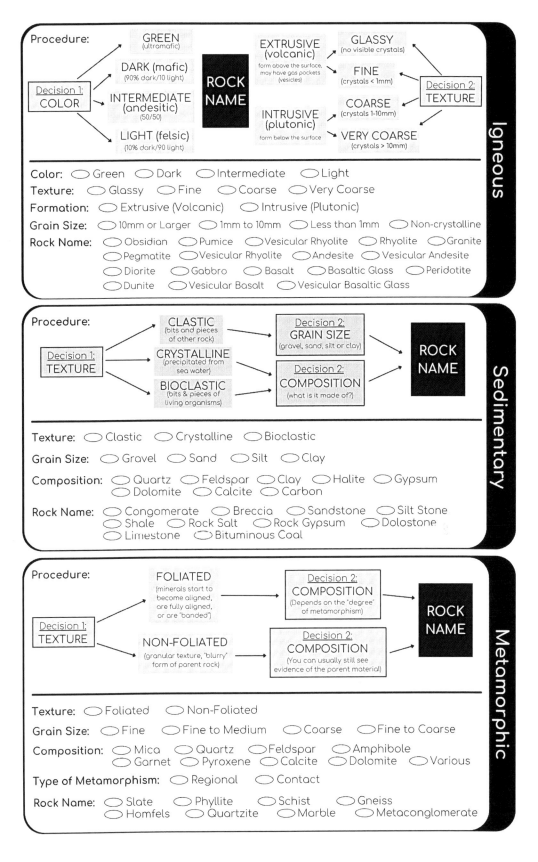

Igneous

Procedure:

Decision 1: COLOR →
- GREEN (ultramafic)
- DARK (mafic) (90% dark/10 light)
- INTERMEDIATE (andesitic) (50/50)
- LIGHT (felsic) (10% dark/90 light)

ROCK NAME

- EXTRUSIVE (volcanic) — form above the surface, may have gas pockets (vesicles)
- INTRUSIVE (plutonic) — form below the surface

Decision 2: TEXTURE →
- GLASSY (no visible crystals)
- FINE (crystals < 1mm)
- COARSE (crystals 1-10mm)
- VERY COARSE (crystals > 10mm)

Color: ◯ Green ◯ Dark ◯ Intermediate ◯ Light

Texture: ◯ Glassy ◯ Fine ◯ Coarse ◯ Very Coarse

Formation: ◯ Extrusive (Volcanic) ◯ Intrusive (Plutonic)

Grain Size: ◯ 10mm or Larger ◯ 1mm to 10mm ◯ Less than 1mm ◯ Non-crystalline

Rock Name: ◯ Obsidian ◯ Pumice ◯ Vesicular Rhyolite ◯ Rhyolite ◯ Granite ◯ Pegmatite ◯ Vesicular Rhyolite ◯ Andesite ◯ Vesicular Andesite ◯ Diorite ◯ Gabbro ◯ Basalt ◯ Basaltic Glass ◯ Peridotite ◯ Dunite ◯ Vesicular Basalt ◯ Vesicular Basaltic Glass

Sedimentary

Procedure:

Decision 1: TEXTURE →
- CLASTIC (bits and pieces of other rock)
- CRYSTALLINE (precipitated from sea water)
- BIOCLASTIC (bits & pieces of living organisms)

Decision 2: GRAIN SIZE (gravel, sand, silt or clay)
Decision 2: COMPOSITION (what is it made of?)

ROCK NAME

Texture: ◯ Clastic ◯ Crystalline ◯ Bioclastic

Grain Size: ◯ Gravel ◯ Sand ◯ Silt ◯ Clay

Composition: ◯ Quartz ◯ Feldspar ◯ Clay ◯ Halite ◯ Gypsum ◯ Dolomite ◯ Calcite ◯ Carbon

Rock Name: ◯ Congomerate ◯ Breccia ◯ Sandstone ◯ Silt Stone ◯ Shale ◯ Rock Salt ◯ Rock Gypsum ◯ Dolostone ◯ Limestone ◯ Bituminous Coal

Metamorphic

Procedure:

Decision 1: TEXTURE →
- FOLIATED (minerals start to become aligned, are fully aligned, or are "banded")
- NON-FOLIATED (granular texture, "blurry" form of parent rock)

Decision 2: COMPOSITION (Depends on the "degree" of metamorphism)
Decision 2: COMPOSITION (You can usually still see evidence of the parent material)

ROCK NAME

Texture: ◯ Foliated ◯ Non-Foliated

Grain Size: ◯ Fine ◯ Fine to Medium ◯ Coarse ◯ Fine to Coarse

Composition: ◯ Mica ◯ Quartz ◯ Feldspar ◯ Amphibole ◯ Garnet ◯ Pyroxene ◯ Calcite ◯ Dolomite ◯ Various

Type of Metamorphism: ◯ Regional ◯ Contact

Rock Name: ◯ Slate ◯ Phyllite ◯ Schist ◯ Gneiss ◯ Homfels ◯ Quartzite ◯ Marble ◯ Metaconglomerate

General

Date: _____ GPS Location: _____

Location: ○ Public Land ○ Private Land ○ Pay-to-Dig Site ○ Quarry
○ Roadcut ○ Outcrop ○ Riverbed ○ Creek Bed ○ Beach
○ Mine Tailing ○ Fresh Overturned Soil ○ Other_____

Weather: ○ Sunny & Clear ○ Cloudy/Overcast ○ Windy ○ Rainy / Drizzle
○ Snow ○ Stormy ○ Fog ○ Drought ○ Other_____

Rock Type: ○ Igneous ○ Sedimentary ○ Metamorphic

Equipment Checklist:
(Rockhounding)
○ Eye Protection ○ Heavy-Duty Gloves ○ Boots / Waterproof
○ First-Aid Kit ○ Hard Hat ○ Rock Hammer / Pick ○ Sieve
○ Colander ○ Small Picks ○ Trowel ○ Small Knife ○ Chisel
○ Small Broom ○ Crack Hammer ○ Pry Bar ○ Sledgehammer
○ Mason's Hammer ○ Shovel ○ Backpack ○ Bucket ○ Map
○ Wrapping Material ○ Small Tubes ○ Boxes / Containers
○ Loupe ○ Magnifying Glass ○ Magnet ○ Compass / GPS

Notes: _____

Mineral Identification

Color: ○ Light ○ Dark Specific Colors: _____

Luster: ○ Metallic ○ Gold ○ Brass ○ Bronze ○ Iron ○ Steel ○ Lead ○ Silver ○ Alum.
○ Non-Metallic ○ Adamantine ○ Vitreous ○ Resinous ○ Pearly ○ Dull ○ Greasy ○ Earthy ○ Silky

Cleavage: ○ 1 Direction ○ 2 Directions at 90° ○ 2 Directions not at 90°
○ 3 Directions at 90° (cubic) ○ 3 Directions not at 90° (rhombohedral)
○ 4 Directions (octahedral) ○ 6 Directions (dodecahedral)

Fracture: ○ Conchoidal (smooth, shell-like, or glass-like breaks) ○ Uneven (irregular, but not conchoidal) ○ Hackly (jagged, as of a metal)
○ Splintery (occurs in aggregates of many slender, brittle crystals) ○ Fibrous (occurs in aggregates of many slender, threadlike crystals)

Crystal Habit: ○ Prismatic ○ Acicular ○ Striated ○ Botryoidal ○ Dendritic
○ Nodular ○ Banded ○ Other_____

Hardness: (Mohs Scale)
○ 1 Talc ○ 2 Gypsum ○ 2.5 Fingernail ○ 3 Calcite ○ 4 Fluorite
○ 5 Apatite ○ 5.5 Glass ○ 6 Feldspar ○ 6.5 Steel File
○ 7 Quartz ○ 8 Topaz ○ 9 Corundrum ○ 10 Diamond

Specific Gravity:
○ Average (like quartz = 2.6 - 2.8)
○ Heavy (like galena = 7.5)
○ Light (lighter than quartz = <2.6)

$$\frac{\text{mass of mineral}}{\text{mass of same volume of water}} = \frac{\text{weight of mineral in air}}{\text{weight of equal volume of water}}$$

Tenacity: ○ Brittle ○ Ductile ○ Elastic ○ Flexible ○ Friable
○ Malleable ○ Sectile

Diaphaneity: ○ Transparent ○ Translucent ○ Opaque

Notes: _____

Notes

_____
_____
_____
_____
_____
_____
_____
_____
_____

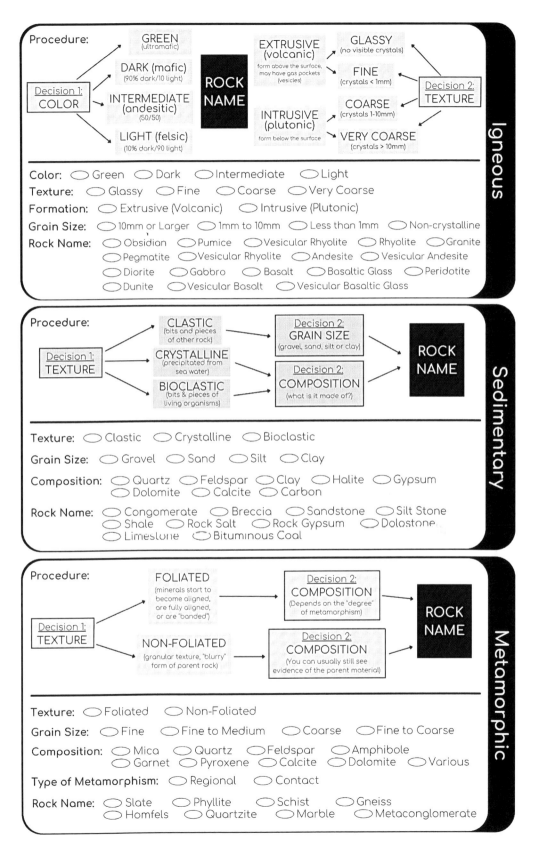

Igneous

Procedure:

Decision 1: COLOR
- GREEN (ultramafic)
- DARK (mafic) (90% dark/10 light)
- INTERMEDIATE (andesitic) (50/50)
- LIGHT (felsic) (10% dark/90 light)

ROCK NAME

EXTRUSIVE (volcanic) — form above the surface, may have gas pockets (vesicles)

INTRUSIVE (plutonic) — form below the surface

Decision 2: TEXTURE
- GLASSY (no visible crystals)
- FINE (crystals < 1mm)
- COARSE (crystals 1-10mm)
- VERY COARSE (crystals > 10mm)

Color: ◯ Green ◯ Dark ◯ Intermediate ◯ Light
Texture: ◯ Glassy ◯ Fine ◯ Coarse ◯ Very Coarse
Formation: ◯ Extrusive (Volcanic) ◯ Intrusive (Plutonic)
Grain Size: ◯ 10mm or Larger ◯ 1mm to 10mm ◯ Less than 1mm ◯ Non-crystalline
Rock Name: ◯ Obsidian ◯ Pumice ◯ Vesicular Rhyolite ◯ Rhyolite ◯ Granite
◯ Pegmatite ◯ Vesicular Rhyolite ◯ Andesite ◯ Vesicular Andesite
◯ Diorite ◯ Gabbro ◯ Basalt ◯ Basaltic Glass ◯ Peridotite
◯ Dunite ◯ Vesicular Basalt ◯ Vesicular Basaltic Glass

Sedimentary

Procedure:

Decision 1: TEXTURE
- CLASTIC (bits and pieces of other rock)
- CRYSTALLINE (precipitated from sea water)
- BIOCLASTIC (bits & pieces of living organisms)

Decision 2: GRAIN SIZE (gravel, sand, silt or clay)

Decision 2: COMPOSITION (what is it made of?)

ROCK NAME

Texture: ◯ Clastic ◯ Crystalline ◯ Bioclastic
Grain Size: ◯ Gravel ◯ Sand ◯ Silt ◯ Clay
Composition: ◯ Quartz ◯ Feldspar ◯ Clay ◯ Halite ◯ Gypsum
◯ Dolomite ◯ Calcite ◯ Carbon
Rock Name: ◯ Congomerate ◯ Breccia ◯ Sandstone ◯ Silt Stone
◯ Shale ◯ Rock Salt ◯ Rock Gypsum ◯ Dolostone
◯ Limestone ◯ Bituminous Coal

Metamorphic

Procedure:

Decision 1: TEXTURE
- FOLIATED (minerals start to become aligned, are fully aligned, or are "banded")
- NON-FOLIATED (granular texture, "blurry" form of parent rock)

Decision 2: COMPOSITION (Depends on the "degree" of metamorphism)

Decision 2: COMPOSITION (You can usually still see evidence of the parent material)

ROCK NAME

Texture: ◯ Foliated ◯ Non-Foliated
Grain Size: ◯ Fine ◯ Fine to Medium ◯ Coarse ◯ Fine to Coarse
Composition: ◯ Mica ◯ Quartz ◯ Feldspar ◯ Amphibole
◯ Garnet ◯ Pyroxene ◯ Calcite ◯ Dolomite ◯ Various
Type of Metamorphism: ◯ Regional ◯ Contact
Rock Name: ◯ Slate ◯ Phyllite ◯ Schist ◯ Gneiss
◯ Homfels ◯ Quartzite ◯ Marble ◯ Metaconglomerate

General

Date: _____ GPS Location: _____

Location: ⚪ Public Land ⚪ Private Land ⚪ Pay-to-Dig Site ⚪ Quarry
⚪ Roadcut ⚪ Outcrop ⚪ Riverbed ⚪ Creek Bed ⚪ Beach
⚪ Mine Tailing ⚪ Fresh Overturned Soil ⚪ Other_____

Weather: ⚪ Sunny & Clear ⚪ Cloudy/Overcast ⚪ Windy ⚪ Rainy / Drizzle
⚪ Snow ⚪ Stormy ⚪ Fog ⚪ Drought ⚪ Other_____

Rock Type: ⚪ Igneous ⚪ Sedimentary ⚪ Metamorphic

Equipment Checklist: (Rockhounding)
⚪ Eye Protection ⚪ Heavy-Duty Gloves ⚪ Boots / Waterproof
⚪ First-Aid Kit ⚪ Hard Hat ⚪ Rock Hammer / Pick ⚪ Sieve
⚪ Colander ⚪ Small Picks ⚪ Trowel ⚪ Small Knife ⚪ Chisel
⚪ Small Broom ⚪ Crack Hammer ⚪ Pry Bar ⚪ Sledgehammer
⚪ Mason's Hammer ⚪ Shovel ⚪ Backpack ⚪ Bucket ⚪ Map
⚪ Wrapping Material ⚪ Small Tubes ⚪ Boxes / Containers
⚪ Loupe ⚪ Magnifying Glass ⚪ Magnet ⚪ Compass / GPS

Notes: _____

Mineral Identification

Color: ⚪ Light ⚪ Dark Specific Colors: _____

Luster: ⚪ Metallic ⚪ Gold ⚪ Brass ⚪ Non-Metallic ⚪ Adamantine ⚪ Vitreous
⚪ Bronze ⚪ Iron ⚪ Resinous ⚪ Pearly ⚪ Dull
⚪ Steel ⚪ Lead ⚪ Greasy ⚪ Earthy ⚪ Silky
⚪ Silver ⚪ Alum.

Cleavage: ⚪ 1 Direction ⚪ 2 Directions at 90° ⚪ 2 Directions not at 90°
⚪ 3 Directions at 90° (cubic) ⚪ 3 Directions not at 90° (rhombohedral)
⚪ 4 Directions (octahedral) ⚪ 6 Directions (dodecahedral)

Fracture: ⚪ Conchoidal (smooth, shell-like, or glass-like breaks) ⚪ Uneven (irregular, but not conchoidal) ⚪ Hackly (jagged, as of a metal)
⚪ Splintery (occurs in aggregates of many slender, brittle crystals) ⚪ Fibrous (occurs in aggregates of many slender, threadlike crystals)

Crystal Habit: ⚪ Prismatic ⚪ Acicular ⚪ Striated ⚪ Botryoidal ⚪ Dendritic
⚪ Nodular ⚪ Banded ⚪ Other_____

Hardness: (Mohs Scale)
⚪ 1 Talc ⚪ 2 Gypsum ⚪ 2.5 Fingernail ⚪ 3 Calcite ⚪ 4 Fluorite
⚪ 5 Apatite ⚪ 5.5 Glass ⚪ 6 Feldspar ⚪ 6.5 Steel File
⚪ 7 Quartz ⚪ 8 Topaz ⚪ 9 Corundrum ⚪ 10 Diamond

Specific Gravity:
⚪ Average (like quartz = 2.6 - 2.8)
⚪ Heavy (like galena = 7.5)
⚪ Light (lighter than quartz = <2.6)

$$\frac{\text{mass of mineral}}{\text{mass of same volume of water}} = \frac{\text{weight of mineral in air}}{\text{weight of equal volume of water}}$$

Tenacity: ⚪ Brittle ⚪ Ductile ⚪ Elastic ⚪ Flexible ⚪ Friable
⚪ Malleable ⚪ Sectile

Diaphaneity: ⚪ Transparent ⚪ Translucent ⚪ Opaque

Notes: _____

Notes

_____
_____
_____
_____
_____
_____
_____
_____
_____
_____

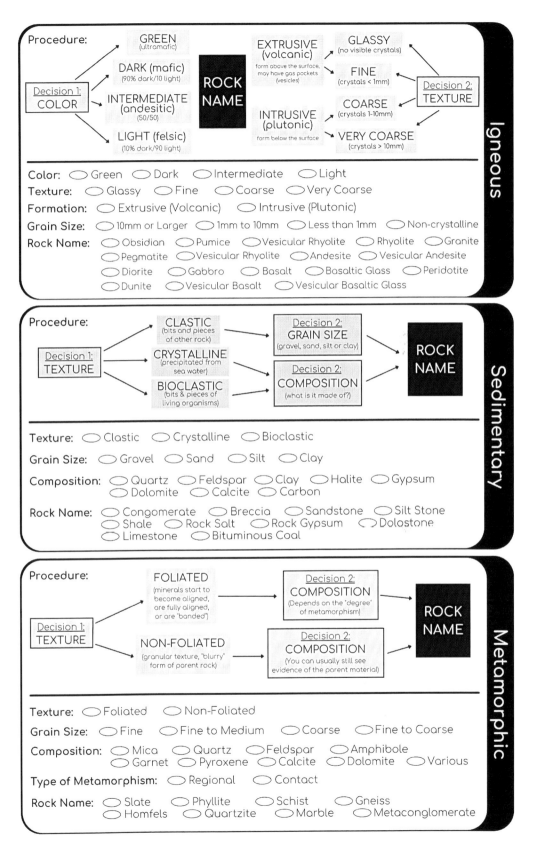

Igneous

Procedure:

Decision 1: COLOR
- GREEN (ultramafic)
- DARK (mafic) (90% dark/10 light)
- INTERMEDIATE (andesitic) (50/50)
- LIGHT (felsic) (10% dark/90 light)

ROCK NAME

EXTRUSIVE (volcanic) — form above the surface, may have gas pockets (vesicles)

INTRUSIVE (plutonic) — form below the surface

Decision 2: TEXTURE
- GLASSY (no visible crystals)
- FINE (crystals < 1mm)
- COARSE (crystals 1-10mm)
- VERY COARSE (crystals > 10mm)

Color: ○ Green ○ Dark ○ Intermediate ○ Light
Texture: ○ Glassy ○ Fine ○ Coarse ○ Very Coarse
Formation: ○ Extrusive (Volcanic) ○ Intrusive (Plutonic)
Grain Size: ○ 10mm or Larger ○ 1mm to 10mm ○ Less than 1mm ○ Non-crystalline
Rock Name: ○ Obsidian ○ Pumice ○ Vesicular Rhyolite ○ Rhyolite ○ Granite
○ Pegmatite ○ Vesicular Rhyolite ○ Andesite ○ Vesicular Andesite
○ Diorite ○ Gabbro ○ Basalt ○ Basaltic Glass ○ Peridotite
○ Dunite ○ Vesicular Basalt ○ Vesicular Basaltic Glass

Sedimentary

Procedure:

Decision 1: TEXTURE
- CLASTIC (bits and pieces of other rock)
- CRYSTALLINE (precipitated from sea water)
- BIOCLASTIC (bits & pieces of living organisms)

Decision 2: GRAIN SIZE (gravel, sand, silt or clay)

Decision 2: COMPOSITION (what is it made of?)

ROCK NAME

Texture: ○ Clastic ○ Crystalline ○ Bioclastic
Grain Size: ○ Gravel ○ Sand ○ Silt ○ Clay
Composition: ○ Quartz ○ Feldspar ○ Clay ○ Halite ○ Gypsum
○ Dolomite ○ Calcite ○ Carbon
Rock Name: ○ Congomerate ○ Breccia ○ Sandstone ○ Silt Stone
○ Shale ○ Rock Salt ○ Rock Gypsum ○ Dolostone
○ Limestone ○ Bituminous Coal

Metamorphic

Procedure:

Decision 1: TEXTURE
- FOLIATED (minerals start to become aligned, are fully aligned, or are "banded")
- NON-FOLIATED (granular texture, "blurry" form of parent rock)

Decision 2: COMPOSITION (Depends on the "degree" of metamorphism)

Decision 2: COMPOSITION (You can usually still see evidence of the parent material)

ROCK NAME

Texture: ○ Foliated ○ Non-Foliated
Grain Size: ○ Fine ○ Fine to Medium ○ Coarse ○ Fine to Coarse
Composition: ○ Mica ○ Quartz ○ Feldspar ○ Amphibole
○ Garnet ○ Pyroxene ○ Calcite ○ Dolomite ○ Various
Type of Metamorphism: ○ Regional ○ Contact
Rock Name: ○ Slate ○ Phyllite ○ Schist ○ Gneiss
○ Homfels ○ Quartzite ○ Marble ○ Metaconglomerate

General

Date: _____ GPS Location: _____

Location: ○ Public Land ○ Private Land ○ Pay-to-Dig Site ○ Quarry
○ Roadcut ○ Outcrop ○ Riverbed ○ Creek Bed ○ Beach
○ Mine Tailing ○ Fresh Overturned Soil ○ Other_____

Weather: ○ Sunny & Clear ○ Cloudy/Overcast ○ Windy ○ Rainy / Drizzle
○ Snow ○ Stormy ○ Fog ○ Drought ○ Other_____

Rock Type: ○ Igneous ○ Sedimentary ○ Metamorphic

Equipment Checklist: (Rockhounding)
○ Eye Protection ○ Heavy-Duty Gloves ○ Boots / Waterproof
○ First-Aid Kit ○ Hard Hat ○ Rock Hammer / Pick ○ Sieve
○ Colander ○ Small Picks ○ Trowel ○ Small Knife ○ Chisel
○ Small Broom ○ Crack Hammer ○ Pry Bar ○ Sledgehammer
○ Mason's Hammer ○ Shovel ○ Backpack ○ Bucket ○ Map
○ Wrapping Material ○ Small Tubes ○ Boxes / Containers
○ Loupe ○ Magnifying Glass ○ Magnet ○ Compass / GPS

Notes: _____

Mineral Identification

Color: ○ Light ○ Dark Specific Colors: _____

Luster: ○ Metallic ○ Gold ○ Brass ○ Non-Metallic ○ Adamantine ○ Vitreous
○ Bronze ○ Iron ○ Resinous ○ Pearly ○ Dull
○ Steel ○ Lead ○ Greasy ○ Earthy ○ Silky
○ Silver ○ Alum.

Cleavage: ○ 1 Direction ○ 2 Directions at 90° ○ 2 Directions not at 90°
○ 3 Directions at 90° (cubic) ○ 3 Directions not at 90° (rhombohedral)
○ 4 Directions (octahedral) ○ 6 Directions (dodecahedral)

Fracture: ○ Conchoidal (smooth, shell-like, or glass-like breaks) ○ Uneven (irregular, but not conchoidal) ○ Hackly (jagged, as of a metal)
○ Splintery (occurs in aggregates of many slender, brittle crystals) ○ Fibrous (occurs in aggregates of many slender, threadlike crystals)

Crystal Habit: ○ Prismatic ○ Acicular ○ Striated ○ Botryoidal ○ Dendritic
○ Nodular ○ Banded ○ Other_____

Hardness: (Mohs Scale)
○ 1 Talc ○ 2 Gypsum ○ 2.5 Fingernail ○ 3 Calcite ○ 4 Fluorite
○ 5 Apatite ○ 5.5 Glass ○ 6 Feldspar ○ 6.5 Steel File
○ 7 Quartz ○ 8 Topaz ○ 9 Corundrum ○ 10 Diamond

Specific Gravity:
○ Average (like quartz = 2.6 - 2.8) ○ Heavy (like galena = 7.5) ○ Light (lighter than quartz = <2.6)

$$\frac{\text{mass of mineral}}{\text{mass of same volume of water}} = \frac{\text{weight of mineral in air}}{\text{weight of equal volume of water}}$$

Tenacity: ○ Brittle ○ Ductile ○ Elastic ○ Flexible ○ Friable
○ Malleable ○ Sectile

Diaphaneity: ○ Transparent ○ Translucent ○ Opaque

Notes: _____

Notes

_____
_____
_____
_____
_____
_____
_____
_____
_____

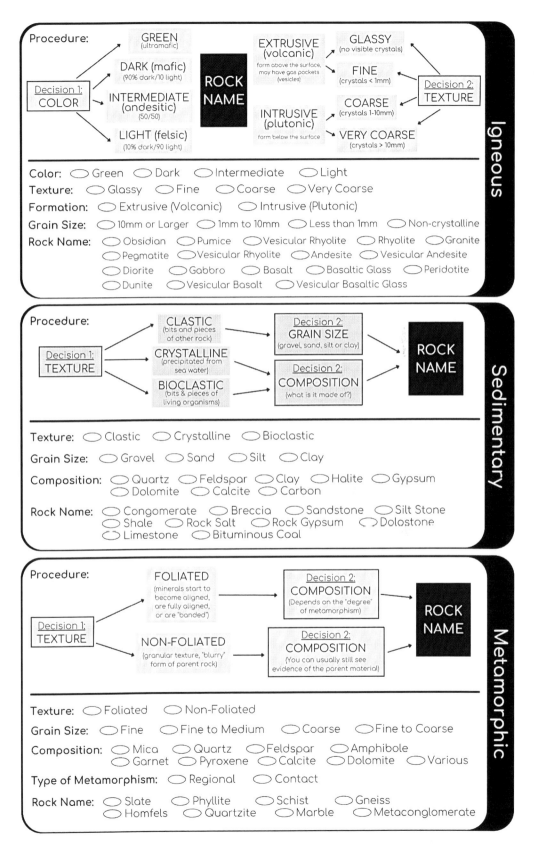

Igneous

Procedure:

Decision 1: COLOR
- GREEN (ultramafic)
- DARK (mafic) (90% dark/10 light)
- INTERMEDIATE (andesitic) (50/50)
- LIGHT (felsic) (10% dark/90 light)

ROCK NAME

- EXTRUSIVE (volcanic) — form above the surface, may have gas pockets (vesicles)
- INTRUSIVE (plutonic) — form below the surface

Decision 2: TEXTURE
- GLASSY (no visible crystals)
- FINE (crystals < 1mm)
- COARSE (crystals 1-10mm)
- VERY COARSE (crystals > 10mm)

Color: ◯ Green ◯ Dark ◯ Intermediate ◯ Light
Texture: ◯ Glassy ◯ Fine ◯ Coarse ◯ Very Coarse
Formation: ◯ Extrusive (Volcanic) ◯ Intrusive (Plutonic)
Grain Size: ◯ 10mm or Larger ◯ 1mm to 10mm ◯ Less than 1mm ◯ Non-crystalline
Rock Name: ◯ Obsidian ◯ Pumice ◯ Vesicular Rhyolite ◯ Rhyolite ◯ Granite
◯ Pegmatite ◯ Vesicular Rhyolite ◯ Andesite ◯ Vesicular Andesite
◯ Diorite ◯ Gabbro ◯ Basalt ◯ Basaltic Glass ◯ Peridotite
◯ Dunite ◯ Vesicular Basalt ◯ Vesicular Basaltic Glass

Sedimentary

Procedure:

Decision 1: TEXTURE
- CLASTIC (bits and pieces of other rock)
- CRYSTALLINE (precipitated from sea water)
- BIOCLASTIC (bits & pieces of living organisms)

Decision 2: GRAIN SIZE (gravel, sand, silt or clay)

Decision 2: COMPOSITION (what is it made of?)

ROCK NAME

Texture: ◯ Clastic ◯ Crystalline ◯ Bioclastic
Grain Size: ◯ Gravel ◯ Sand ◯ Silt ◯ Clay
Composition: ◯ Quartz ◯ Feldspar ◯ Clay ◯ Halite ◯ Gypsum
◯ Dolomite ◯ Calcite ◯ Carbon
Rock Name: ◯ Congomerate ◯ Breccia ◯ Sandstone ◯ Silt Stone
◯ Shale ◯ Rock Salt ◯ Rock Gypsum ◯ Dolostone
◯ Limestone ◯ Bituminous Coal

Metamorphic

Procedure:

Decision 1: TEXTURE
- FOLIATED (minerals start to become aligned, are fully aligned, or are "banded")
- NON-FOLIATED (granular texture, "blurry" form of parent rock)

Decision 2: COMPOSITION (Depends on the "degree" of metamorphism)

Decision 2: COMPOSITION (You can usually still see evidence of the parent material)

ROCK NAME

Texture: ◯ Foliated ◯ Non-Foliated
Grain Size: ◯ Fine ◯ Fine to Medium ◯ Coarse ◯ Fine to Coarse
Composition: ◯ Mica ◯ Quartz ◯ Feldspar ◯ Amphibole
◯ Garnet ◯ Pyroxene ◯ Calcite ◯ Dolomite ◯ Various
Type of Metamorphism: ◯ Regional ◯ Contact
Rock Name: ◯ Slate ◯ Phyllite ◯ Schist ◯ Gneiss
◯ Homfels ◯ Quartzite ◯ Marble ◯ Metaconglomerate

General

Date: _____   GPS Location: _____

Location: ⊙ Public Land ⊙ Private Land ⊙ Pay-to-Dig Site ⊙ Quarry
⊙ Roadcut ⊙ Outcrop ⊙ Riverbed ⊙ Creek Bed ⊙ Beach
⊙ Mine Tailing ⊙ Fresh Overturned Soil ⊙ Other_____

Weather: ⊙ Sunny & Clear ⊙ Cloudy/Overcast ⊙ Windy ⊙ Rainy / Drizzle
⊙ Snow ⊙ Stormy ⊙ Fog ⊙ Drought ⊙ Other_____

Rock Type: ⊙ Igneous ⊙ Sedimentary ⊙ Metamorphic

Equipment Checklist:
(Rockhounding)
⊙ Eye Protection ⊙ Heavy-Duty Gloves ⊙ Boots / Waterproof
⊙ First-Aid Kit ⊙ Hard Hat ⊙ Rock Hammer / Pick ⊙ Sieve
⊙ Colander ⊙ Small Picks ⊙ Trowel ⊙ Small Knife ⊙ Chisel
⊙ Small Broom ⊙ Crack Hammer ⊙ Pry Bar ⊙ Sledgehammer
⊙ Mason's Hammer ⊙ Shovel ⊙ Backpack ⊙ Bucket ⊙ Map
⊙ Wrapping Material ⊙ Small Tubes ⊙ Boxes / Containers
⊙ Loupe ⊙ Magnifying Glass ⊙ Magnet ⊙ Compass / GPS

Notes: _____

Mineral Identification

Color: ⊙ Light ⊙ Dark Specific Colors: _____

Luster: ⊙ Metallic ⊙ Gold ⊙ Brass ⊙ Bronze ⊙ Iron ⊙ Steel ⊙ Lead ⊙ Silver ⊙ Alum.
⊙ Non-Metallic ⊙ Adamantine ⊙ Vitreous ⊙ Resinous ⊙ Pearly ⊙ Dull ⊙ Greasy ⊙ Earthy ⊙ Silky

Cleavage: ⊙ 1 Direction ⊙ 2 Directions at 90° ⊙ 2 Directions not at 90°
⊙ 3 Directions at 90° (cubic) ⊙ 3 Directions not at 90° (rhombohedral)
⊙ 4 Directions (octahedral) ⊙ 6 Directions (dodecahedral)

Fracture: ⊙ Conchoidal (smooth, shell-like, or glass-like breaks) ⊙ Uneven (irregular, but not conchoidal) ⊙ Hackly (jagged, as of a metal)
⊙ Splintery (occurs in aggregates of many slender, brittle crystals) ⊙ Fibrous (occurs in aggregates of many slender, threadlike crystals)

Crystal Habit: ⊙ Prismatic ⊙ Acicular ⊙ Striated ⊙ Botryoidal ⊙ Dendritic
⊙ Nodular ⊙ Banded ⊙ Other_____

Hardness: (Mohs Scale)
⊙ 1 Talc ⊙ 2 Gypsum ⊙ 2.5 Fingernail ⊙ 3 Calcite ⊙ 4 Fluorite
⊙ 5 Apatite ⊙ 5.5 Glass ⊙ 6 Feldspar ⊙ 6.5 Steel File
⊙ 7 Quartz ⊙ 8 Topaz ⊙ 9 Corundrum ⊙ 10 Diamond

Specific Gravity:
⊙ Average (like quartz = 2.6 - 2.8)
⊙ Heavy (like galeno = 7.5)
⊙ Light (lighter than quartz = <2.6)

$$\frac{\text{mass of mineral}}{\text{mass of same volume of water}} = \frac{\text{weight of mineral in air}}{\text{weight of equal volume of water}}$$

Tenacity: ⊙ Brittle ⊙ Ductile ⊙ Elastic ⊙ Flexible ⊙ Friable
⊙ Malleable ⊙ Sectile

Diaphaneity: ⊙ Transparent ⊙ Translucent ⊙ Opaque

Notes: _____

Notes

_____
_____
_____
_____
_____
_____
_____
_____
_____

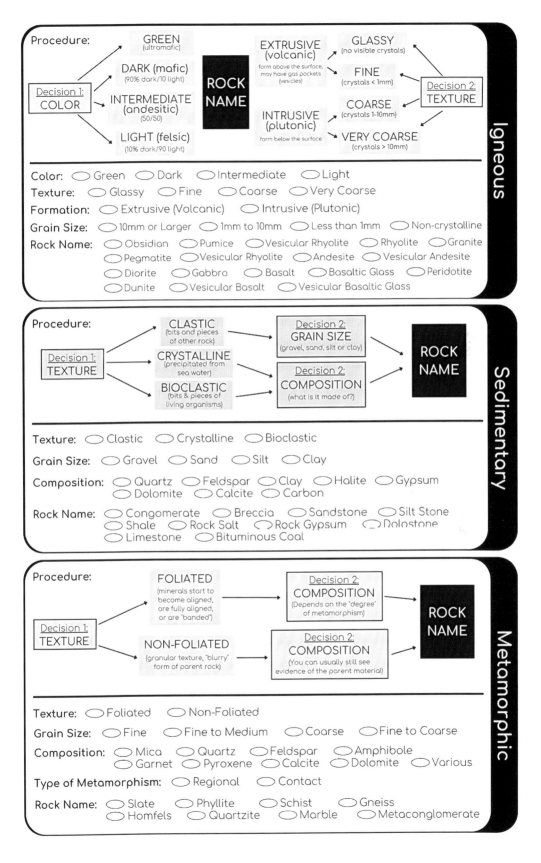

Igneous

Procedure:

Decision 1: COLOR
- GREEN (ultramafic)
- DARK (mafic) (90% dark/10 light)
- INTERMEDIATE (andesitic) (50/50)
- LIGHT (felsic) (10% dark/90 light)

ROCK NAME

- EXTRUSIVE (volcanic) form above the surface, may have gas pockets (vesicles)
- INTRUSIVE (plutonic) form below the surface

Decision 2: TEXTURE
- GLASSY (no visible crystals)
- FINE (crystals < 1mm)
- COARSE (crystals 1-10mm)
- VERY COARSE (crystals > 10mm)

Color: ◯ Green ◯ Dark ◯ Intermediate ◯ Light
Texture: ◯ Glassy ◯ Fine ◯ Coarse ◯ Very Coarse
Formation: ◯ Extrusive (Volcanic) ◯ Intrusive (Plutonic)
Grain Size: ◯ 10mm or Larger ◯ 1mm to 10mm ◯ Less than 1mm ◯ Non-crystalline
Rock Name: ◯ Obsidian ◯ Pumice ◯ Vesicular Rhyolite ◯ Rhyolite ◯ Granite
◯ Pegmatite ◯ Vesicular Rhyolite ◯ Andesite ◯ Vesicular Andesite
◯ Diorite ◯ Gabbro ◯ Basalt ◯ Basaltic Glass ◯ Peridotite
◯ Dunite ◯ Vesicular Basalt ◯ Vesicular Basaltic Glass

Sedimentary

Procedure:

Decision 1: TEXTURE
- CLASTIC (bits and pieces of other rock)
- CRYSTALLINE (precipitated from sea water)
- BIOCLASTIC (bits & pieces of living organisms)

Decision 2: GRAIN SIZE (gravel, sand, silt or clay)

Decision 2: COMPOSITION (what is it made of?)

ROCK NAME

Texture: ◯ Clastic ◯ Crystalline ◯ Bioclastic
Grain Size: ◯ Gravel ◯ Sand ◯ Silt ◯ Clay
Composition: ◯ Quartz ◯ Feldspar ◯ Clay ◯ Halite ◯ Gypsum
◯ Dolomite ◯ Calcite ◯ Carbon
Rock Name: ◯ Congomerate ◯ Breccia ◯ Sandstone ◯ Silt Stone
◯ Shale ◯ Rock Salt ◯ Rock Gypsum ◯ Dolostone
◯ Limestone ◯ Bituminous Coal

Metamorphic

Procedure:

Decision 1: TEXTURE
- FOLIATED (minerals start to become aligned, are fully aligned, or are "banded")
- NON-FOLIATED (granular texture, "blurry" form of parent rock)

Decision 2: COMPOSITION (Depends on the "degree" of metamorphism)

Decision 2: COMPOSITION (You can usually still see evidence of the parent material)

ROCK NAME

Texture: ◯ Foliated ◯ Non-Foliated
Grain Size: ◯ Fine ◯ Fine to Medium ◯ Coarse ◯ Fine to Coarse
Composition: ◯ Mica ◯ Quartz ◯ Feldspar ◯ Amphibole
◯ Garnet ◯ Pyroxene ◯ Calcite ◯ Dolomite ◯ Various
Type of Metamorphism: ◯ Regional ◯ Contact
Rock Name: ◯ Slate ◯ Phyllite ◯ Schist ◯ Gneiss
◯ Homfels ◯ Quartzite ◯ Marble ◯ Metaconglomerate

General

Date: _____ GPS Location: _____

Location: ○ Public Land ○ Private Land ○ Pay-to-Dig Site ○ Quarry
○ Roadcut ○ Outcrop ○ Riverbed ○ Creek Bed ○ Beach
○ Mine Tailing ○ Fresh Overturned Soil ○ Other_____

Weather: ○ Sunny & Clear ○ Cloudy/Overcast ○ Windy ○ Rainy / Drizzle
○ Snow ○ Stormy ○ Fog ○ Drought ○ Other_____

Rock Type: ○ Igneous ○ Sedimentary ○ Metamorphic

Equipment ○ Eye Protection ○ Heavy-Duty Gloves ○ Boots / Waterproof
Checklist: ○ First-Aid Kit ○ Hard Hat ○ Rock Hammer / Pick ○ Sieve
(Rockhounding) ○ Colander ○ Small Picks ○ Trowel ○ Small Knife ○ Chisel
○ Small Broom ○ Crack Hammer ○ Pry Bar ○ Sledgehammer
○ Mason's Hammer ○ Shovel ○ Backpack ○ Bucket ○ Map
○ Wrapping Material ○ Small Tubes ○ Boxes / Containers
○ Loupe ○ Magnifying Glass ○ Magnet ○ Compass / GPS

Notes: _____

Mineral Identification

Color: ○ Light ○ Dark Specific Colors: _____

Luster: ○ Metallic ○ Gold ○ Brass   ○ Non-Metallic ○ Adamantine ○ Vitreous
                    ○ Bronze ○ Iron   ○ Resinous ○ Pearly ○ Dull
                    ○ Steel ○ Lead   ○ Greasy ○ Earthy ○ Silky
                    ○ Silver ○ Alum.

Cleavage: ○ 1 Direction ○ 2 Directions at 90° ○ 2 Directions not at 90°
○ 3 Directions at 90° (cubic) ○ 3 Directions not at 90° (rhombohedral)
○ 4 Directions (octahedral) ○ 6 Directions (dodecahedral)

Fracture: ○ Conchoidal (smooth, shell-like, or glass-like breaks) ○ Uneven (irregular, but not conchoidal) ○ Hackly (jagged, as of a metal)
○ Splintery (occurs in aggregates of many slender, brittle crystals) ○ Fibrous (occurs in aggregates of many slender, threadlike crystals)

Crystal ○ Prismatic ○ Acicular ○ Striated ○ Botryoidal ○ Dendritic
Habit: ○ Nodular ○ Banded ○ Other_____

Hardness: ○ 1 Talc ○ 2 Gypsum ○ 2.5 Fingernail ○ 3 Calcite ○ 4 Fluorite
(Mohs Scale) ○ 5 Apatite ○ 5.5 Glass ○ 6 Feldspar ○ 6.5 Steel File
○ 7 Quartz ○ 8 Topaz ○ 9 Corundrum ○ 10 Diamond

Specific ○ Average (like quartz = 2.6 - 2.8) $\dfrac{\text{mass of mineral}}{\text{mass of same volume of water}} = \dfrac{\text{weight of mineral in air}}{\text{weight of equal volume of water}}$
Gravity: ○ Heavy (like galena = 7.5)
○ Light (lighter than quartz = <2.6)

Tenacity: ○ Brittle ○ Ductile ○ Elastic ○ Flexible ○ Friable
○ Malleable ○ Sectile

Diaphaneity: ○ Transparent ○ Translucent ○ Opaque

Notes: _____

Notes

_____
_____
_____
_____
_____
_____
_____
_____
_____

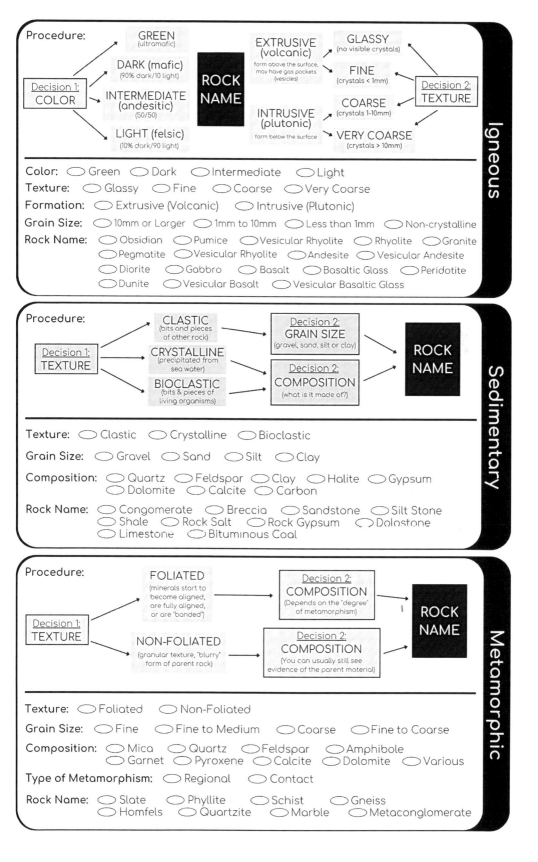

Igneous

Procedure:

Decision 1: COLOR →
- GREEN (ultramafic)
- DARK (mafic) (90% dark/10 light)
- INTERMEDIATE (andesitic) (50/50)
- LIGHT (felsic) (10% dark/90 light)

→ ROCK NAME

EXTRUSIVE (volcanic) — form above the surface, may have gas pockets (vesicles)

INTRUSIVE (plutonic) — form below the surface

- GLASSY (no visible crystals)
- FINE (crystals < 1mm)
- COARSE (crystals 1-10mm)
- VERY COARSE (crystals > 10mm)

Decision 2: TEXTURE

Color: ◯ Green ◯ Dark ◯ Intermediate ◯ Light
Texture: ◯ Glassy ◯ Fine ◯ Coarse ◯ Very Coarse
Formation: ◯ Extrusive (Volcanic) ◯ Intrusive (Plutonic)
Grain Size: ◯ 10mm or Larger ◯ 1mm to 10mm ◯ Less than 1mm ◯ Non-crystalline
Rock Name: ◯ Obsidian ◯ Pumice ◯ Vesicular Rhyolite ◯ Rhyolite ◯ Granite
◯ Pegmatite ◯ Vesicular Rhyolite ◯ Andesite ◯ Vesicular Andesite
◯ Diorite ◯ Gabbro ◯ Basalt ◯ Basaltic Glass ◯ Peridotite
◯ Dunite ◯ Vesicular Basalt ◯ Vesicular Basaltic Glass

Sedimentary

Procedure:

Decision 1: TEXTURE →
- CLASTIC (bits and pieces of other rock)
- CRYSTALLINE (precipitated from sea water)
- BIOCLASTIC (bits & pieces of living organisms)

→ Decision 2: GRAIN SIZE (gravel, sand, silt or clay)
→ Decision 2: COMPOSITION (what is it made of?)

→ ROCK NAME

Texture: ◯ Clastic ◯ Crystalline ◯ Bioclastic
Grain Size: ◯ Gravel ◯ Sand ◯ Silt ◯ Clay
Composition: ◯ Quartz ◯ Feldspar ◯ Clay ◯ Halite ◯ Gypsum
◯ Dolomite ◯ Calcite ◯ Carbon
Rock Name: ◯ Congomerate ◯ Breccia ◯ Sandstone ◯ Silt Stone
◯ Shale ◯ Rock Salt ◯ Rock Gypsum ◯ Dolostone
◯ Limestone ◯ Bituminous Coal

Metamorphic

Procedure:

Decision 1: TEXTURE →
- FOLIATED (minerals start to become aligned, are fully aligned, or are "banded")
- NON-FOLIATED (granular texture, "blurry" form of parent rock)

→ Decision 2: COMPOSITION (Depends on the "degree" of metamorphism)
→ Decision 2: COMPOSITION (You can usually still see evidence of the parent material)

→ ROCK NAME

Texture: ◯ Foliated ◯ Non-Foliated
Grain Size: ◯ Fine ◯ Fine to Medium ◯ Coarse ◯ Fine to Coarse
Composition: ◯ Mica ◯ Quartz ◯ Feldspar ◯ Amphibole
◯ Garnet ◯ Pyroxene ◯ Calcite ◯ Dolomite ◯ Various
Type of Metamorphism: ◯ Regional ◯ Contact
Rock Name: ◯ Slate ◯ Phyllite ◯ Schist ◯ Gneiss
◯ Homfels ◯ Quartzite ◯ Marble ◯ Metaconglomerate

General

Date: _____ GPS Location: _____

Location:
- ◯ Public Land ◯ Private Land ◯ Pay-to-Dig Site ◯ Quarry
- ◯ Roadcut ◯ Outcrop ◯ Riverbed ◯ Creek Bed ◯ Beach
- ◯ Mine Tailing ◯ Fresh Overturned Soil ◯ Other_____

Weather:
- ◯ Sunny & Clear ◯ Cloudy/Overcast ◯ Windy ◯ Rainy / Drizzle
- ◯ Snow ◯ Stormy ◯ Fog ◯ Drought ◯ Other_____

Rock Type: ◯ Igneous ◯ Sedimentary ◯ Metamorphic

Equipment Checklist: (Rockhounding)
- ◯ Eye Protection ◯ Heavy-Duty Gloves ◯ Boots / Waterproof
- ◯ First-Aid Kit ◯ Hard Hat ◯ Rock Hammer / Pick ◯ Sieve
- ◯ Colander ◯ Small Picks ◯ Trowel ◯ Small Knife ◯ Chisel
- ◯ Small Broom ◯ Crack Hammer ◯ Pry Bar ◯ Sledgehammer
- ◯ Mason's Hammer ◯ Shovel ◯ Backpack ◯ Bucket ◯ Map
- ◯ Wrapping Material ◯ Small Tubes ◯ Boxes / Containers
- ◯ Loupe ◯ Magnifying Glass ◯ Magnet ◯ Compass / GPS

Notes: _____

Mineral Identification

Color: ◯ Light ◯ Dark Specific Colors: _____

Luster:
- ◯ Metallic ◯ Gold ◯ Brass ◯ Bronze ◯ Iron ◯ Steel ◯ Lead ◯ Silver ◯ Alum.
- ◯ Non-Metallic ◯ Adamantine ◯ Vitreous ◯ Resinous ◯ Pearly ◯ Dull ◯ Greasy ◯ Earthy ◯ Silky

Cleavage:
- ◯ 1 Direction ◯ 2 Directions at 90° ◯ 2 Directions not at 90°
- ◯ 3 Directions at 90° (cubic) ◯ 3 Directions not at 90° (rhombohedral)
- ◯ 4 Directions (octahedral) ◯ 6 Directions (dodecahedral)

Fracture:
- ◯ Conchoidal (smooth, shell-like, or glass-like breaks) ◯ Uneven (irregular, but not conchoidal) ◯ Hackly (jagged, as of a metal)
- ◯ Splintery (occurs in aggregates of many slender, brittle crystals) ◯ Fibrous (occurs in aggregates of many slender, threadlike crystals)

Crystal Habit:
- ◯ Prismatic ◯ Acicular ◯ Striated ◯ Botryoidal ◯ Dendritic
- ◯ Nodular ◯ Banded ◯ Other_____

Hardness: (Mohs Scale)
- ◯ 1 Talc ◯ 2 Gypsum ◯ 2.5 Fingernail ◯ 3 Calcite ◯ 4 Fluorite
- ◯ 5 Apatite ◯ 5.5 Glass ◯ 6 Feldspar ◯ 6.5 Steel File
- ◯ 7 Quartz ◯ 8 Topaz ◯ 9 Corundrum ◯ 10 Diamond

Specific Gravity:
- ◯ Average (like quartz = 2.6 - 2.8)
- ◯ Heavy (like galena = 7.5)
- ◯ Light (lighter than quartz = <2.6)

$$\frac{\text{mass of mineral}}{\text{mass of same volume of water}} = \frac{\text{weight of mineral in air}}{\text{weight of equal volume of water}}$$

Tenacity:
- ◯ Brittle ◯ Ductile ◯ Elastic ◯ Flexible ◯ Friable
- ◯ Malleable ◯ Sectile

Diaphaneity: ◯ Transparent ◯ Translucent ◯ Opaque

Notes: _____

Notes

_____
_____
_____
_____
_____
_____
_____
_____
_____

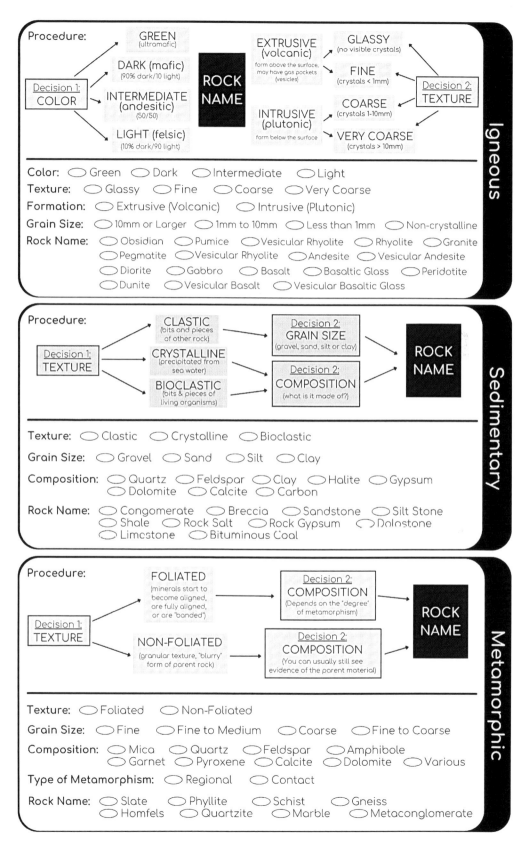

Igneous

Procedure:

Decision 1: COLOR
- GREEN (ultramafic)
- DARK (mafic) (90% dark/10 light)
- INTERMEDIATE (andesitic) (50/50)
- LIGHT (felsic) (10% dark/90 light)

ROCK NAME

EXTRUSIVE (volcanic) — form above the surface, may have gas pockets (vesicles)

INTRUSIVE (plutonic) — form below the surface

Decision 2: TEXTURE
- GLASSY (no visible crystals)
- FINE (crystals < 1mm)
- COARSE (crystals 1-10mm)
- VERY COARSE (crystals > 10mm)

Color: ◯ Green ◯ Dark ◯ Intermediate ◯ Light

Texture: ◯ Glassy ◯ Fine ◯ Coarse ◯ Very Coarse

Formation: ◯ Extrusive (Volcanic) ◯ Intrusive (Plutonic)

Grain Size: ◯ 10mm or Larger ◯ 1mm to 10mm ◯ Less than 1mm ◯ Non-crystalline

Rock Name: ◯ Obsidian ◯ Pumice ◯ Vesicular Rhyolite ◯ Rhyolite ◯ Granite
◯ Pegmatite ◯ Vesicular Rhyolite ◯ Andesite ◯ Vesicular Andesite
◯ Diorite ◯ Gabbro ◯ Basalt ◯ Basaltic Glass ◯ Peridotite
◯ Dunite ◯ Vesicular Basalt ◯ Vesicular Basaltic Glass

Sedimentary

Procedure:

Decision 1: TEXTURE
- CLASTIC (bits and pieces of other rock)
- CRYSTALLINE (precipitated from sea water)
- BIOCLASTIC (bits & pieces of living organisms)

Decision 2: GRAIN SIZE (gravel, sand, silt or clay)

Decision 2: COMPOSITION (what is it made of?)

ROCK NAME

Texture: ◯ Clastic ◯ Crystalline ◯ Bioclastic

Grain Size: ◯ Gravel ◯ Sand ◯ Silt ◯ Clay

Composition: ◯ Quartz ◯ Feldspar ◯ Clay ◯ Halite ◯ Gypsum
◯ Dolomite ◯ Calcite ◯ Carbon

Rock Name: ◯ Congomerate ◯ Breccia ◯ Sandstone ◯ Silt Stone
◯ Shale ◯ Rock Salt ◯ Rock Gypsum ◯ Dolostone
◯ Limestone ◯ Bituminous Coal

Metamorphic

Procedure:

Decision 1: TEXTURE
- FOLIATED (minerals start to become aligned, are fully aligned, or are "banded")
- NON-FOLIATED (granular texture, "blurry" form of parent rock)

Decision 2: COMPOSITION (Depends on the "degree" of metamorphism)

Decision 2: COMPOSITION (You can usually still see evidence of the parent material)

ROCK NAME

Texture: ◯ Foliated ◯ Non-Foliated

Grain Size: ◯ Fine ◯ Fine to Medium ◯ Coarse ◯ Fine to Coarse

Composition: ◯ Mica ◯ Quartz ◯ Feldspar ◯ Amphibole
◯ Garnet ◯ Pyroxene ◯ Calcite ◯ Dolomite ◯ Various

Type of Metamorphism: ◯ Regional ◯ Contact

Rock Name: ◯ Slate ◯ Phyllite ◯ Schist ◯ Gneiss
◯ Homfels ◯ Quartzite ◯ Marble ◯ Metaconglomerate

General

Date: _____ GPS Location: _____

Location: ○ Public Land ○ Private Land ○ Pay-to-Dig Site ○ Quarry
○ Roadcut ○ Outcrop ○ Riverbed ○ Creek Bed ○ Beach
○ Mine Tailing ○ Fresh Overturned Soil ○ Other_____

Weather: ○ Sunny & Clear ○ Cloudy/Overcast ○ Windy ○ Rainy / Drizzle
○ Snow ○ Stormy ○ Fog ○ Drought ○ Other_____

Rock Type: ○ Igneous ○ Sedimentary ○ Metamorphic

Equipment Checklist:
(Rockhounding)
○ Eye Protection ○ Heavy-Duty Gloves ○ Boots / Waterproof
○ First-Aid Kit ○ Hard Hat ○ Rock Hammer / Pick ○ Sieve
○ Colander ○ Small Picks ○ Trowel ○ Small Knife ○ Chisel
○ Small Broom ○ Crack Hammer ○ Pry Bar ○ Sledgehammer
○ Mason's Hammer ○ Shovel ○ Backpack ○ Bucket ○ Map
○ Wrapping Material ○ Small Tubes ○ Boxes / Containers
○ Loupe ○ Magnifying Glass ○ Magnet ○ Compass / GPS

Notes: _____

Mineral Identification

Color: ○ Light ○ Dark Specific Colors: _____

Luster: ○ Metallic ○ Gold ○ Brass
○ Bronze ○ Iron
○ Steel ○ Lead
○ Silver ○ Alum.
○ Non-Metallic ○ Adamantine ○ Vitreous
○ Resinous ○ Pearly ○ Dull
○ Greasy ○ Earthy ○ Silky

Cleavage: ○ 1 Direction ○ 2 Directions at 90° ○ 2 Directions not at 90°
○ 3 Directions at 90° (cubic) ○ 3 Directions not at 90° (rhombohedral)
○ 4 Directions (octahedral) ○ 6 Directions (dodecahedral)

Fracture: ○ Conchoidal (smooth, shell-like, or glass-like breaks) ○ Uneven (irregular, but not conchoidal) ○ Hackly (jagged, as of a metal)
○ Splintery (occurs in aggregates of many slender, brittle crystals) ○ Fibrous (occurs in aggregates of many slender, threadlike crystals)

Crystal Habit: ○ Prismatic ○ Acicular ○ Striated ○ Botryoidal ○ Dendritic
○ Nodular ○ Banded ○ Other_____

Hardness: (Mohs Scale)
○ 1 Talc ○ 2 Gypsum ○ 2.5 Fingernail ○ 3 Calcite ○ 4 Fluorite
○ 5 Apatite ○ 5.5 Glass ○ 6 Feldspar ○ 6.5 Steel File
○ 7 Quartz ○ 8 Topaz ○ 9 Corundrum ○ 10 Diamond

Specific Gravity:
○ Average (like quartz = 2.6 - 2.8)
○ Heavy (like galena = 7.5)
○ Light (lighter than quartz = <2.6)

$$\frac{\text{mass of mineral}}{\text{mass of same volume of water}} = \frac{\text{weight of mineral in air}}{\text{weight of equal volume of water}}$$

Tenacity: ○ Brittle ○ Ductile ○ Elastic ○ Flexible ○ Friable
○ Malleable ○ Sectile

Diaphaneity: ○ Transparent ○ Translucent ○ Opaque

Notes: _____

Notes

_____
_____
_____
_____
_____
_____
_____
_____
_____
_____

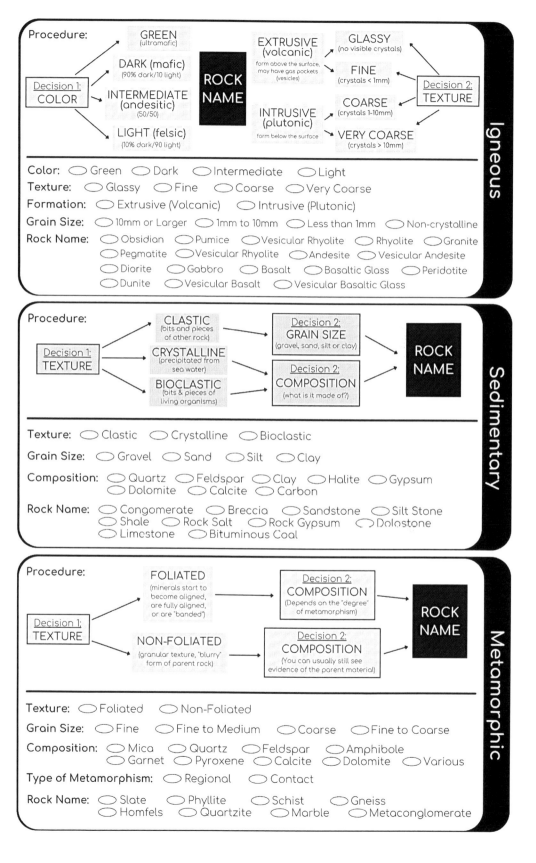

Igneous

Procedure:

Decision 1: COLOR →
- GREEN (ultramafic)
- DARK (mafic) (90% dark/10 light)
- INTERMEDIATE (andesitic) (50/50)
- LIGHT (felsic) (10% dark/90 light)

ROCK NAME

EXTRUSIVE (volcanic) — form above the surface, may have gas pockets (vesicles)

INTRUSIVE (plutonic) — form below the surface

- GLASSY (no visible crystals)
- FINE (crystals < 1mm)
- COARSE (crystals 1-10mm)
- VERY COARSE (crystals > 10mm)

Decision 2: TEXTURE

Color: ◯ Green ◯ Dark ◯ Intermediate ◯ Light

Texture: ◯ Glassy ◯ Fine ◯ Coarse ◯ Very Coarse

Formation: ◯ Extrusive (Volcanic) ◯ Intrusive (Plutonic)

Grain Size: ◯ 10mm or Larger ◯ 1mm to 10mm ◯ Less than 1mm ◯ Non-crystalline

Rock Name: ◯ Obsidian ◯ Pumice ◯ Vesicular Rhyolite ◯ Rhyolite ◯ Granite ◯ Pegmatite ◯ Vesicular Rhyolite ◯ Andesite ◯ Vesicular Andesite ◯ Diorite ◯ Gabbro ◯ Basalt ◯ Basaltic Glass ◯ Peridotite ◯ Dunite ◯ Vesicular Basalt ◯ Vesicular Basaltic Glass

Sedimentary

Procedure:

Decision 1: TEXTURE →
- CLASTIC (bits and pieces of other rock)
- CRYSTALLINE (precipitated from sea water)
- BIOCLASTIC (bits & pieces of living organisms)

Decision 2: GRAIN SIZE (gravel, sand, silt or clay)

Decision 2: COMPOSITION (what is it made of?)

ROCK NAME

Texture: ◯ Clastic ◯ Crystalline ◯ Bioclastic

Grain Size: ◯ Gravel ◯ Sand ◯ Silt ◯ Clay

Composition: ◯ Quartz ◯ Feldspar ◯ Clay ◯ Halite ◯ Gypsum ◯ Dolomite ◯ Calcite ◯ Carbon

Rock Name: ◯ Congomerate ◯ Breccia ◯ Sandstone ◯ Silt Stone ◯ Shale ◯ Rock Salt ◯ Rock Gypsum ◯ Dolostone ◯ Limestone ◯ Bituminous Coal

Metamorphic

Procedure:

Decision 1: TEXTURE →
- FOLIATED (minerals start to become aligned, are fully aligned, or are "banded")
- NON-FOLIATED (granular texture, "blurry" form of parent rock)

Decision 2: COMPOSITION (Depends on the "degree" of metamorphism)

Decision 2: COMPOSITION (You can usually still see evidence of the parent material)

ROCK NAME

Texture: ◯ Foliated ◯ Non-Foliated

Grain Size: ◯ Fine ◯ Fine to Medium ◯ Coarse ◯ Fine to Coarse

Composition: ◯ Mica ◯ Quartz ◯ Feldspar ◯ Amphibole ◯ Garnet ◯ Pyroxene ◯ Calcite ◯ Dolomite ◯ Various

Type of Metamorphism: ◯ Regional ◯ Contact

Rock Name: ◯ Slate ◯ Phyllite ◯ Schist ◯ Gneiss ◯ Homfels ◯ Quartzite ◯ Marble ◯ Metaconglomerate

General

Date: _____ GPS Location: _____

Location: ⃝ Public Land ⃝ Private Land ⃝ Pay-to-Dig Site ⃝ Quarry
⃝ Roadcut ⃝ Outcrop ⃝ Riverbed ⃝ Creek Bed ⃝ Beach
⃝ Mine Tailing ⃝ Fresh Overturned Soil ⃝ Other_____

Weather: ⃝ Sunny & Clear ⃝ Cloudy/Overcast ⃝ Windy ⃝ Rainy / Drizzle
⃝ Snow ⃝ Stormy ⃝ Fog ⃝ Drought ⃝ Other_____

Rock Type: ⃝ Igneous ⃝ Sedimentary ⃝ Metamorphic

Equipment Checklist: (Rockhounding)
⃝ Eye Protection ⃝ Heavy-Duty Gloves ⃝ Boots / Waterproof
⃝ First-Aid Kit ⃝ Hard Hat ⃝ Rock Hammer / Pick ⃝ Sieve
⃝ Colander ⃝ Small Picks ⃝ Trowel ⃝ Small Knife ⃝ Chisel
⃝ Small Broom ⃝ Crack Hammer ⃝ Pry Bar ⃝ Sledgehammer
⃝ Mason's Hammer ⃝ Shovel ⃝ Backpack ⃝ Bucket ⃝ Map
⃝ Wrapping Material ⃝ Small Tubes ⃝ Boxes / Containers
⃝ Loupe ⃝ Magnifying Glass ⃝ Magnet ⃝ Compass / GPS

Notes: _____

Mineral Identification

Color: ⃝ Light ⃝ Dark Specific Colors: _____

Luster: ⃝ Metallic ⃝ Gold ⃝ Brass ⃝ Bronze ⃝ Iron ⃝ Steel ⃝ Lead ⃝ Silver ⃝ Alum.
⃝ Non-Metallic ⃝ Adamantine ⃝ Vitreous ⃝ Resinous ⃝ Pearly ⃝ Dull ⃝ Greasy ⃝ Earthy ⃝ Silky

Cleavage: ⃝ 1 Direction ⃝ 2 Directions at 90° ⃝ 2 Directions not at 90°
⃝ 3 Directions at 90° (cubic) ⃝ 3 Directions not at 90° (rhombohedral)
⃝ 4 Directions (octahedral) ⃝ 6 Directions (dodecahedral)

Fracture: ⃝ Conchoidal (smooth, shell-like, or glass-like breaks) ⃝ Uneven (irregular, but not conchoidal) ⃝ Hackly (jagged, as of a metal)
⃝ Splintery (occurs in aggregates of many slender, brittle crystals) ⃝ Fibrous (occurs in aggregates of many slender, threadlike crystals)

Crystal Habit: ⃝ Prismatic ⃝ Acicular ⃝ Striated ⃝ Botryoidal ⃝ Dendritic
⃝ Nodular ⃝ Banded ⃝ Other_____

Hardness: (Mohs Scale)
⃝ 1 Talc ⃝ 2 Gypsum ⃝ 2.5 Fingernail ⃝ 3 Calcite ⃝ 4 Fluorite
⃝ 5 Apatite ⃝ 5.5 Glass ⃝ 6 Feldspar ⃝ 6.5 Steel File
⃝ 7 Quartz ⃝ 8 Topaz ⃝ 9 Corundrum ⃝ 10 Diamond

Specific Gravity:
⃝ Average (like quartz = 2.6 - 2.8)
⃝ Heavy (like galena = 7.5)
⃝ Light (lighter than quartz = <2.6)

$$\frac{\text{mass of mineral}}{\text{mass of same volume of water}} = \frac{\text{weight of mineral in air}}{\text{weight of equal volume of water}}$$

Tenacity: ⃝ Brittle ⃝ Ductile ⃝ Elastic ⃝ Flexible ⃝ Friable
⃝ Malleable ⃝ Sectile

Diaphaneity: ⃝ Transparent ⃝ Translucent ⃝ Opaque

Notes: _____

Notes

_____
_____
_____
_____
_____
_____
_____
_____
_____

Igneous

Procedure:

Decision 1: **COLOR**
- GREEN (ultramafic)
- DARK (mafic) (90% dark/10 light)
- INTERMEDIATE (andesitic) (50/50)
- LIGHT (felsic) (10% dark/90 light)

ROCK NAME

- EXTRUSIVE (volcanic) — form above the surface, may have gas pockets (vesicles)
  - GLASSY (no visible crystals)
  - FINE (crystals < 1mm)
- INTRUSIVE (plutonic) — form below the surface
  - COARSE (crystals 1-10mm)
  - VERY COARSE (crystals > 10mm)

Decision 2: **TEXTURE**

Color: ◯ Green ◯ Dark ◯ Intermediate ◯ Light

Texture: ◯ Glassy ◯ Fine ◯ Coarse ◯ Very Coarse

Formation: ◯ Extrusive (Volcanic) ◯ Intrusive (Plutonic)

Grain Size: ◯ 10mm or Larger ◯ 1mm to 10mm ◯ Less than 1mm ◯ Non-crystalline

Rock Name: ◯ Obsidian ◯ Pumice ◯ Vesicular Rhyolite ◯ Rhyolite ◯ Granite
◯ Pegmatite ◯ Vesicular Rhyolite ◯ Andesite ◯ Vesicular Andesite
◯ Diorite ◯ Gabbro ◯ Basalt ◯ Basaltic Glass ◯ Peridotite
◯ Dunite ◯ Vesicular Basalt ◯ Vesicular Basaltic Glass

Sedimentary

Procedure:

Decision 1: **TEXTURE**
- CLASTIC (bits and pieces of other rock)
- CRYSTALLINE (precipitated from sea water)
- BIOCLASTIC (bits & pieces of living organisms)

Decision 2: **GRAIN SIZE** (gravel, sand, silt or clay)

Decision 2: **COMPOSITION** (what is it made of?)

ROCK NAME

Texture: ◯ Clastic ◯ Crystalline ◯ Bioclastic

Grain Size: ◯ Gravel ◯ Sand ◯ Silt ◯ Clay

Composition: ◯ Quartz ◯ Feldspar ◯ Clay ◯ Halite ◯ Gypsum
◯ Dolomite ◯ Calcite ◯ Carbon

Rock Name: ◯ Congomerate ◯ Breccia ◯ Sandstone ◯ Silt Stone
◯ Shale ◯ Rock Salt ◯ Rock Gypsum ◯ Dolostone
◯ Limestone ◯ Bituminous Coal

Metamorphic

Procedure:

Decision 1: **TEXTURE**
- FOLIATED (minerals start to become aligned, are fully aligned, or are "banded")
- NON-FOLIATED (granular texture, "blurry" form of parent rock)

Decision 2: **COMPOSITION** (Depends on the "degree" of metamorphism)

Decision 2: **COMPOSITION** (You can usually still see evidence of the parent material)

ROCK NAME

Texture: ◯ Foliated ◯ Non-Foliated

Grain Size: ◯ Fine ◯ Fine to Medium ◯ Coarse ◯ Fine to Coarse

Composition: ◯ Mica ◯ Quartz ◯ Feldspar ◯ Amphibole
◯ Garnet ◯ Pyroxene ◯ Calcite ◯ Dolomite ◯ Various

Type of Metamorphism: ◯ Regional ◯ Contact

Rock Name: ◯ Slate ◯ Phyllite ◯ Schist ◯ Gneiss
◯ Homfels ◯ Quartzite ◯ Marble ◯ Metaconglomerate

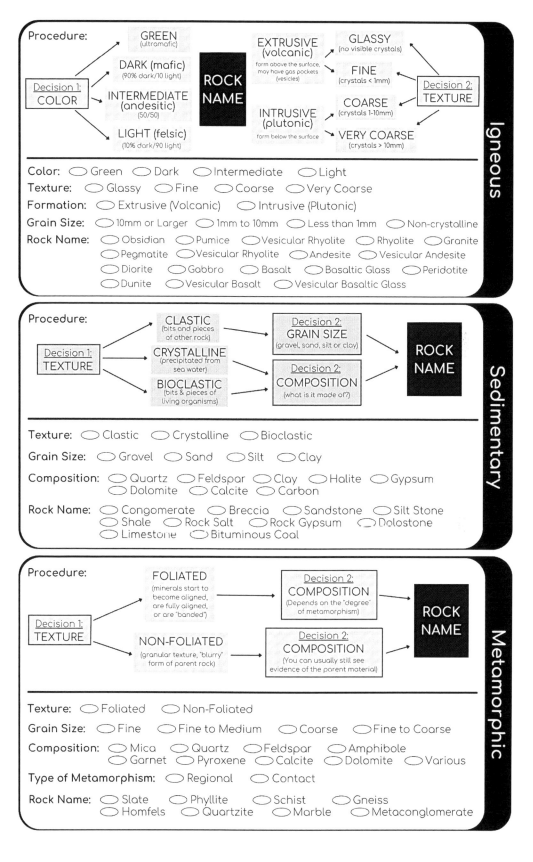

General

Date: _____ GPS Location: _____

Location:
- ◯ Public Land ◯ Private Land ◯ Pay-to-Dig Site ◯ Quarry
- ◯ Roadcut ◯ Outcrop ◯ Riverbed ◯ Creek Bed ◯ Beach
- ◯ Mine Tailing ◯ Fresh Overturned Soil ◯ Other_____

Weather:
- ◯ Sunny & Clear ◯ Cloudy/Overcast ◯ Windy ◯ Rainy / Drizzle
- ◯ Snow ◯ Stormy ◯ Fog ◯ Drought ◯ Other_____

Rock Type: ◯ Igneous ◯ Sedimentary ◯ Metamorphic

Equipment Checklist:
(Rockhounding)
- ◯ Eye Protection ◯ Heavy-Duty Gloves ◯ Boots / Waterproof
- ◯ First-Aid Kit ◯ Hard Hat ◯ Rock Hammer / Pick ◯ Sieve
- ◯ Colander ◯ Small Picks ◯ Trowel ◯ Small Knife ◯ Chisel
- ◯ Small Broom ◯ Crack Hammer ◯ Pry Bar ◯ Sledgehammer
- ◯ Mason's Hammer ◯ Shovel ◯ Backpack ◯ Bucket ◯ Map
- ◯ Wrapping Material ◯ Small Tubes ◯ Boxes / Containers
- ◯ Loupe ◯ Magnifying Glass ◯ Magnet ◯ Compass / GPS

Notes: _____

Mineral Identification

Color: ◯ Light ◯ Dark Specific Colors: _____

Luster:
- ◯ Metallic ◯ Gold ◯ Brass ◯ Bronze ◯ Iron ◯ Steel ◯ Lead ◯ Silver ◯ Alum.
- ◯ Non-Metallic ◯ Adamantine ◯ Vitreous ◯ Resinous ◯ Pearly ◯ Dull ◯ Greasy ◯ Earthy ◯ Silky

Cleavage:
- ◯ 1 Direction ◯ 2 Directions at 90° ◯ 2 Directions not at 90°
- ◯ 3 Directions at 90° (cubic) ◯ 3 Directions not at 90° (rhombohedral)
- ◯ 4 Directions (octahedral) ◯ 6 Directions (dodecahedral)

Fracture:
- ◯ Conchoidal (smooth, shell-like, or glass-like breaks) ◯ Uneven (irregular, but not conchoidal) ◯ Hackly (jagged, as of a metal)
- ◯ Splintery (occurs in aggregates of many slender, brittle crystals) ◯ Fibrous (occurs in aggregates of many slender, threadlike crystals)

Crystal Habit:
- ◯ Prismatic ◯ Acicular ◯ Striated ◯ Botryoidal ◯ Dendritic
- ◯ Nodular ◯ Banded ◯ Other_____

Hardness: (Mohs Scale)
- ◯ 1 Talc ◯ 2 Gypsum ◯ 2.5 Fingernail ◯ 3 Calcite ◯ 4 Fluorite
- ◯ 5 Apatite ◯ 5.5 Glass ◯ 6 Feldspar ◯ 6.5 Steel File
- ◯ 7 Quartz ◯ 8 Topaz ◯ 9 Corundrum ◯ 10 Diamond

Specific Gravity:
- ◯ Average (like quartz = 2.6 - 2.8)
- ◯ Heavy (like galena = 7.5)
- ◯ Light (lighter than quartz = <2.6)

$$\frac{\text{mass of mineral}}{\text{mass of same volume of water}} = \frac{\text{weight of mineral in air}}{\text{weight of equal volume of water}}$$

Tenacity:
- ◯ Brittle ◯ Ductile ◯ Elastic ◯ Flexible ◯ Friable
- ◯ Malleable ◯ Sectile

Diaphaneity: ◯ Transparent ◯ Translucent ◯ Opaque

Notes: _____

Notes

_____
_____
_____
_____
_____
_____
_____
_____
_____
_____

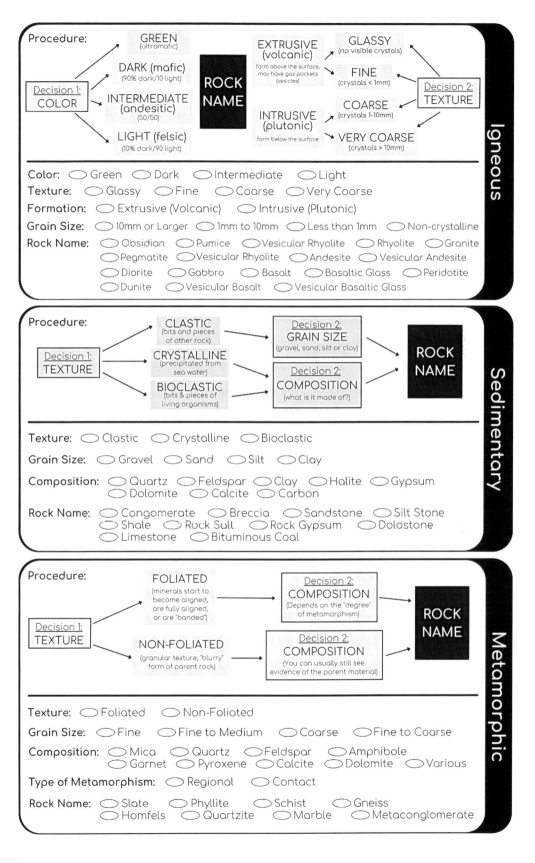

Igneous

Procedure:

Decision 1: COLOR
- GREEN (ultramafic)
- DARK (mafic) (90% dark/10 light)
- INTERMEDIATE (andesitic) (50/50)
- LIGHT (felsic) (10% dark/90 light)

ROCK NAME

- EXTRUSIVE (volcanic) form above the surface, may have gas pockets (vesicles)
- INTRUSIVE (plutonic) form below the surface

Decision 2: TEXTURE
- GLASSY (no visible crystals)
- FINE (crystals < 1mm)
- COARSE (crystals 1-10mm)
- VERY COARSE (crystals > 10mm)

Color: ◯ Green ◯ Dark ◯ Intermediate ◯ Light
Texture: ◯ Glassy ◯ Fine ◯ Coarse ◯ Very Coarse
Formation: ◯ Extrusive (Volcanic) ◯ Intrusive (Plutonic)
Grain Size: ◯ 10mm or Larger ◯ 1mm to 10mm ◯ Less than 1mm ◯ Non-crystalline
Rock Name: ◯ Obsidian ◯ Pumice ◯ Vesicular Rhyolite ◯ Rhyolite ◯ Granite ◯ Pegmatite ◯ Vesicular Rhyolite ◯ Andesite ◯ Vesicular Andesite ◯ Diorite ◯ Gabbro ◯ Basalt ◯ Basaltic Glass ◯ Peridotite ◯ Dunite ◯ Vesicular Basalt ◯ Vesicular Basaltic Glass

Sedimentary

Procedure:

Decision 1: TEXTURE
- CLASTIC (bits and pieces of other rock)
- CRYSTALLINE (precipitated from sea water)
- BIOCLASTIC (bits & pieces of living organisms)

Decision 2: GRAIN SIZE (gravel, sand, silt or clay)
Decision 2: COMPOSITION (what is it made of?)

ROCK NAME

Texture: ◯ Clastic ◯ Crystalline ◯ Bioclastic
Grain Size: ◯ Gravel ◯ Sand ◯ Silt ◯ Clay
Composition: ◯ Quartz ◯ Feldspar ◯ Clay ◯ Halite ◯ Gypsum ◯ Dolomite ◯ Calcite ◯ Carbon
Rock Name: ◯ Congomerate ◯ Breccia ◯ Sandstone ◯ Silt Stone ◯ Shale ◯ Rock Salt ◯ Rock Gypsum ◯ Dolostone ◯ Limestone ◯ Bituminous Coal

Metamorphic

Procedure:

Decision 1: TEXTURE
- FOLIATED (minerals start to become aligned, are fully aligned, or are "banded")
- NON-FOLIATED (granular texture, "blurry" form of parent rock)

Decision 2: COMPOSITION (Depends on the "degree" of metamorphism)
Decision 2: COMPOSITION (You can usually still see evidence of the parent material)

ROCK NAME

Texture: ◯ Foliated ◯ Non-Foliated
Grain Size: ◯ Fine ◯ Fine to Medium ◯ Coarse ◯ Fine to Coarse
Composition: ◯ Mica ◯ Quartz ◯ Feldspar ◯ Amphibole ◯ Garnet ◯ Pyroxene ◯ Calcite ◯ Dolomite ◯ Various
Type of Metamorphism: ◯ Regional ◯ Contact
Rock Name: ◯ Slate ◯ Phyllite ◯ Schist ◯ Gneiss ◯ Hornfels ◯ Quartzite ◯ Marble ◯ Metaconglomerate

General

Date: _____ GPS Location: _____

Location: ◯ Public Land ◯ Private Land ◯ Pay-to-Dig Site ◯ Quarry
◯ Roadcut ◯ Outcrop ◯ Riverbed ◯ Creek Bed ◯ Beach
◯ Mine Tailing ◯ Fresh Overturned Soil ◯ Other_____

Weather: ◯ Sunny & Clear ◯ Cloudy/Overcast ◯ Windy ◯ Rainy / Drizzle
◯ Snow ◯ Stormy ◯ Fog ◯ Drought ◯ Other_____

Rock Type: ◯ Igneous ◯ Sedimentary ◯ Metamorphic

Equipment Checklist:
(Rockhounding)
◯ Eye Protection ◯ Heavy-Duty Gloves ◯ Boots / Waterproof
◯ First-Aid Kit ◯ Hard Hat ◯ Rock Hammer / Pick ◯ Sieve
◯ Colander ◯ Small Picks ◯ Trowel ◯ Small Knife ◯ Chisel
◯ Small Broom ◯ Crack Hammer ◯ Pry Bar ◯ Sledgehammer
◯ Mason's Hammer ◯ Shovel ◯ Backpack ◯ Bucket ◯ Map
◯ Wrapping Material ◯ Small Tubes ◯ Boxes / Containers
◯ Loupe ◯ Magnifying Glass ◯ Magnet ◯ Compass / GPS

Notes: _____

Mineral Identification

Color: ◯ Light ◯ Dark Specific Colors: _____

Luster: ◯ Metallic ◯ Gold ◯ Brass ◯ Non-Metallic ◯ Adamantine ◯ Vitreous
◯ Bronze ◯ Iron ◯ Resinous ◯ Pearly ◯ Dull
◯ Steel ◯ Lead ◯ Greasy ◯ Earthy ◯ Silky
◯ Silver ◯ Alum.

Cleavage: ◯ 1 Direction ◯ 2 Directions at 90° ◯ 2 Directions not at 90°
◯ 3 Directions at 90° (cubic) ◯ 3 Directions not at 90° (rhombohedral)
◯ 4 Directions (octahedral) ◯ 6 Directions (dodecahedral)

Fracture: ◯ Conchoidal (smooth, shell-like, or glass-like breaks) ◯ Uneven (irregular, but not conchoidal) ◯ Hackly (jagged, as of a metal)
◯ Splintery (occurs in aggregates of many slender, brittle crystals) ◯ Fibrous (occurs in aggregates of many slender, threadlike crystals)

Crystal Habit: ◯ Prismatic ◯ Acicular ◯ Striated ◯ Botryoidal ◯ Dendritic
◯ Nodular ◯ Banded ◯ Other_____

Hardness: (Mohs Scale)
◯ 1 Talc ◯ 2 Gypsum ◯ 2.5 Fingernail ◯ 3 Calcite ◯ 4 Fluorite
◯ 5 Apatite ◯ 5.5 Glass ◯ 6 Feldspar ◯ 6.5 Steel File
◯ 7 Quartz ◯ 8 Topaz ◯ 9 Corundrum ◯ 10 Diamond

Specific Gravity:
◯ Average (like quartz = 2.6 - 2.8)
◯ Heavy (like galena = 7.5)
◯ Light (lighter than quartz = <2.6)

$$\frac{\text{mass of mineral}}{\text{mass of same volume of water}} = \frac{\text{weight of mineral in air}}{\text{weight of equal volume of water}}$$

Tenacity: ◯ Brittle ◯ Ductile ◯ Elastic ◯ Flexible ◯ Friable
◯ Malleable ◯ Sectile

Diaphaneity: ◯ Transparent ◯ Translucent ◯ Opaque

Notes: _____

Notes

_____
_____
_____
_____
_____
_____
_____
_____
_____
_____

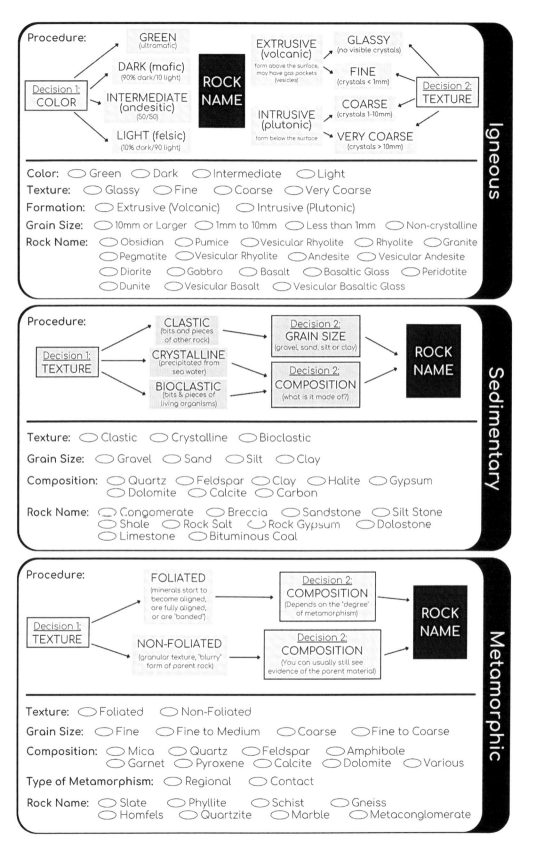

Igneous

Procedure:

Decision 1: COLOR →
- GREEN (ultramafic)
- DARK (mafic) (90% dark/10 light)
- INTERMEDIATE (andesitic) (50/50)
- LIGHT (felsic) (10% dark/90 light)

ROCK NAME

EXTRUSIVE (volcanic) — form above the surface, may have gas pockets (vesicles)

INTRUSIVE (plutonic) — form below the surface

Decision 2: TEXTURE →
- GLASSY (no visible crystals)
- FINE (crystals < 1mm)
- COARSE (crystals 1-10mm)
- VERY COARSE (crystals > 10mm)

Color: ◯ Green ◯ Dark ◯ Intermediate ◯ Light

Texture: ◯ Glassy ◯ Fine ◯ Coarse ◯ Very Coarse

Formation: ◯ Extrusive (Volcanic) ◯ Intrusive (Plutonic)

Grain Size: ◯ 10mm or Larger ◯ 1mm to 10mm ◯ Less than 1mm ◯ Non-crystalline

Rock Name: ◯ Obsidian ◯ Pumice ◯ Vesicular Rhyolite ◯ Rhyolite ◯ Granite
◯ Pegmatite ◯ Vesicular Rhyolite ◯ Andesite ◯ Vesicular Andesite
◯ Diorite ◯ Gabbro ◯ Basalt ◯ Basaltic Glass ◯ Peridotite
◯ Dunite ◯ Vesicular Basalt ◯ Vesicular Basaltic Glass

Sedimentary

Procedure:

Decision 1: TEXTURE →
- CLASTIC (bits and pieces of other rock)
- CRYSTALLINE (precipitated from sea water)
- BIOCLASTIC (bits & pieces of living organisms)

Decision 2: GRAIN SIZE (gravel, sand, silt or clay)

Decision 2: COMPOSITION (what is it made of?)

ROCK NAME

Texture: ◯ Clastic ◯ Crystalline ◯ Bioclastic

Grain Size: ◯ Gravel ◯ Sand ◯ Silt ◯ Clay

Composition: ◯ Quartz ◯ Feldspar ◯ Clay ◯ Halite ◯ Gypsum
◯ Dolomite ◯ Calcite ◯ Carbon

Rock Name: ◯ Conglomerate ◯ Breccia ◯ Sandstone ◯ Silt Stone
◯ Shale ◯ Rock Salt ◯ Rock Gypsum ◯ Dolostone
◯ Limestone ◯ Bituminous Coal

Metamorphic

Procedure:

Decision 1: TEXTURE →
- FOLIATED (minerals start to become aligned, are fully aligned, or are "banded")
- NON-FOLIATED (granular texture, "blurry" form of parent rock)

Decision 2: COMPOSITION (Depends on the "degree" of metamorphism)

Decision 2: COMPOSITION (You can usually still see evidence of the parent material)

ROCK NAME

Texture: ◯ Foliated ◯ Non-Foliated

Grain Size: ◯ Fine ◯ Fine to Medium ◯ Coarse ◯ Fine to Coarse

Composition: ◯ Mica ◯ Quartz ◯ Feldspar ◯ Amphibole
◯ Garnet ◯ Pyroxene ◯ Calcite ◯ Dolomite ◯ Various

Type of Metamorphism: ◯ Regional ◯ Contact

Rock Name: ◯ Slate ◯ Phyllite ◯ Schist ◯ Gneiss
◯ Homfels ◯ Quartzite ◯ Marble ◯ Metaconglomerate

General

Date: _____ GPS Location: _____

Location: ⭘ Public Land ⭘ Private Land ⭘ Pay-to-Dig Site ⭘ Quarry
⭘ Roadcut ⭘ Outcrop ⭘ Riverbed ⭘ Creek Bed ⭘ Beach
⭘ Mine Tailing ⭘ Fresh Overturned Soil ⭘ Other_____

Weather: ⭘ Sunny & Clear ⭘ Cloudy/Overcast ⭘ Windy ⭘ Rainy / Drizzle
⭘ Snow ⭘ Stormy ⭘ Fog ⭘ Drought ⭘ Other_____

Rock Type: ⭘ Igneous ⭘ Sedimentary ⭘ Metamorphic

Equipment Checklist:
(Rockhounding)
⭘ Eye Protection ⭘ Heavy-Duty Gloves ⭘ Boots / Waterproof
⭘ First-Aid Kit ⭘ Hard Hat ⭘ Rock Hammer / Pick ⭘ Sieve
⭘ Colander ⭘ Small Picks ⭘ Trowel ⭘ Small Knife ⭘ Chisel
⭘ Small Broom ⭘ Crack Hammer ⭘ Pry Bar ⭘ Sledgehammer
⭘ Mason's Hammer ⭘ Shovel ⭘ Backpack ⭘ Bucket ⭘ Map
⭘ Wrapping Material ⭘ Small Tubes ⭘ Boxes / Containers
⭘ Loupe ⭘ Magnifying Glass ⭘ Magnet ⭘ Compass / GPS

Notes: _____

Mineral Identification

Color: ⭘ Light ⭘ Dark Specific Colors: _____

Luster: ⭘ Metallic ⭘ Gold ⭘ Brass ⭘ Non-Metallic ⭘ Adamantine ⭘ Vitreous
⭘ Bronze ⭘ Iron ⭘ Resinous ⭘ Pearly ⭘ Dull
⭘ Steel ⭘ Lead ⭘ Greasy ⭘ Earthy ⭘ Silky
⭘ Silver ⭘ Alum.

Cleavage: ⭘ 1 Direction ⭘ 2 Directions at 90° ⭘ 2 Directions not at 90°
⭘ 3 Directions at 90° (cubic) ⭘ 3 Directions not at 90° (rhombohedral)
⭘ 4 Directions (octahedral) ⭘ 6 Directions (dodecahedral)

Fracture: ⭘ Conchoidal (smooth, shell-like, or glass-like breaks) ⭘ Uneven (irregular, but not conchoidal) ⭘ Hackly (jagged, as of a metal)
⭘ Splintery (occurs in aggregates of many slender, brittle crystals) ⭘ Fibrous (occurs in aggregates of many slender, threadlike crystals)

Crystal Habit: ⭘ Prismatic ⭘ Acicular ⭘ Striated ⭘ Botryoidal ⭘ Dendritic
⭘ Nodular ⭘ Banded ⭘ Other_____

Hardness:
(Mohs Scale)
⭘ 1 Talc ⭘ 2 Gypsum ⭘ 2.5 Fingernail ⭘ 3 Calcite ⭘ 4 Fluorite
⭘ 5 Apatite ⭘ 5.5 Glass ⭘ 6 Feldspar ⭘ 6.5 Steel File
⭘ 7 Quartz ⭘ 8 Topaz ⭘ 9 Corundrum ⭘ 10 Diamond

Specific Gravity:
⭘ Average (like quartz = 2.6 - 2.8)
⭘ Heavy (like galena = 7.5)
⭘ Light (lighter than quartz = <2.6)

$$\frac{\text{mass of mineral}}{\text{mass of same volume of water}} = \frac{\text{weight of mineral in air}}{\text{weight of equal volume of water}}$$

Tenacity: ⭘ Brittle ⭘ Ductile ⭘ Elastic ⭘ Flexible ⭘ Friable
⭘ Malleable ⭘ Sectile

Diaphaneity: ⭘ Transparent ⭘ Translucent ⭘ Opaque

Notes:_____

Notes

_____
_____
_____
_____
_____
_____
_____
_____
_____
_____

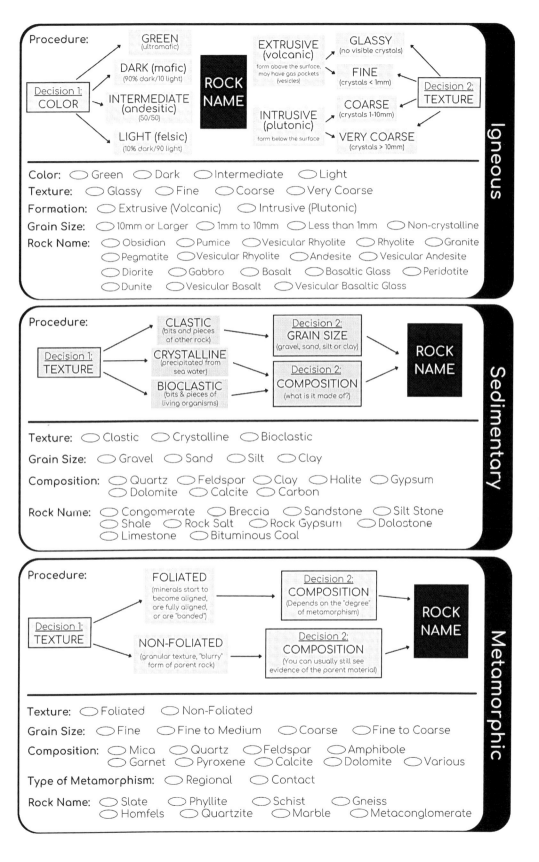

Igneous

Procedure:

Decision 1: COLOR
- GREEN (ultramafic)
- DARK (mafic) (90% dark/10 light)
- INTERMEDIATE (andesitic) (50/50)
- LIGHT (felsic) (10% dark/90 light)

ROCK NAME

- EXTRUSIVE (volcanic) — form above the surface, may have gas pockets (vesicles)
- INTRUSIVE (plutonic) — form below the surface

Decision 2: TEXTURE
- GLASSY (no visible crystals)
- FINE (crystals < 1mm)
- COARSE (crystals 1-10mm)
- VERY COARSE (crystals > 10mm)

Color: ○ Green ○ Dark ○ Intermediate ○ Light

Texture: ○ Glassy ○ Fine ○ Coarse ○ Very Coarse

Formation: ○ Extrusive (Volcanic) ○ Intrusive (Plutonic)

Grain Size: ○ 10mm or Larger ○ 1mm to 10mm ○ Less than 1mm ○ Non-crystalline

Rock Name: ○ Obsidian ○ Pumice ○ Vesicular Rhyolite ○ Rhyolite ○ Granite ○ Pegmatite ○ Vesicular Rhyolite ○ Andesite ○ Vesicular Andesite ○ Diorite ○ Gabbro ○ Basalt ○ Basaltic Glass ○ Peridotite ○ Dunite ○ Vesicular Basalt ○ Vesicular Basaltic Glass

Sedimentary

Procedure:

Decision 1: TEXTURE
- CLASTIC (bits and pieces of other rock)
- CRYSTALLINE (precipitated from sea water)
- BIOCLASTIC (bits & pieces of living organisms)

Decision 2: GRAIN SIZE (gravel, sand, silt or clay)

Decision 2: COMPOSITION (what is it made of?)

ROCK NAME

Texture: ○ Clastic ○ Crystalline ○ Bioclastic

Grain Size: ○ Gravel ○ Sand ○ Silt ○ Clay

Composition: ○ Quartz ○ Feldspar ○ Clay ○ Halite ○ Gypsum ○ Dolomite ○ Calcite ○ Carbon

Rock Name: ○ Conglomerate ○ Breccia ○ Sandstone ○ Silt Stone ○ Shale ○ Rock Salt ○ Rock Gypsum ○ Dolostone ○ Limestone ○ Bituminous Coal

Metamorphic

Procedure:

Decision 1: TEXTURE
- FOLIATED (minerals start to become aligned, are fully aligned, or are "banded")
- NON-FOLIATED (granular texture, "blurry" form of parent rock)

Decision 2: COMPOSITION (Depends on the "degree" of metamorphism)

Decision 2: COMPOSITION (You can usually still see evidence of the parent material)

ROCK NAME

Texture: ○ Foliated ○ Non-Foliated

Grain Size: ○ Fine ○ Fine to Medium ○ Coarse ○ Fine to Coarse

Composition: ○ Mica ○ Quartz ○ Feldspar ○ Amphibole ○ Garnet ○ Pyroxene ○ Calcite ○ Dolomite ○ Various

Type of Metamorphism: ○ Regional ○ Contact

Rock Name: ○ Slate ○ Phyllite ○ Schist ○ Gneiss ○ Hornfels ○ Quartzite ○ Marble ○ Metaconglomerate

General

Date: _____ GPS Location: _____

Location: ◯ Public Land ◯ Private Land ◯ Pay-to-Dig Site ◯ Quarry
◯ Roadcut ◯ Outcrop ◯ Riverbed ◯ Creek Bed ◯ Beach
◯ Mine Tailing ◯ Fresh Overturned Soil ◯ Other_____

Weather: ◯ Sunny & Clear ◯ Cloudy/Overcast ◯ Windy ◯ Rainy / Drizzle
◯ Snow ◯ Stormy ◯ Fog ◯ Drought ◯ Other_____

Rock Type: ◯ Igneous ◯ Sedimentary ◯ Metamorphic

Equipment Checklist:
(Rockhounding)
◯ Eye Protection ◯ Heavy-Duty Gloves ◯ Boots / Waterproof
◯ First-Aid Kit ◯ Hard Hat ◯ Rock Hammer / Pick ◯ Sieve
◯ Colander ◯ Small Picks ◯ Trowel ◯ Small Knife ◯ Chisel
◯ Small Broom ◯ Crack Hammer ◯ Pry Bar ◯ Sledgehammer
◯ Mason's Hammer ◯ Shovel ◯ Backpack ◯ Bucket ◯ Map
◯ Wrapping Material ◯ Small Tubes ◯ Boxes / Containers
◯ Loupe ◯ Magnifying Glass ◯ Magnet ◯ Compass / GPS

Notes: _____

Mineral Identification

Color: ◯ Light ◯ Dark Specific Colors: _____

Luster: ◯ Metallic ◯ Gold ◯ Brass ◯ Non-Metallic ◯ Adamantine ◯ Vitreous
◯ Bronze ◯ Iron   ◯ Resinous ◯ Pearly ◯ Dull
◯ Steel ◯ Lead   ◯ Greasy ◯ Earthy ◯ Silky
◯ Silver ◯ Alum.

Cleavage: ◯ 1 Direction ◯ 2 Directions at 90° ◯ 2 Directions not at 90°
◯ 3 Directions at 90° (cubic) ◯ 3 Directions not at 90° (rhombohedral)
◯ 4 Directions (octahedral) ◯ 6 Directions (dodecahedral)

Fracture: ◯ Conchoidal (smooth, shell-like, or glass-like breaks) ◯ Uneven (irregular, but not conchoidal) ◯ Hackly (jagged, as of a metal)
◯ Splintery (occurs in aggregates of many slender, brittle crystals) ◯ Fibrous (occurs in aggregates of many slender, threadlike crystals)

Crystal Habit: ◯ Prismatic ◯ Acicular ◯ Striated ◯ Botryoidal ◯ Dendritic
◯ Nodular ◯ Banded ◯ Other_____

Hardness: (Mohs Scale)
◯ 1 Talc ◯ 2 Gypsum ◯ 2.5 Fingernail ◯ 3 Calcite ◯ 4 Fluorite
◯ 5 Apatite ◯ 5.5 Glass ◯ 6 Feldspar ◯ 6.5 Steel File
◯ 7 Quartz ◯ 8 Topaz ◯ 9 Corundrum ◯ 10 Diamond

Specific Gravity:
◯ Average (like quartz = 2.6 - 2.8)
◯ Heavy (like galena = 7.5)
◯ Light (lighter than quartz = <2.6)

mass of mineral / mass of same volume of water = weight of mineral in air / weight of equal volume of water

Tenacity: ◯ Brittle ◯ Ductile ◯ Elastic ◯ Flexible ◯ Friable
◯ Malleable ◯ Sectile

Diaphaneity: ◯ Transparent ◯ Translucent ◯ Opaque

Notes: _____

Notes

_____
_____
_____
_____
_____
_____
_____
_____
_____
_____

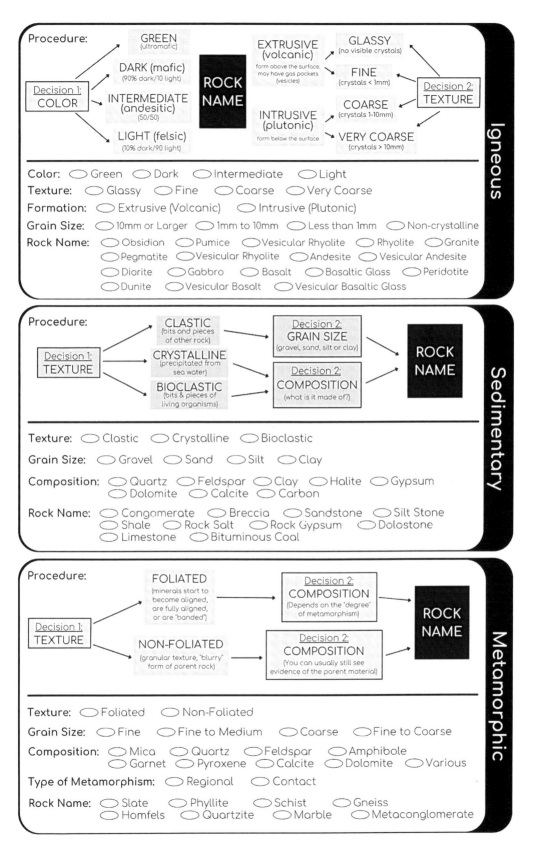

General

Date: _____ GPS Location: _____

Location: ⚪ Public Land ⚪ Private Land ⚪ Pay-to-Dig Site ⚪ Quarry
⚪ Roadcut ⚪ Outcrop ⚪ Riverbed ⚪ Creek Bed ⚪ Beach
⚪ Mine Tailing ⚪ Fresh Overturned Soil ⚪ Other_____

Weather: ⚪ Sunny & Clear ⚪ Cloudy/Overcast ⚪ Windy ⚪ Rainy / Drizzle
⚪ Snow ⚪ Stormy ⚪ Fog ⚪ Drought ⚪ Other_____

Rock Type: ⚪ Igneous ⚪ Sedimentary ⚪ Metamorphic

Equipment Checklist:
(Rockhounding)
⚪ Eye Protection ⚪ Heavy-Duty Gloves ⚪ Boots / Waterproof
⚪ First-Aid Kit ⚪ Hard Hat ⚪ Rock Hammer / Pick ⚪ Sieve
⚪ Colander ⚪ Small Picks ⚪ Trowel ⚪ Small Knife ⚪ Chisel
⚪ Small Broom ⚪ Crack Hammer ⚪ Pry Bar ⚪ Sledgehammer
⚪ Mason's Hammer ⚪ Shovel ⚪ Backpack ⚪ Bucket ⚪ Map
⚪ Wrapping Material ⚪ Small Tubes ⚪ Boxes / Containers
⚪ Loupe ⚪ Magnifying Glass ⚪ Magnet ⚪ Compass / GPS

Notes: _____

Mineral Identification

Color: ⚪ Light ⚪ Dark Specific Colors: _____

Luster: ⚪ Metallic ⚪ Gold ⚪ Brass ⚪ Non-Metallic ⚪ Adamantine ⚪ Vitreous
⚪ Bronze ⚪ Iron ⚪ Resinous ⚪ Pearly ⚪ Dull
⚪ Steel ⚪ Lead ⚪ Greasy ⚪ Earthy ⚪ Silky
⚪ Silver ⚪ Alum.

Cleavage: ⚪ 1 Direction ⚪ 2 Directions at 90° ⚪ 2 Directions not at 90°
⚪ 3 Directions at 90° (cubic) ⚪ 3 Directions not at 90° (rhombohedral)
⚪ 4 Directions (octahedral) ⚪ 6 Directions (dodecahedral)

Fracture: ⚪ Conchoidal (smooth, shell-like, or glass-like breaks) ⚪ Uneven (irregular, but not conchoidal) ⚪ Hackly (jagged, as of a metal)
⚪ Splintery (occurs in aggregates of many slender, brittle crystals) ⚪ Fibrous (occurs in aggregates of many slender, threadlike crystals)

Crystal Habit: ⚪ Prismatic ⚪ Acicular ⚪ Striated ⚪ Botryoidal ⚪ Dendritic
⚪ Nodular ⚪ Banded ⚪ Other_____

Hardness: (Mohs Scale)
⚪ 1 Talc ⚪ 2 Gypsum ⚪ 2.5 Fingernail ⚪ 3 Calcite ⚪ 4 Fluorite
⚪ 5 Apatite ⚪ 5.5 Glass ⚪ 6 Feldspar ⚪ 6.5 Steel File
⚪ 7 Quartz ⚪ 8 Topaz ⚪ 9 Corundrum ⚪ 10 Diamond

Specific Gravity:
⚪ Average (like quartz = 2.6 - 2.8) $\frac{\text{mass of mineral}}{\text{mass of same volume of water}} = \frac{\text{weight of mineral in air}}{\text{weight of equal volume of water}}$
⚪ Heavy (like galena = 7.5)
⚪ Light (lighter than quartz = <2.6)

Tenacity: ⚪ Brittle ⚪ Ductile ⚪ Elastic ⚪ Flexible ⚪ Friable
⚪ Malleable ⚪ Sectile

Diaphaneity: ⚪ Transparent ⚪ Translucent ⚪ Opaque

Notes: _____

Notes

_____
_____
_____
_____
_____
_____
_____
_____
_____
_____

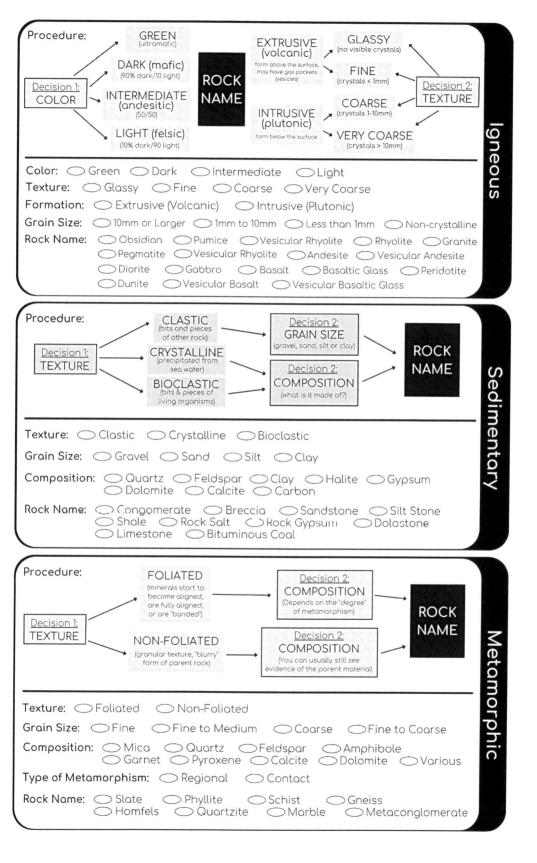

Igneous

Procedure:

Decision 1: COLOR →
- GREEN (ultramafic)
- DARK (mafic) (90% dark/10 light)
- INTERMEDIATE (andesitic) (50/50)
- LIGHT (felsic) (10% dark/90 light)

ROCK NAME

EXTRUSIVE (volcanic) — form above the surface, may have gas pockets (vesicles)

INTRUSIVE (plutonic) — form below the surface

Decision 2: TEXTURE →
- GLASSY (no visible crystals)
- FINE (crystals < 1mm)
- COARSE (crystals 1-10mm)
- VERY COARSE (crystals > 10mm)

Color: ◯ Green ◯ Dark ◯ Intermediate ◯ Light

Texture: ◯ Glassy ◯ Fine ◯ Coarse ◯ Very Coarse

Formation: ◯ Extrusive (Volcanic) ◯ Intrusive (Plutonic)

Grain Size: ◯ 10mm or Larger ◯ 1mm to 10mm ◯ Less than 1mm ◯ Non-crystalline

Rock Name: ◯ Obsidian ◯ Pumice ◯ Vesicular Rhyolite ◯ Rhyolite ◯ Granite
◯ Pegmatite ◯ Vesicular Rhyolite ◯ Andesite ◯ Vesicular Andesite
◯ Diorite ◯ Gabbro ◯ Basalt ◯ Basaltic Glass ◯ Peridotite
◯ Dunite ◯ Vesicular Basalt ◯ Vesicular Basaltic Glass

Sedimentary

Procedure:

Decision 1: TEXTURE →
- CLASTIC (bits and pieces of other rock) → Decision 2: GRAIN SIZE (gravel, sand, silt or clay)
- CRYSTALLINE (precipitated from sea water)
- BIOCLASTIC (bits & pieces of living organisms) → Decision 2: COMPOSITION (what is it made of?)

ROCK NAME

Texture: ◯ Clastic ◯ Crystalline ◯ Bioclastic

Grain Size: ◯ Gravel ◯ Sand ◯ Silt ◯ Clay

Composition: ◯ Quartz ◯ Feldspar ◯ Clay ◯ Halite ◯ Gypsum
◯ Dolomite ◯ Calcite ◯ Carbon

Rock Name: ◯ Conglomerate ◯ Breccia ◯ Sandstone ◯ Silt Stone
◯ Shale ◯ Rock Salt ◯ Rock Gypsum ◯ Dolostone
◯ Limestone ◯ Bituminous Coal

Metamorphic

Procedure:

Decision 1: TEXTURE →
- FOLIATED (minerals start to become aligned, are fully aligned, or are "banded") → Decision 2: COMPOSITION (Depends on the "degree" of metamorphism)
- NON-FOLIATED (granular texture, "blurry" form of parent rock) → Decision 2: COMPOSITION (You can usually still see evidence of the parent material)

ROCK NAME

Texture: ◯ Foliated ◯ Non-Foliated

Grain Size: ◯ Fine ◯ Fine to Medium ◯ Coarse ◯ Fine to Coarse

Composition: ◯ Mica ◯ Quartz ◯ Feldspar ◯ Amphibole
◯ Garnet ◯ Pyroxene ◯ Calcite ◯ Dolomite ◯ Various

Type of Metamorphism: ◯ Regional ◯ Contact

Rock Name: ◯ Slate ◯ Phyllite ◯ Schist ◯ Gneiss
◯ Homfels ◯ Quartzite ◯ Marble ◯ Metaconglomerate

Date: _____ GPS Location: _____

Location: ○ Public Land ○ Private Land ○ Pay-to-Dig Site ○ Quarry
○ Roadcut ○ Outcrop ○ Riverbed ○ Creek Bed ○ Beach
○ Mine Tailing ○ Fresh Overturned Soil ○ Other_____

Weather: ○ Sunny & Clear ○ Cloudy/Overcast ○ Windy ○ Rainy / Drizzle
○ Snow ○ Stormy ○ Fog ○ Drought ○ Other_____

Rock Type: ○ Igneous ○ Sedimentary ○ Metamorphic

Equipment Checklist: (Rockhounding)
○ Eye Protection ○ Heavy-Duty Gloves ○ Boots / Waterproof
○ First-Aid Kit ○ Hard Hat ○ Rock Hammer / Pick ○ Sieve
○ Colander ○ Small Picks ○ Trowel ○ Small Knife ○ Chisel
○ Small Broom ○ Crack Hammer ○ Pry Bar ○ Sledgehammer
○ Mason's Hammer ○ Shovel ○ Backpack ○ Bucket ○ Map
○ Wrapping Material ○ Small Tubes ○ Boxes / Containers
○ Loupe ○ Magnifying Glass ○ Magnet ○ Compass / GPS

Notes: _____

Color: ○ Light ○ Dark Specific Colors: _____

Luster: ○ Metallic ○ Gold ○ Brass ○ Bronze ○ Iron ○ Steel ○ Lead ○ Silver ○ Alum.
○ Non-Metallic ○ Adamantine ○ Vitreous ○ Resinous ○ Pearly ○ Dull ○ Greasy ○ Earthy ○ Silky

Cleavage: ○ 1 Direction ○ 2 Directions at 90° ○ 2 Directions not at 90°
○ 3 Directions at 90° (cubic) ○ 3 Directions not at 90° (rhombohedral)
○ 4 Directions (octahedral) ○ 6 Directions (dodecahedral)

Fracture: ○ Conchoidal (smooth, shell-like, or glass-like breaks) ○ Uneven (irregular, but not conchoidal) ○ Hackly (jagged, as of a metal)
○ Splintery (occurs in aggregates of many slender, brittle crystals) ○ Fibrous (occurs in aggregates of many slender, threadlike crystals)

Crystal Habit: ○ Prismatic ○ Acicular ○ Striated ○ Botryoidal ○ Dendritic
○ Nodular ○ Banded ○ Other_____

Hardness: (Mohs Scale)
○ 1 Talc ○ 2 Gypsum ○ 2.5 Fingernail ○ 3 Calcite ○ 4 Fluorite
○ 5 Apatite ○ 5.5 Glass ○ 6 Feldspar ○ 6.5 Steel File
○ 7 Quartz ○ 8 Topaz ○ 9 Corundrum ○ 10 Diamond

Specific Gravity: ○ Average (like quartz = 2.6 - 2.8) ○ Heavy (like galena = 7.5) ○ Light (lighter than quartz = <2.6)

$$\frac{\text{mass of mineral}}{\text{mass of same volume of water}} = \frac{\text{weight of mineral in air}}{\text{weight of equal volume of water}}$$

Tenacity: ○ Brittle ○ Ductile ○ Elastic ○ Flexible ○ Friable
○ Malleable ○ Sectile

Diaphaneity: ○ Transparent ○ Translucent ○ Opaque

Notes: _____

_____
_____
_____
_____
_____
_____
_____
_____
_____

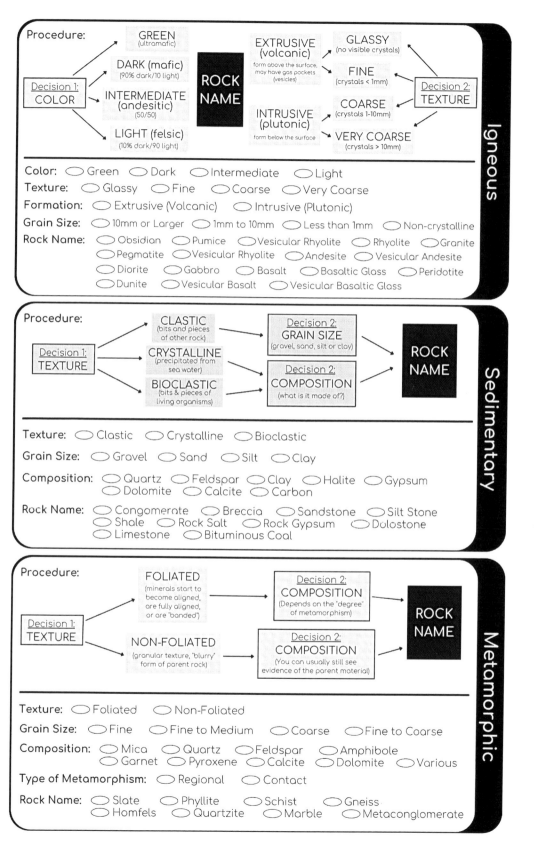

Igneous

Procedure:

Decision 1: COLOR →
- GREEN (ultramafic)
- DARK (mafic) (90% dark/10 light)
- INTERMEDIATE (andesitic) (50/50)
- LIGHT (felsic) (10% dark/90 light)

ROCK NAME

EXTRUSIVE (volcanic) — form above the surface, may have gas pockets (vesicles)

INTRUSIVE (plutonic) — form below the surface

Decision 2: TEXTURE →
- GLASSY (no visible crystals)
- FINE (crystals < 1mm)
- COARSE (crystals 1-10mm)
- VERY COARSE (crystals > 10mm)

Color: ◯ Green ◯ Dark ◯ Intermediate ◯ Light

Texture: ◯ Glassy ◯ Fine ◯ Coarse ◯ Very Coarse

Formation: ◯ Extrusive (Volcanic) ◯ Intrusive (Plutonic)

Grain Size: ◯ 10mm or Larger ◯ 1mm to 10mm ◯ Less than 1mm ◯ Non-crystalline

Rock Name: ◯ Obsidian ◯ Pumice ◯ Vesicular Rhyolite ◯ Rhyolite ◯ Granite
◯ Pegmatite ◯ Vesicular Rhyolite ◯ Andesite ◯ Vesicular Andesite
◯ Diorite ◯ Gabbro ◯ Basalt ◯ Basaltic Glass ◯ Peridotite
◯ Dunite ◯ Vesicular Basalt ◯ Vesicular Basaltic Glass

Sedimentary

Procedure:

Decision 1: TEXTURE →
- CLASTIC (bits and pieces of other rock)
- CRYSTALLINE (precipitated from sea water)
- BIOCLASTIC (bits & pieces of living organisms)

Decision 2: GRAIN SIZE (gravel, sand, silt or clay)

Decision 2: COMPOSITION (what is it made of?)

→ ROCK NAME

Texture: ◯ Clastic ◯ Crystalline ◯ Bioclastic

Grain Size: ◯ Gravel ◯ Sand ◯ Silt ◯ Clay

Composition: ◯ Quartz ◯ Feldspar ◯ Clay ◯ Halite ◯ Gypsum
◯ Dolomite ◯ Calcite ◯ Carbon

Rock Name: ◯ Conglomerate ◯ Breccia ◯ Sandstone ◯ Silt Stone
◯ Shale ◯ Rock Salt ◯ Rock Gypsum ◯ Dolostone
◯ Limestone ◯ Bituminous Coal

Metamorphic

Procedure:

Decision 1: TEXTURE →
- FOLIATED (minerals start to become aligned, are fully aligned, or are "banded")
- NON-FOLIATED (granular texture, "blurry" form of parent rock)

Decision 2: COMPOSITION (Depends on the "degree" of metamorphism)

Decision 2: COMPOSITION (You can usually still see evidence of the parent material)

→ ROCK NAME

Texture: ◯ Foliated ◯ Non-Foliated

Grain Size: ◯ Fine ◯ Fine to Medium ◯ Coarse ◯ Fine to Coarse

Composition: ◯ Mica ◯ Quartz ◯ Feldspar ◯ Amphibole
◯ Garnet ◯ Pyroxene ◯ Calcite ◯ Dolomite ◯ Various

Type of Metamorphism: ◯ Regional ◯ Contact

Rock Name: ◯ Slate ◯ Phyllite ◯ Schist ◯ Gneiss
◯ Hornfels ◯ Quartzite ◯ Marble ◯ Metaconglomerate

General

Date: _____   GPS Location: _____

Location: ○ Public Land ○ Private Land ○ Pay-to-Dig Site ○ Quarry
○ Roadcut ○ Outcrop ○ Riverbed ○ Creek Bed ○ Beach
○ Mine Tailing ○ Fresh Overturned Soil ○ Other_____

Weather: ○ Sunny & Clear ○ Cloudy/Overcast ○ Windy ○ Rainy / Drizzle
○ Snow ○ Stormy ○ Fog ○ Drought ○ Other_____

Rock Type: ○ Igneous ○ Sedimentary ○ Metamorphic

Equipment Checklist:
(Rockhounding)
○ Eye Protection ○ Heavy-Duty Gloves ○ Boots / Waterproof
○ First-Aid Kit ○ Hard Hat ○ Rock Hammer / Pick ○ Sieve
○ Colander ○ Small Picks ○ Trowel ○ Small Knife ○ Chisel
○ Small Broom ○ Crack Hammer ○ Pry Bar ○ Sledgehammer
○ Mason's Hammer ○ Shovel ○ Backpack ○ Bucket ○ Map
○ Wrapping Material ○ Small Tubes ○ Boxes / Containers
○ Loupe ○ Magnifying Glass ○ Magnet ○ Compass / GPS

Notes: _____

Mineral Identification

Color: ○ Light ○ Dark Specific Colors: _____

Luster: ○ Metallic ○ Gold ○ Brass ○ Non-Metallic ○ Adamantine ○ Vitreous
○ Bronze ○ Iron ○ Resinous ○ Pearly ○ Dull
○ Steel ○ Lead ○ Greasy ○ Earthy ○ Silky
○ Silver ○ Alum.

Cleavage: ○ 1 Direction ○ 2 Directions at 90° ○ 2 Directions not at 90°
○ 3 Directions at 90° (cubic) ○ 3 Directions not at 90° (rhombohedral)
○ 4 Directions (octahedral) ○ 6 Directions (dodecahedral)

Fracture: ○ Conchoidal (smooth, shell-like, or glass-like breaks) ○ Uneven (irregular, but not conchoidal) ○ Hackly (jagged, as of a metal)
○ Splintery (occurs in aggregates of many slender, brittle crystals) ○ Fibrous (occurs in aggregates of many slender, threadlike crystals)

Crystal Habit: ○ Prismatic ○ Acicular ○ Striated ○ Botryoidal ○ Dendritic
○ Nodular ○ Banded ○ Other_____

Hardness: (Mohs Scale)
○ 1 Talc ○ 2 Gypsum ○ 2.5 Fingernail ○ 3 Calcite ○ 4 Fluorite
○ 5 Apatite ○ 5.5 Glass ○ 6 Feldspar ○ 6.5 Steel File
○ 7 Quartz ○ 8 Topaz ○ 9 Corundrum ○ 10 Diamond

Specific Gravity: ○ Average (like quartz = 2.6 - 2.8) ○ Heavy (like galena = 7.5) ○ Light (lighter than quartz = <2.6)

$$\frac{\text{mass of mineral}}{\text{mass of same volume of water}} = \frac{\text{weight of mineral in air}}{\text{weight of equal volume of water}}$$

Tenacity: ○ Brittle ○ Ductile ○ Elastic ○ Flexible ○ Friable
○ Malleable ○ Sectile

Diaphaneity: ○ Transparent ○ Translucent ○ Opaque

Notes: _____

Notes

_____
_____
_____
_____
_____
_____
_____
_____
_____

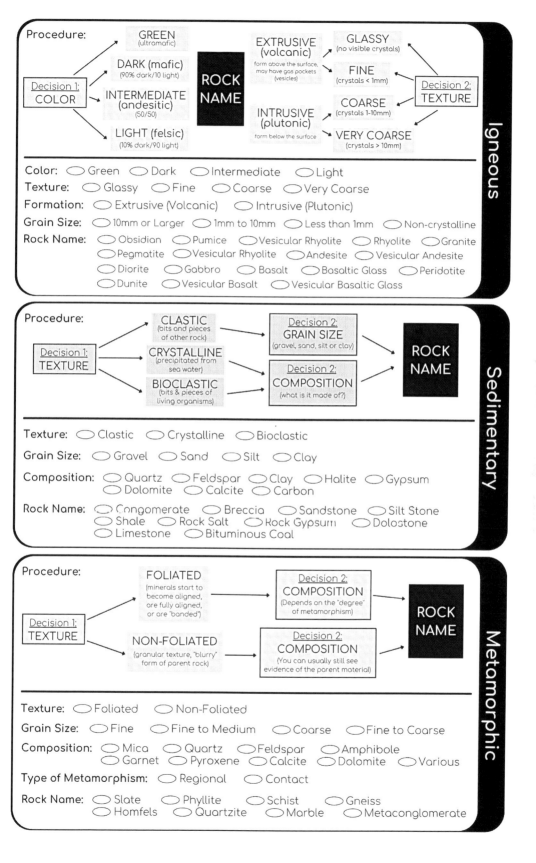

Igneous

Procedure:

Decision 1: COLOR →
- GREEN (ultramafic)
- DARK (mafic) (90% dark/10 light)
- INTERMEDIATE (andesitic) (50/50)
- LIGHT (felsic) (10% dark/90 light)

ROCK NAME

EXTRUSIVE (volcanic) — form above the surface, may have gas pockets (vesicles)
INTRUSIVE (plutonic) — form below the surface

Decision 2: TEXTURE →
- GLASSY (no visible crystals)
- FINE (crystals < 1mm)
- COARSE (crystals 1-10mm)
- VERY COARSE (crystals > 10mm)

Color: ◯ Green ◯ Dark ◯ Intermediate ◯ Light
Texture: ◯ Glassy ◯ Fine ◯ Coarse ◯ Very Coarse
Formation: ◯ Extrusive (Volcanic) ◯ Intrusive (Plutonic)
Grain Size: ◯ 10mm or Larger ◯ 1mm to 10mm ◯ Less than 1mm ◯ Non-crystalline
Rock Name: ◯ Obsidian ◯ Pumice ◯ Vesicular Rhyolite ◯ Rhyolite ◯ Granite ◯ Pegmatite ◯ Vesicular Rhyolite ◯ Andesite ◯ Vesicular Andesite ◯ Diorite ◯ Gabbro ◯ Basalt ◯ Basaltic Glass ◯ Peridotite ◯ Dunite ◯ Vesicular Basalt ◯ Vesicular Basaltic Glass

Sedimentary

Procedure:

Decision 1: TEXTURE →
- CLASTIC (bits and pieces of other rock)
- CRYSTALLINE (precipitated from sea water)
- BIOCLASTIC (bits & pieces of living organisms)

Decision 2: GRAIN SIZE (gravel, sand, silt or clay)
Decision 2: COMPOSITION (what is it made of?)

ROCK NAME

Texture: ◯ Clastic ◯ Crystalline ◯ Bioclastic
Grain Size: ◯ Gravel ◯ Sand ◯ Silt ◯ Clay
Composition: ◯ Quartz ◯ Feldspar ◯ Clay ◯ Halite ◯ Gypsum ◯ Dolomite ◯ Calcite ◯ Carbon
Rock Name: ◯ Conglomerate ◯ Breccia ◯ Sandstone ◯ Silt Stone ◯ Shale ◯ Rock Salt ◯ Rock Gypsum ◯ Dolostone ◯ Limestone ◯ Bituminous Coal

Metamorphic

Procedure:

Decision 1: TEXTURE →
- FOLIATED (minerals start to become aligned, are fully aligned, or are "banded")
- NON-FOLIATED (granular texture, "blurry" form of parent rock)

Decision 2: COMPOSITION (Depends on the "degree" of metamorphism)
Decision 2: COMPOSITION (You can usually still see evidence of the parent material)

ROCK NAME

Texture: ◯ Foliated ◯ Non-Foliated
Grain Size: ◯ Fine ◯ Fine to Medium ◯ Coarse ◯ Fine to Coarse
Composition: ◯ Mica ◯ Quartz ◯ Feldspar ◯ Amphibole ◯ Garnet ◯ Pyroxene ◯ Calcite ◯ Dolomite ◯ Various
Type of Metamorphism: ◯ Regional ◯ Contact
Rock Name: ◯ Slate ◯ Phyllite ◯ Schist ◯ Gneiss ◯ Hornfels ◯ Quartzite ◯ Marble ◯ Metaconglomerate

General

Date: _____ GPS Location: _____

Location: ○ Public Land ○ Private Land ○ Pay-to-Dig Site ○ Quarry
○ Roadcut ○ Outcrop ○ Riverbed ○ Creek Bed ○ Beach
○ Mine Tailing ○ Fresh Overturned Soil ○ Other_____

Weather: ○ Sunny & Clear ○ Cloudy/Overcast ○ Windy ○ Rainy / Drizzle
○ Snow ○ Stormy ○ Fog ○ Drought ○ Other_____

Rock Type: ○ Igneous ○ Sedimentary ○ Metamorphic

Equipment Checklist:
(Rockhounding)
○ Eye Protection ○ Heavy-Duty Gloves ○ Boots / Waterproof
○ First-Aid Kit ○ Hard Hat ○ Rock Hammer / Pick ○ Sieve
○ Colander ○ Small Picks ○ Trowel ○ Small Knife ○ Chisel
○ Small Broom ○ Crack Hammer ○ Pry Bar ○ Sledgehammer
○ Mason's Hammer ○ Shovel ○ Backpack ○ Bucket ○ Map
○ Wrapping Material ○ Small Tubes ○ Boxes / Containers
○ Loupe ○ Magnifying Glass ○ Magnet ○ Compass / GPS

Notes: _____

Mineral Identification

Color: ○ Light ○ Dark (Specific Colors: _____

Luster: ○ Metallic ○ Gold ○ Brass
○ Bronze ○ Iron
○ Steel ○ Lead
○ Silver ○ Alum.
○ Non-Metallic ○ Adamantine ○ Vitreous
○ Resinous ○ Pearly ○ Dull
○ Greasy ○ Earthy ○ Silky

Cleavage: ○ 1 Direction ○ 2 Directions at 90° ○ 2 Directions not at 90°
○ 3 Directions at 90° (cubic) ○ 3 Directions not at 90° (rhombohedral)
○ 4 Directions (octahedral) ○ 6 Directions (dodecahedral)

Fracture: ○ Conchoidal (smooth, shell-like, or glass-like breaks) ○ Uneven (irregular, but not conchoidal) ○ Hackly (jagged, as of a metal)
○ Splintery (occurs in aggregates of many slender, brittle crystals) ○ Fibrous (occurs in aggregates of many slender, threadlike crystals)

Crystal Habit: ○ Prismatic ○ Acicular ○ Striated ○ Botryoidal ○ Dendritic
○ Nodular ○ Banded ○ Other_____

Hardness: (Mohs Scale)
○ 1 Talc ○ 2 Gypsum ○ 2.5 Fingernail ○ 3 Calcite ○ 4 Fluorite
○ 5 Apatite ○ 5.5 Glass ○ 6 Feldspar ○ 6.5 Steel File
○ 7 Quartz ○ 8 Topaz ○ 9 Corundrum ○ 10 Diamond

Specific Gravity:
○ Average (like quartz = 2.6 - 2.8)
○ Heavy (like galena = 7.5)
○ Light (lighter than quartz = <2.6)

$$\frac{\text{mass of mineral}}{\text{mass of same volume of water}} = \frac{\text{weight of mineral in air}}{\text{weight of equal volume of water}}$$

Tenacity: ○ Brittle ○ Ductile ○ Elastic ○ Flexible ○ Friable
○ Malleable ○ Sectile

Diaphaneity: ○ Transparent ○ Translucent ○ Opaque

Notes: _____

Notes

_____
_____
_____
_____
_____
_____
_____
_____
_____
_____

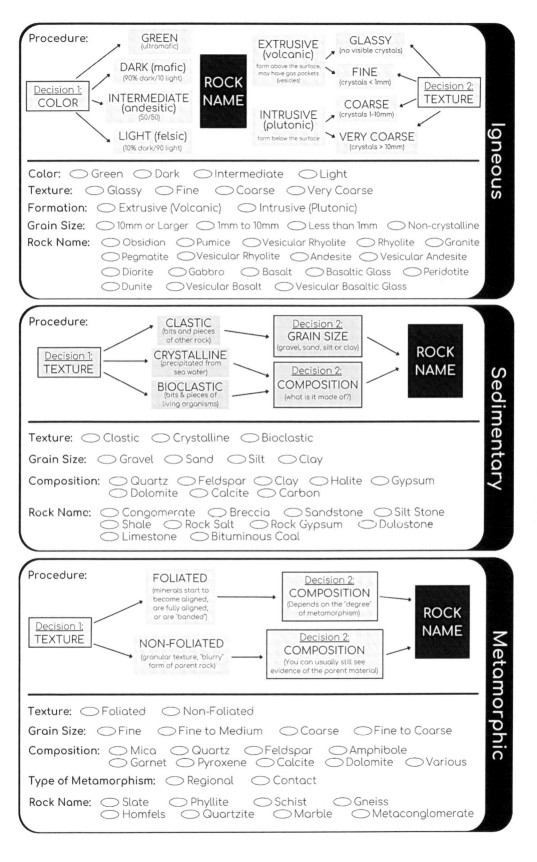

Igneous

Procedure:

Decision 1: COLOR →
- GREEN (ultramafic)
- DARK (mafic) (90% dark/10 light)
- INTERMEDIATE (andesitic) (50/50)
- LIGHT (felsic) (10% dark/90 light)

ROCK NAME

EXTRUSIVE (volcanic) — form above the surface, may have gas pockets (vesicles)
INTRUSIVE (plutonic) — form below the surface

Decision 2: TEXTURE →
- GLASSY (no visible crystals)
- FINE (crystals < 1mm)
- COARSE (crystals 1-10mm)
- VERY COARSE (crystals > 10mm)

Color: ◯ Green ◯ Dark ◯ Intermediate ◯ Light

Texture: ◯ Glassy ◯ Fine ◯ Coarse ◯ Very Coarse

Formation: ◯ Extrusive (Volcanic) ◯ Intrusive (Plutonic)

Grain Size: ◯ 10mm or Larger ◯ 1mm to 10mm ◯ Less than 1mm ◯ Non-crystalline

Rock Name: ◯ Obsidian ◯ Pumice ◯ Vesicular Rhyolite ◯ Rhyolite ◯ Granite
◯ Pegmatite ◯ Vesicular Rhyolite ◯ Andesite ◯ Vesicular Andesite
◯ Diorite ◯ Gabbro ◯ Basalt ◯ Basaltic Glass ◯ Peridotite
◯ Dunite ◯ Vesicular Basalt ◯ Vesicular Basaltic Glass

Sedimentary

Procedure:

Decision 1: TEXTURE →
- CLASTIC (bits and pieces of other rock)
- CRYSTALLINE (precipitated from sea water)
- BIOCLASTIC (bits & pieces of living organisms)

Decision 2: GRAIN SIZE (gravel, sand, silt or clay)
Decision 2: COMPOSITION (what is it made of?)

ROCK NAME

Texture: ◯ Clastic ◯ Crystalline ◯ Bioclastic

Grain Size: ◯ Gravel ◯ Sand ◯ Silt ◯ Clay

Composition: ◯ Quartz ◯ Feldspar ◯ Clay ◯ Halite ◯ Gypsum
◯ Dolomite ◯ Calcite ◯ Carbon

Rock Name: ◯ Conglomerate ◯ Breccia ◯ Sandstone ◯ Silt Stone
◯ Shale ◯ Rock Salt ◯ Rock Gypsum ◯ Dolostone
◯ Limestone ◯ Bituminous Coal

Metamorphic

Procedure:

Decision 1: TEXTURE →
- FOLIATED (minerals start to become aligned, are fully aligned, or are "banded")
- NON-FOLIATED (granular texture, "blurry" form of parent rock)

Decision 2: COMPOSITION (Depends on the "degree" of metamorphism)
Decision 2: COMPOSITION (You can usually still see evidence of the parent material)

ROCK NAME

Texture: ◯ Foliated ◯ Non-Foliated

Grain Size: ◯ Fine ◯ Fine to Medium ◯ Coarse ◯ Fine to Coarse

Composition: ◯ Mica ◯ Quartz ◯ Feldspar ◯ Amphibole
◯ Garnet ◯ Pyroxene ◯ Calcite ◯ Dolomite ◯ Various

Type of Metamorphism: ◯ Regional ◯ Contact

Rock Name: ◯ Slate ◯ Phyllite ◯ Schist ◯ Gneiss
◯ Hornfels ◯ Quartzite ◯ Marble ◯ Metaconglomerate

General

Date: _____ GPS Location: _____

Location:
- ○ Public Land ○ Private Land ○ Pay-to-Dig Site ○ Quarry
- ○ Roadcut ○ Outcrop ○ Riverbed ○ Creek Bed ○ Beach
- ○ Mine Tailing ○ Fresh Overturned Soil ○ Other_____

Weather:
- ○ Sunny & Clear ○ Cloudy/Overcast ○ Windy ○ Rainy / Drizzle
- ○ Snow ○ Stormy ○ Fog ○ Drought ○ Other_____

Rock Type: ○ Igneous ○ Sedimentary ○ Metamorphic

Equipment Checklist: (Rockhounding)
- ○ Eye Protection ○ Heavy-Duty Gloves ○ Boots / Waterproof
- ○ First-Aid Kit ○ Hard Hat ○ Rock Hammer / Pick ○ Sieve
- ○ Colander ○ Small Picks ○ Trowel ○ Small Knife ○ Chisel
- ○ Small Broom ○ Crack Hammer ○ Pry Bar ○ Sledgehammer
- ○ Mason's Hammer ○ Shovel ○ Backpack ○ Bucket ○ Map
- ○ Wrapping Material ○ Small Tubes ○ Boxes / Containers
- ○ Loupe ○ Magnifying Glass ○ Magnet ○ Compass / GPS

Notes: _____

Mineral Identification

Color: ○ Light ○ Dark Specific Colors: _____

Luster:
- ○ Metallic ○ Gold ○ Brass ○ Bronze ○ Iron ○ Steel ○ Lead ○ Silver ○ Alum.
- ○ Non-Metallic ○ Adamantine ○ Vitreous ○ Resinous ○ Pearly ○ Dull ○ Greasy ○ Earthy ○ Silky

Cleavage:
- ○ 1 Direction ○ 2 Directions at 90° ○ 2 Directions not at 90°
- ○ 3 Directions at 90° (cubic) ○ 3 Directions not at 90° (rhombohedral)
- ○ 4 Directions (octahedral) ○ 6 Directions (dodecahedral)

Fracture:
- ○ Conchoidal (smooth, shell-like, or glass-like breaks) ○ Uneven (irregular, but not conchoidal) ○ Hackly (jagged, as of a metal)
- ○ Splintery (occurs in aggregates of many slender, brittle crystals) ○ Fibrous (occurs in aggregates of many slender, threadlike crystals)

Crystal Habit:
- ○ Prismatic ○ Acicular ○ Striated ○ Botryoidal ○ Dendritic
- ○ Nodular ○ Banded ○ Other_____

Hardness: (Mohs Scale)
- ○ 1 Talc ○ 2 Gypsum ○ 2.5 Fingernail ○ 3 Calcite ○ 4 Fluorite
- ○ 5 Apatite ○ 5.5 Glass ○ 6 Feldspar ○ 6.5 Steel File
- ○ 7 Quartz ○ 8 Topaz ○ 9 Corundrum ○ 10 Diamond

Specific Gravity:
- ○ Average (like quartz = 2.6 - 2.8)
- ○ Heavy (like galena = 7.5)
- ○ Light (lighter than quartz = <2.6)

$$\frac{\text{mass of mineral}}{\text{mass of same volume of water}} = \frac{\text{weight of mineral in air}}{\text{weight of equal volume of water}}$$

Tenacity:
- ○ Brittle ○ Ductile ○ Elastic ○ Flexible ○ Friable
- ○ Malleable ○ Sectile

Diaphaneity: ○ Transparent ○ Translucent ○ Opaque

Notes: _____

Notes

_____
_____
_____
_____
_____
_____
_____
_____
_____
_____

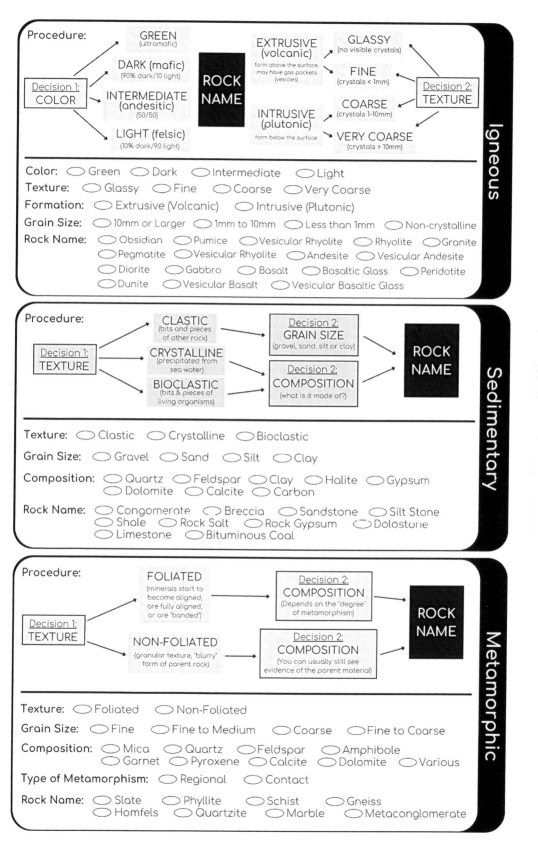

Igneous

Procedure:

Decision 1: COLOR
- GREEN (ultramafic)
- DARK (mafic) (90% dark/10 light)
- INTERMEDIATE (andesitic) (50/50)
- LIGHT (felsic) (10% dark/90 light)

EXTRUSIVE (volcanic) — form above the surface, may have gas pockets (vesicles)

INTRUSIVE (plutonic) — form below the surface

ROCK NAME

Decision 2: TEXTURE
- GLASSY (no visible crystals)
- FINE (crystals < 1mm)
- COARSE (crystals 1-10mm)
- VERY COARSE (crystals > 10mm)

Color: ◯ Green ◯ Dark ◯ Intermediate ◯ Light

Texture: ◯ Glassy ◯ Fine ◯ Coarse ◯ Very Coarse

Formation: ◯ Extrusive (Volcanic) ◯ Intrusive (Plutonic)

Grain Size: ◯ 10mm or Larger ◯ 1mm to 10mm ◯ Less than 1mm ◯ Non-crystalline

Rock Name: ◯ Obsidian ◯ Pumice ◯ Vesicular Rhyolite ◯ Rhyolite ◯ Granite
◯ Pegmatite ◯ Vesicular Rhyolite ◯ Andesite ◯ Vesicular Andesite
◯ Diorite ◯ Gabbro ◯ Basalt ◯ Basaltic Glass ◯ Peridotite
◯ Dunite ◯ Vesicular Basalt ◯ Vesicular Basaltic Glass

Sedimentary

Procedure:

Decision 1: TEXTURE
- CLASTIC (bits and pieces of other rock)
- CRYSTALLINE (precipitated from sea water)
- BIOCLASTIC (bits & pieces of living organisms)

Decision 2: GRAIN SIZE (gravel, sand, silt or clay)

Decision 2: COMPOSITION (what is it made of?)

ROCK NAME

Texture: ◯ Clastic ◯ Crystalline ◯ Bioclastic

Grain Size: ◯ Gravel ◯ Sand ◯ Silt ◯ Clay

Composition: ◯ Quartz ◯ Feldspar ◯ Clay ◯ Halite ◯ Gypsum
◯ Dolomite ◯ Calcite ◯ Carbon

Rock Name: ◯ Congomerate ◯ Breccia ◯ Sandstone ◯ Silt Stone
◯ Shale ◯ Rock Salt ◯ Rock Gypsum ◯ Dolostone
◯ Limestone ◯ Bituminous Coal

Metamorphic

Procedure:

Decision 1: TEXTURE
- FOLIATED (minerals start to become aligned, are fully aligned, or are "banded")
- NON-FOLIATED (granular texture, "blurry" form of parent rock)

Decision 2: COMPOSITION (Depends on the "degree" of metamorphism)

Decision 2: COMPOSITION (You can usually still see evidence of the parent material)

ROCK NAME

Texture: ◯ Foliated ◯ Non-Foliated

Grain Size: ◯ Fine ◯ Fine to Medium ◯ Coarse ◯ Fine to Coarse

Composition: ◯ Mica ◯ Quartz ◯ Feldspar ◯ Amphibole
◯ Garnet ◯ Pyroxene ◯ Calcite ◯ Dolomite ◯ Various

Type of Metamorphism: ◯ Regional ◯ Contact

Rock Name: ◯ Slate ◯ Phyllite ◯ Schist ◯ Gneiss
◯ Homfels ◯ Quartzite ◯ Marble ◯ Metaconglomerate

General

Date: _____   GPS Location: _____

Location:
- ○ Public Land ○ Private Land ○ Pay-to-Dig Site ○ Quarry
- ○ Roadcut ○ Outcrop ○ Riverbed ○ Creek Bed ○ Beach
- ○ Mine Tailing ○ Fresh Overturned Soil ○ Other_____

Weather:
- ○ Sunny & Clear ○ Cloudy/Overcast ○ Windy ○ Rainy / Drizzle
- ○ Snow ○ Stormy ○ Fog ○ Drought ○ Other_____

Rock Type: ○ Igneous ○ Sedimentary ○ Metamorphic

Equipment Checklist: (Rockhounding)
- ○ Eye Protection ○ Heavy-Duty Gloves ○ Boots / Waterproof
- ○ First-Aid Kit ○ Hard Hat ○ Rock Hammer / Pick ○ Sieve
- ○ Colander ○ Small Picks ○ Trowel ○ Small Knife ○ Chisel
- ○ Small Broom ○ Crack Hammer ○ Pry Bar ○ Sledgehammer
- ○ Mason's Hammer ○ Shovel ○ Backpack ○ Bucket ○ Map
- ○ Wrapping Material ○ Small Tubes ○ Boxes / Containers
- ○ Loupe ○ Magnifying Glass ○ Magnet ○ Compass / GPS

Notes: _____

Mineral Identification

Color: ○ Light ○ Dark Specific Colors: _____

Luster:
- Metallic: ○ ○ Gold ○ Brass ○ Bronze ○ Iron ○ Steel ○ Lead ○ Silver ○ Alum.
- Non-Metallic: ○ ○ Adamantine ○ Vitreous ○ Resinous ○ Pearly ○ Dull ○ Greasy ○ Earthy ○ Silky

Cleavage:
- ○ 1 Direction ○ 2 Directions at 90° ○ 2 Directions not at 90°
- ○ 3 Directions at 90° (cubic) ○ 3 Directions not at 90° (rhombohedral)
- ○ 4 Directions (octahedral) ○ 6 Directions (dodecahedral)

Fracture:
- ○ Conchoidal (smooth, shell-like, or glass-like breaks) ○ Uneven (irregular, but not conchoidal) ○ Hackly (jagged, as of a metal)
- ○ Splintery (occurs in aggregates of many slender, brittle crystals) ○ Fibrous (occurs in aggregates of many slender, threadlike crystals)

Crystal Habit:
- ○ Prismatic ○ Acicular ○ Striated ○ Botryoidal ○ Dendritic
- ○ Nodular ○ Banded ○ Other_____

Hardness: (Mohs Scale)
- ○ 1 Talc ○ 2 Gypsum ○ 2.5 Fingernail ○ 3 Calcite ○ 4 Fluorite
- ○ 5 Apatite ○ 5.5 Glass ○ 6 Feldspar ○ 6.5 Steel File
- ○ 7 Quartz ○ 8 Topaz ○ 9 Corundrum ○ 10 Diamond

Specific Gravity:
- ○ Average (like quartz = 2.6 - 2.8)
- ○ Heavy (like galena = 7.5)
- ○ Light (lighter than quartz = <2.6)

$$\frac{\text{mass of mineral}}{\text{mass of same volume of water}} = \frac{\text{weight of mineral in air}}{\text{weight of equal volume of water}}$$

Tenacity:
- ○ Brittle ○ Ductile ○ Elastic ○ Flexible ○ Friable
- ○ Malleable ○ Sectile

Diaphaneity: ○ Transparent ○ Translucent ○ Opaque

Notes: _____

Notes

_____
_____
_____
_____
_____
_____
_____
_____
_____

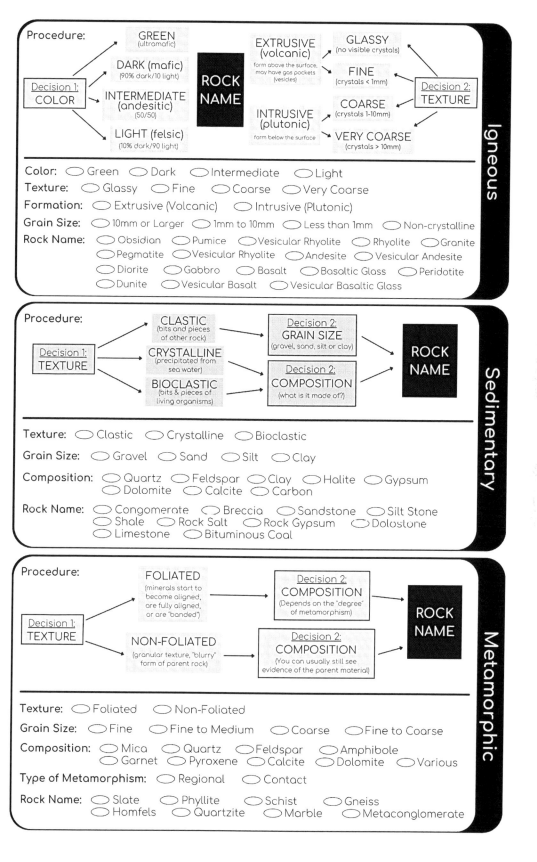

Igneous

Procedure:

Decision 1: COLOR →
- GREEN (ultramafic)
- DARK (mafic) (90% dark/10 light)
- INTERMEDIATE (andesitic) (50/50)
- LIGHT (felsic) (10% dark/90 light)

ROCK NAME

EXTRUSIVE (volcanic) — form above the surface, may have gas pockets (vesicles) →
INTRUSIVE (plutonic) — form below the surface →

Decision 2: TEXTURE →
- GLASSY (no visible crystals)
- FINE (crystals < 1mm)
- COARSE (crystals 1-10mm)
- VERY COARSE (crystals > 10mm)

Color: ○ Green ○ Dark ○ Intermediate ○ Light

Texture: ○ Glassy ○ Fine ○ Coarse ○ Very Coarse

Formation: ○ Extrusive (Volcanic) ○ Intrusive (Plutonic)

Grain Size: ○ 10mm or Larger ○ 1mm to 10mm ○ Less than 1mm ○ Non-crystalline

Rock Name: ○ Obsidian ○ Pumice ○ Vesicular Rhyolite ○ Rhyolite ○ Granite ○ Pegmatite ○ Vesicular Rhyolite ○ Andesite ○ Vesicular Andesite ○ Diorite ○ Gabbro ○ Basalt ○ Basaltic Glass ○ Peridotite ○ Dunite ○ Vesicular Basalt ○ Vesicular Basaltic Glass

Sedimentary

Procedure:

Decision 1: TEXTURE →
- CLASTIC (bits and pieces of other rock) → Decision 2: GRAIN SIZE (gravel, sand, silt or clay) →
- CRYSTALLINE (precipitated from sea water) → Decision 2: COMPOSITION (what is it made of?) →
- BIOCLASTIC (bits & pieces of living organisms) →

ROCK NAME

Texture: ○ Clastic ○ Crystalline ○ Bioclastic

Grain Size: ○ Gravel ○ Sand ○ Silt ○ Clay

Composition: ○ Quartz ○ Feldspar ○ Clay ○ Halite ○ Gypsum ○ Dolomite ○ Calcite ○ Carbon

Rock Name: ○ Conglomerate ○ Breccia ○ Sandstone ○ Silt Stone ○ Shale ○ Rock Salt ○ Rock Gypsum ○ Dolostone ○ Limestone ○ Bituminous Coal

Metamorphic

Procedure:

Decision 1: TEXTURE →
- FOLIATED (minerals start to become aligned, are fully aligned, or are "banded") → Decision 2: COMPOSITION (Depends on the "degree" of metamorphism) →
- NON-FOLIATED (granular texture, "blurry" form of parent rock) → Decision 2: COMPOSITION (You can usually still see evidence of the parent material) →

ROCK NAME

Texture: ○ Foliated ○ Non-Foliated

Grain Size: ○ Fine ○ Fine to Medium ○ Coarse ○ Fine to Coarse

Composition: ○ Mica ○ Quartz ○ Feldspar ○ Amphibole ○ Garnet ○ Pyroxene ○ Calcite ○ Dolomite ○ Various

Type of Metamorphism: ○ Regional ○ Contact

Rock Name: ○ Slate ○ Phyllite ○ Schist ○ Gneiss ○ Homfels ○ Quartzite ○ Marble ○ Metaconglomerate

General

Date: _____ GPS Location: _____

Location: ◯ Public Land   ◯ Private Land   ◯ Pay-to-Dig Site   ◯ Quarry
◯ Roadcut   ◯ Outcrop   ◯ Riverbed   ◯ Creek Bed   ◯ Beach
◯ Mine Tailing   ◯ Fresh Overturned Soil   ◯ Other_____

Weather: ◯ Sunny & Clear   ◯ Cloudy/Overcast   ◯ Windy   ◯ Rainy / Drizzle
◯ Snow   ◯ Stormy   ◯ Fog   ◯ Drought   ◯ Other_____

Rock Type: ◯ Igneous   ◯ Sedimentary   ◯ Metamorphic

Equipment   ◯ Eye Protection   ◯ Heavy-Duty Gloves   ◯ Boots / Waterproof
Checklist: ◯ First-Aid Kit   ◯ Hard Hat   ◯ Rock Hammer / Pick   ◯ Sieve
(Rockhounding)   ◯ Colander   ◯ Small Picks   ◯ Trowel   ◯ Small Knife   ◯ Chisel
◯ Small Broom   ◯ Crack Hammer   ◯ Pry Bar   ◯ Sledgehammer
◯ Mason's Hammer   ◯ Shovel   ◯ Backpack   ◯ Bucket   ◯ Map
◯ Wrapping Material   ◯ Small Tubes   ◯ Boxes / Containers
◯ Loupe   ◯ Magnifying Glass   ◯ Magnet   ◯ Compass / GPS

Notes: _____

Mineral Identification

Color: ◯ Light   ◯ Dark   Specific Colors: _____

Luster: ◯ Metallic   ◯ Gold   ◯ Brass   ◯ Non-Metallic   ◯ Adamantine   ◯ Vitreous
◯ Bronze   ◯ Iron   ◯ Resinous   ◯ Pearly   ◯ Dull
◯ Steel   ◯ Lead   ◯ Greasy   ◯ Earthy   ◯ Silky
◯ Silver   ◯ Alum.

Cleavage: ◯ 1 Direction   ◯ 2 Directions at 90°   ◯ 2 Directions not at 90°
◯ 3 Directions at 90° (cubic)   ◯ 3 Directions not at 90° (rhombohedral)
◯ 4 Directions (octahedral)   ◯ 6 Directions (dodecahedral)

Fracture: ◯ Conchoidal (smooth, shell-like, or glass-like breaks)   ◯ Uneven (irregular, but not conchoidal)   ◯ Hackly (jagged, as of a metal)
◯ Splintery (occurs in aggregates of many slender, brittle crystals)   ◯ Fibrous (occurs in aggregates of many slender, threadlike crystals)

Crystal   ◯ Prismatic   ◯ Acicular   ◯ Striated   ◯ Botryoidal   ◯ Dendritic
Habit: ◯ Nodular   ◯ Banded   ◯ Other_____

Hardness: ◯ 1 Talc   ◯ 2 Gypsum   ◯ 2.5 Fingernail   ◯ 3 Calcite   ◯ 4 Fluorite
(Mohs Scale)   ◯ 5 Apatite   ◯ 5.5 Glass   ◯ 6 Feldspar   ◯ 6.5 Steel File
◯ 7 Quartz   ◯ 8 Topaz   ◯ 9 Corundrum   ◯ 10 Diamond

Specific   ◯ Average (like quartz = 2.6 - 2.8) $\frac{\text{mass of mineral}}{\text{mass of same volume of water}} = \frac{\text{weight of mineral in air}}{\text{weight of equal volume of water}}$
Gravity: ◯ Heavy (like galena = 7.5)
◯ Light (lighter than quartz = <2.6)

Tenacity: ◯ Brittle   ◯ Ductile   ◯ Elastic   ◯ Flexible   ◯ Friable
◯ Malleable   ◯ Sectile

Diaphaneity: ◯ Transparent   ◯ Translucent   ◯ Opaque

Notes: _____

Notes

_____
_____
_____
_____
_____
_____
_____
_____
_____

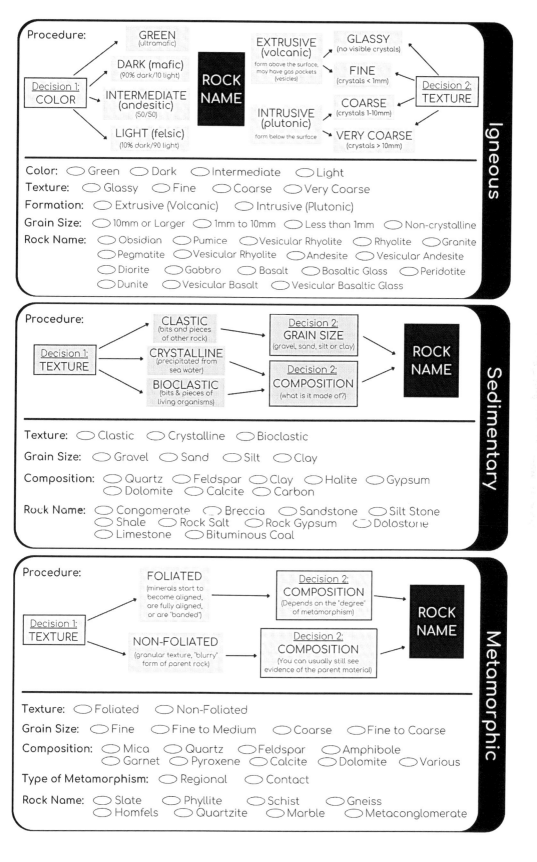

Igneous

Procedure:

Decision 1: COLOR →
- GREEN (ultramafic)
- DARK (mafic) (90% dark/10 light)
- INTERMEDIATE (andesitic) (50/50)
- LIGHT (felsic) (10% dark/90 light)

ROCK NAME

EXTRUSIVE (volcanic) — form above the surface, may have gas pockets (vesicles)
INTRUSIVE (plutonic) — form below the surface

- GLASSY (no visible crystals)
- FINE (crystals < 1mm)
- COARSE (crystals 1-10mm)
- VERY COARSE (crystals > 10mm)

Decision 2: TEXTURE

Color: ◯ Green ◯ Dark ◯ Intermediate ◯ Light

Texture: ◯ Glassy ◯ Fine ◯ Coarse ◯ Very Coarse

Formation: ◯ Extrusive (Volcanic) ◯ Intrusive (Plutonic)

Grain Size: ◯ 10mm or Larger ◯ 1mm to 10mm ◯ Less than 1mm ◯ Non-crystalline

Rock Name: ◯ Obsidian ◯ Pumice ◯ Vesicular Rhyolite ◯ Rhyolite ◯ Granite
◯ Pegmatite ◯ Vesicular Rhyolite ◯ Andesite ◯ Vesicular Andesite
◯ Diorite ◯ Gabbro ◯ Basalt ◯ Basaltic Glass ◯ Peridotite
◯ Dunite ◯ Vesicular Basalt ◯ Vesicular Basaltic Glass

Sedimentary

Procedure:

Decision 1: TEXTURE →
- CLASTIC (bits and pieces of other rock)
- CRYSTALLINE (precipitated from sea water)
- BIOCLASTIC (bits & pieces of living organisms)

Decision 2: GRAIN SIZE (gravel, sand, silt or clay)
Decision 2: COMPOSITION (what is it made of?)

ROCK NAME

Texture: ◯ Clastic ◯ Crystalline ◯ Bioclastic

Grain Size: ◯ Gravel ◯ Sand ◯ Silt ◯ Clay

Composition: ◯ Quartz ◯ Feldspar ◯ Clay ◯ Halite ◯ Gypsum
◯ Dolomite ◯ Calcite ◯ Carbon

Rock Name: ◯ Congomerate ◯ Breccia ◯ Sandstone ◯ Silt Stone
◯ Shale ◯ Rock Salt ◯ Rock Gypsum ◯ Dolostone
◯ Limestone ◯ Bituminous Coal

Metamorphic

Procedure:

Decision 1: TEXTURE →
- FOLIATED (minerals start to become aligned, are fully aligned, or are "banded")
- NON-FOLIATED (granular texture, "blurry" form of parent rock)

Decision 2: COMPOSITION (Depends on the "degree" of metamorphism)
Decision 2: COMPOSITION (You can usually still see evidence of the parent material)

ROCK NAME

Texture: ◯ Foliated ◯ Non-Foliated

Grain Size: ◯ Fine ◯ Fine to Medium ◯ Coarse ◯ Fine to Coarse

Composition: ◯ Mica ◯ Quartz ◯ Feldspar ◯ Amphibole
◯ Garnet ◯ Pyroxene ◯ Calcite ◯ Dolomite ◯ Various

Type of Metamorphism: ◯ Regional ◯ Contact

Rock Name: ◯ Slate ◯ Phyllite ◯ Schist ◯ Gneiss
◯ Homfels ◯ Quartzite ◯ Marble ◯ Metaconglomerate

General

Date: _____ GPS Location: _____

Location: ○ Public Land   ○ Private Land   ○ Pay-to-Dig Site   ○ Quarry
○ Roadcut   ○ Outcrop   ○ Riverbed   ○ Creek Bed   ○ Beach
○ Mine Tailing   ○ Fresh Overturned Soil   ○ Other_____

Weather: ○ Sunny & Clear   ○ Cloudy/Overcast   ○ Windy   ○ Rainy / Drizzle
○ Snow   ○ Stormy   ○ Fog   ○ Drought   ○ Other_____

Rock Type: ○ Igneous   ○ Sedimentary   ○ Metamorphic

Equipment Checklist: ○ Eye Protection   ○ Heavy-Duty Gloves   ○ Boots / Waterproof
(Rockhounding) ○ First-Aid Kit   ○ Hard Hat   ○ Rock Hammer / Pick   ○ Sieve
○ Colander   ○ Small Picks   ○ Trowel   ○ Small Knife   ○ Chisel
○ Small Broom   ○ Crack Hammer   ○ Pry Bar   ○ Sledgehammer
○ Mason's Hammer   ○ Shovel   ○ Backpack   ○ Bucket   ○ Map
○ Wrapping Material   ○ Small Tubes   ○ Boxes / Containers
○ Loupe   ○ Magnifying Glass   ○ Magnet   ○ Compass / GPS

Notes: _____

Mineral Identification

Color: ○ Light   ○ Dark   Specific Colors: _____

Luster: ○ Metallic ○ Gold ○ Brass   ○ Non-Metallic ○ Adamantine ○ Vitreous
○ Bronze ○ Iron   ○ Resinous ○ Pearly ○ Dull
○ Steel ○ Lead   ○ Greasy ○ Earthy ○ Silky
○ Silver ○ Alum.

Cleavage: ○ 1 Direction   ○ 2 Directions at 90°   ○ 2 Directions not at 90°
○ 3 Directions at 90° (cubic)   ○ 3 Directions not at 90° (rhombohedral)
○ 4 Directions (octahedral)   ○ 6 Directions (dodecahedral)

Fracture: ○ Conchoidal (smooth, shell-like, or glass-like breaks)   ○ Uneven (irregular, but not conchoidal)   ○ Hackly (jagged, as of a metal)
○ Splintery (occurs in aggregates of many slender, brittle crystals)   ○ Fibrous (occurs in aggregates of many slender, threadlike crystals)

Crystal Habit: ○ Prismatic   ○ Acicular   ○ Striated   ○ Botryoidal   ○ Dendritic
○ Nodular   ○ Banded   ○ Other_____

Hardness: ○ 1 Talc   ○ 2 Gypsum   ○ 2.5 Fingernail   ○ 3 Calcite   ○ 4 Fluorite
(Mohs Scale) ○ 5 Apatite   ○ 5.5 Glass   ○ 6 Feldspar   ○ 6.5 Steel File
○ 7 Quartz   ○ 8 Topaz   ○ 9 Corundrum   ○ 10 Diamond

Specific Gravity: ○ Average (like quartz = 2.6 - 2.8)
○ Heavy (like galena = 7.5)
○ Light (lighter than quartz = <2.6)

$$\frac{mass\ of\ mineral}{mass\ of\ same\ volume\ of\ water} = \frac{weight\ of\ mineral\ in\ air}{weight\ of\ equal\ volume\ of\ water}$$

Tenacity: ○ Brittle   ○ Ductile   ○ Elastic   ○ Flexible   ○ Friable
○ Malleable   ○ Sectile

Diaphaneity: ○ Transparent   ○ Translucent   ○ Opaque

Notes: _____

Notes

_____
_____
_____
_____
_____
_____
_____
_____
_____
_____

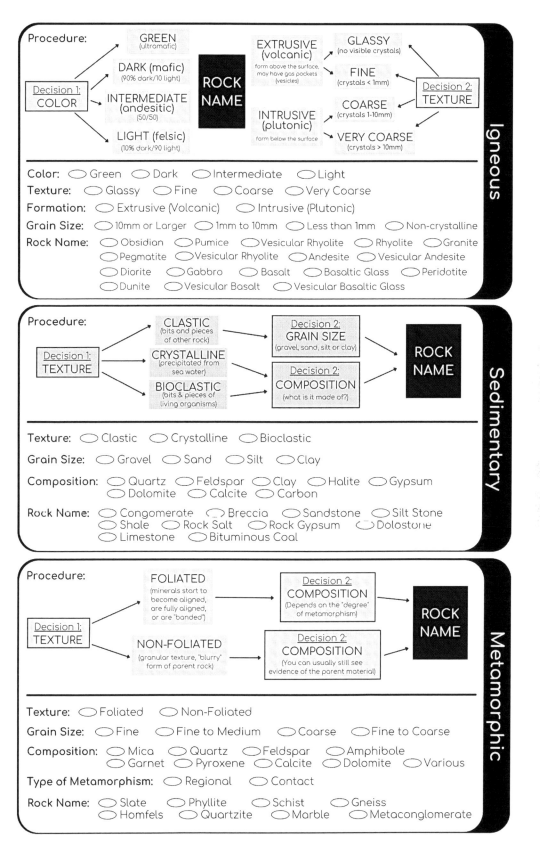

Igneous

Procedure:

Decision 1: COLOR →
- GREEN (ultramafic)
- DARK (mafic) (90% dark/10 light)
- INTERMEDIATE (andesitic) (50/50)
- LIGHT (felsic) (10% dark/90 light)

ROCK NAME

EXTRUSIVE (volcanic) — form above the surface, may have gas pockets (vesicles)

INTRUSIVE (plutonic) — form below the surface

- GLASSY (no visible crystals)
- FINE (crystals < 1mm)
- COARSE (crystals 1-10mm)
- VERY COARSE (crystals > 10mm)

Decision 2: TEXTURE

Color: ◯ Green ◯ Dark ◯ Intermediate ◯ Light

Texture: ◯ Glassy ◯ Fine ◯ Coarse ◯ Very Coarse

Formation: ◯ Extrusive (Volcanic) ◯ Intrusive (Plutonic)

Grain Size: ◯ 10mm or Larger ◯ 1mm to 10mm ◯ Less than 1mm ◯ Non-crystalline

Rock Name: ◯ Obsidian ◯ Pumice ◯ Vesicular Rhyolite ◯ Rhyolite ◯ Granite
◯ Pegmatite ◯ Vesicular Rhyolite ◯ Andesite ◯ Vesicular Andesite
◯ Diorite ◯ Gabbro ◯ Basalt ◯ Basaltic Glass ◯ Peridotite
◯ Dunite ◯ Vesicular Basalt ◯ Vesicular Basaltic Glass

Sedimentary

Procedure:

Decision 1: TEXTURE →
- CLASTIC (bits and pieces of other rock)
- CRYSTALLINE (precipitated from sea water)
- BIOCLASTIC (bits & pieces of living organisms)

Decision 2: GRAIN SIZE (gravel, sand, silt or clay)

Decision 2: COMPOSITION (what is it made of?)

ROCK NAME

Texture: ◯ Clastic ◯ Crystalline ◯ Bioclastic

Grain Size: ◯ Gravel ◯ Sand ◯ Silt ◯ Clay

Composition: ◯ Quartz ◯ Feldspar ◯ Clay ◯ Halite ◯ Gypsum
◯ Dolomite ◯ Calcite ◯ Carbon

Rock Name: ◯ Conglomerate ◯ Breccia ◯ Sandstone ◯ Silt Stone
◯ Shale ◯ Rock Salt ◯ Rock Gypsum ◯ Dolostone
◯ Limestone ◯ Bituminous Coal

Metamorphic

Procedure:

Decision 1: TEXTURE →
- FOLIATED (minerals start to become aligned, are fully aligned, or are "banded")
- NON-FOLIATED (granular texture, "blurry" form of parent rock)

Decision 2: COMPOSITION (Depends on the "degree" of metamorphism)

Decision 2: COMPOSITION (You can usually still see evidence of the parent material)

ROCK NAME

Texture: ◯ Foliated ◯ Non-Foliated

Grain Size: ◯ Fine ◯ Fine to Medium ◯ Coarse ◯ Fine to Coarse

Composition: ◯ Mica ◯ Quartz ◯ Feldspar ◯ Amphibole
◯ Garnet ◯ Pyroxene ◯ Calcite ◯ Dolomite ◯ Various

Type of Metamorphism: ◯ Regional ◯ Contact

Rock Name: ◯ Slate ◯ Phyllite ◯ Schist ◯ Gneiss
◯ Homfels ◯ Quartzite ◯ Marble ◯ Metaconglomerate

General

Date: _____   GPS Location: _____

Location:
- ◯ Public Land ◯ Private Land ◯ Pay-to-Dig Site ◯ Quarry
- ◯ Roadcut ◯ Outcrop ◯ Riverbed ◯ Creek Bed ◯ Beach
- ◯ Mine Tailing ◯ Fresh Overturned Soil ◯ Other_____

Weather:
- ◯ Sunny & Clear ◯ Cloudy/Overcast ◯ Windy ◯ Rainy / Drizzle
- ◯ Snow ◯ Stormy ◯ Fog ◯ Drought ◯ Other_____

Rock Type: ◯ Igneous ◯ Sedimentary ◯ Metamorphic

Equipment Checklist: (Rockhounding)
- ◯ Eye Protection ◯ Heavy-Duty Gloves ◯ Boots / Waterproof
- ◯ First-Aid Kit ◯ Hard Hat ◯ Rock Hammer / Pick ◯ Sieve
- ◯ Colander ◯ Small Picks ◯ Trowel ◯ Small Knife ◯ Chisel
- ◯ Small Broom ◯ Crack Hammer ◯ Pry Bar ◯ Sledgehammer
- ◯ Mason's Hammer ◯ Shovel ◯ Backpack ◯ Bucket ◯ Map
- ◯ Wrapping Material ◯ Small Tubes ◯ Boxes / Containers
- ◯ Loupe ◯ Magnifying Glass ◯ Magnet ◯ Compass / GPS

Notes: _____

Mineral Identification

Color: ◯ Light ◯ Dark Specific Colors: _____

Luster:
- ◯ Metallic ◯ Gold ◯ Brass ◯ Bronze ◯ Iron ◯ Steel ◯ Lead ◯ Silver ◯ Alum.
- ◯ Non-Metallic ◯ Adamantine ◯ Vitreous ◯ Resinous ◯ Pearly ◯ Dull ◯ Greasy ◯ Earthy ◯ Silky

Cleavage:
- ◯ 1 Direction ◯ 2 Directions at 90° ◯ 2 Directions not at 90°
- ◯ 3 Directions at 90° (cubic) ◯ 3 Directions not at 90° (rhombohedral)
- ◯ 4 Directions (octahedral) ◯ 6 Directions (dodecahedral)

Fracture:
- ◯ Conchoidal (smooth, shell-like, or glass-like breaks) ◯ Uneven (irregular, but not conchoidal) ◯ Hackly (jagged, as of a metal)
- ◯ Splintery (occurs in aggregates of many slender, brittle crystals) ◯ Fibrous (occurs in aggregates of many slender, threadlike crystals)

Crystal Habit:
- ◯ Prismatic ◯ Acicular ◯ Striated ◯ Botryoidal ◯ Dendritic
- ◯ Nodular ◯ Banded ◯ Other_____

Hardness: (Mohs Scale)
- ◯ 1 Talc ◯ 2 Gypsum ◯ 2.5 Fingernail ◯ 3 Calcite ◯ 4 Fluorite
- ◯ 5 Apatite ◯ 5.5 Glass ◯ 6 Feldspar ◯ 6.5 Steel File
- ◯ 7 Quartz ◯ 8 Topaz ◯ 9 Corundrum ◯ 10 Diamond

Specific Gravity:
- ◯ Average (like quartz = 2.6 - 2.8)
- ◯ Heavy (like galena = 7.5)
- ◯ Light (lighter than quartz = <2.6)

$$\frac{\text{mass of mineral}}{\text{mass of same volume of water}} = \frac{\text{weight of mineral in air}}{\text{weight of equal volume of water}}$$

Tenacity:
- ◯ Brittle ◯ Ductile ◯ Elastic ◯ Flexible ◯ Friable
- ◯ Malleable ◯ Sectile

Diaphaneity: ◯ Transparent ◯ Translucent ◯ Opaque

Notes: _____

Notes

_____
_____
_____
_____
_____
_____
_____
_____
_____

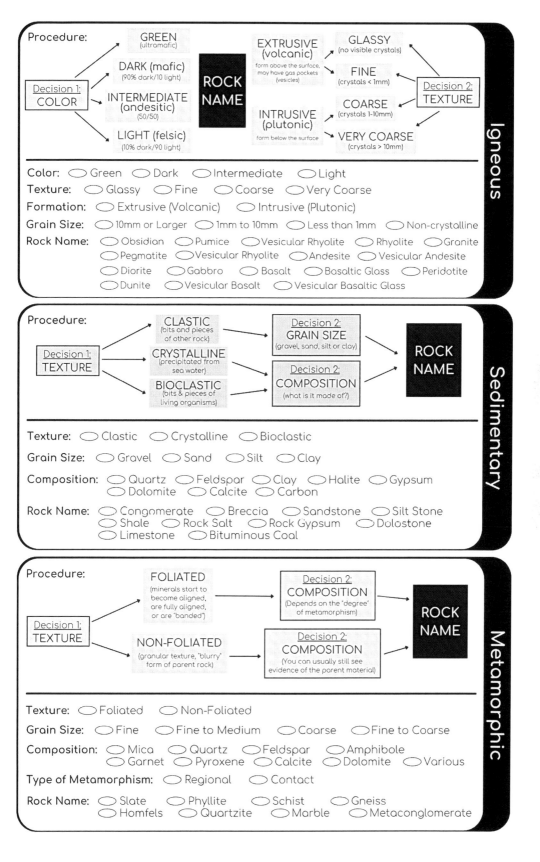

Igneous

Procedure:

Decision 1: COLOR
- GREEN (ultramafic)
- DARK (mafic) (90% dark/10 light)
- INTERMEDIATE (andesitic) (50/50)
- LIGHT (felsic) (10% dark/90 light)

ROCK NAME

EXTRUSIVE (volcanic) — form above the surface, may have gas pockets (vesicles)

INTRUSIVE (plutonic) — form below the surface

Decision 2: TEXTURE
- GLASSY (no visible crystals)
- FINE (crystals < 1mm)
- COARSE (crystals 1-10mm)
- VERY COARSE (crystals > 10mm)

Color: ○ Green ○ Dark ○ Intermediate ○ Light

Texture: ○ Glassy ○ Fine ○ Coarse ○ Very Coarse

Formation: ○ Extrusive (Volcanic) ○ Intrusive (Plutonic)

Grain Size: ○ 10mm or Larger ○ 1mm to 10mm ○ Less than 1mm ○ Non-crystalline

Rock Name: ○ Obsidian ○ Pumice ○ Vesicular Rhyolite ○ Rhyolite ○ Granite
○ Pegmatite ○ Vesicular Rhyolite ○ Andesite ○ Vesicular Andesite
○ Diorite ○ Gabbro ○ Basalt ○ Basaltic Glass ○ Peridotite
○ Dunite ○ Vesicular Basalt ○ Vesicular Basaltic Glass

Sedimentary

Procedure:

Decision 1: TEXTURE
- CLASTIC (bits and pieces of other rock)
- CRYSTALLINE (precipitated from sea water)
- BIOCLASTIC (bits & pieces of living organisms)

Decision 2: GRAIN SIZE (gravel, sand, silt or clay)

Decision 2: COMPOSITION (what is it made of?)

ROCK NAME

Texture: ○ Clastic ○ Crystalline ○ Bioclastic

Grain Size: ○ Gravel ○ Sand ○ Silt ○ Clay

Composition: ○ Quartz ○ Feldspar ○ Clay ○ Halite ○ Gypsum
○ Dolomite ○ Calcite ○ Carbon

Rock Name: ○ Congomerate ○ Breccia ○ Sandstone ○ Silt Stone
○ Shale ○ Rock Salt ○ Rock Gypsum ○ Dolostone
○ Limestone ○ Bituminous Coal

Metamorphic

Procedure:

Decision 1: TEXTURE
- FOLIATED (minerals start to become aligned, are fully aligned, or are "banded")
- NON-FOLIATED (granular texture, "blurry" form of parent rock)

Decision 2: COMPOSITION (Depends on the "degree" of metamorphism)

Decision 2: COMPOSITION (You can usually still see evidence of the parent material)

ROCK NAME

Texture: ○ Foliated ○ Non-Foliated

Grain Size: ○ Fine ○ Fine to Medium ○ Coarse ○ Fine to Coarse

Composition: ○ Mica ○ Quartz ○ Feldspar ○ Amphibole
○ Garnet ○ Pyroxene ○ Calcite ○ Dolomite ○ Various

Type of Metamorphism: ○ Regional ○ Contact

Rock Name: ○ Slate ○ Phyllite ○ Schist ○ Gneiss
○ Hornfels ○ Quartzite ○ Marble ○ Metaconglomerate

General

Date: _____ GPS Location: _____

Location: ⃝ Public Land ⃝ Private Land ⃝ Pay-to-Dig Site ⃝ Quarry
⃝ Roadcut ⃝ Outcrop ⃝ Riverbed ⃝ Creek Bed ⃝ Beach
⃝ Mine Tailing ⃝ Fresh Overturned Soil ⃝ Other_____

Weather: ⃝ Sunny & Clear ⃝ Cloudy/Overcast ⃝ Windy ⃝ Rainy / Drizzle
⃝ Snow ⃝ Stormy ⃝ Fog ⃝ Drought ⃝ Other_____

Rock Type: ⃝ Igneous ⃝ Sedimentary ⃝ Metamorphic

Equipment Checklist:
(Rockhounding)
⃝ Eye Protection ⃝ Heavy-Duty Gloves ⃝ Boots / Waterproof
⃝ First-Aid Kit ⃝ Hard Hat ⃝ Rock Hammer / Pick ⃝ Sieve
⃝ Colander ⃝ Small Picks ⃝ Trowel ⃝ Small Knife ⃝ Chisel
⃝ Small Broom ⃝ Crack Hammer ⃝ Pry Bar ⃝ Sledgehammer
⃝ Mason's Hammer ⃝ Shovel ⃝ Backpack ⃝ Bucket ⃝ Map
⃝ Wrapping Material ⃝ Small Tubes ⃝ Boxes / Containers
⃝ Loupe ⃝ Magnifying Glass ⃝ Magnet ⃝ Compass / GPS

Notes: _____

Mineral Identification

Color: ⃝ Light ⃝ Dark Specific Colors: _____

Luster: ⃝ Metallic ⃝ Gold ⃝ Brass ⃝ Non-Metallic ⃝ Adamantine ⃝ Vitreous
⃝ Bronze ⃝ Iron ⃝ Resinous ⃝ Pearly ⃝ Dull
⃝ Steel ⃝ Lead ⃝ Greasy ⃝ Earthy ⃝ Silky
⃝ Silver ⃝ Alum.

Cleavage: ⃝ 1 Direction ⃝ 2 Directions at 90° ⃝ 2 Directions not at 90°
⃝ 3 Directions at 90° (cubic) ⃝ 3 Directions not at 90° (rhombohedral)
⃝ 4 Directions (octahedral) ⃝ 6 Directions (dodecahedral)

Fracture: ⃝ Conchoidal (smooth, shell-like, or glass-like breaks) ⃝ Uneven (irregular, but not conchoidal) ⃝ Hackly (jagged, as of a metal)
⃝ Splintery (occurs in aggregates of many slender, brittle crystals) ⃝ Fibrous (occurs in aggregates of many slender, threadlike crystals)

Crystal Habit: ⃝ Prismatic ⃝ Acicular ⃝ Striated ⃝ Botryoidal ⃝ Dendritic
⃝ Nodular ⃝ Banded ⃝ Other_____

Hardness: (Mohs Scale)
⃝ 1 Talc ⃝ 2 Gypsum ⃝ 2.5 Fingernail ⃝ 3 Calcite ⃝ 4 Fluorite
⃝ 5 Apatite ⃝ 5.5 Glass ⃝ 6 Feldspar ⃝ 6.5 Steel File
⃝ 7 Quartz ⃝ 8 Topaz ⃝ 9 Corundrum ⃝ 10 Diamond

Specific Gravity: ⃝ Average (like quartz = 2.6 - 2.8) ⃝ Heavy (like galena = 7.5) ⃝ Light (lighter than quartz = <2.6)

$$\frac{\text{mass of mineral}}{\text{mass of same volume of water}} = \frac{\text{weight of mineral in air}}{\text{weight of equal volume of water}}$$

Tenacity: ⃝ Brittle ⃝ Ductile ⃝ Elastic ⃝ Flexible ⃝ Friable
⃝ Malleable ⃝ Sectile

Diaphaneity: ⃝ Transparent ⃝ Translucent ⃝ Opaque

Notes: _____

Notes

_____
_____
_____
_____
_____
_____
_____
_____
_____
_____

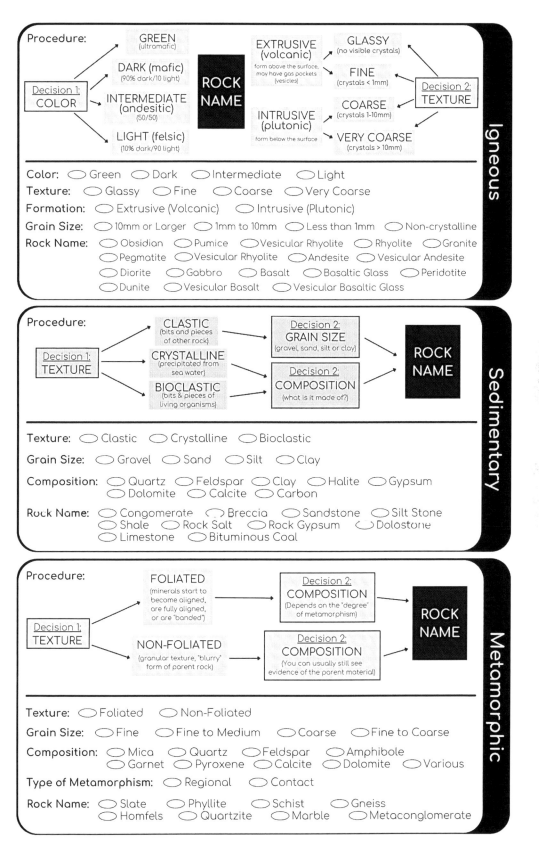

Igneous

Procedure:

Decision 1: COLOR
- GREEN (ultramafic)
- DARK (mafic) (90% dark/10 light)
- INTERMEDIATE (andesitic) (50/50)
- LIGHT (felsic) (10% dark/90 light)

ROCK NAME

EXTRUSIVE (volcanic) — form above the surface, may have gas pockets (vesicles)

INTRUSIVE (plutonic) — form below the surface

Decision 2: TEXTURE
- GLASSY (no visible crystals)
- FINE (crystals < 1mm)
- COARSE (crystals 1-10mm)
- VERY COARSE (crystals > 10mm)

Color: ◯ Green ◯ Dark ◯ Intermediate ◯ Light

Texture: ◯ Glassy ◯ Fine ◯ Coarse ◯ Very Coarse

Formation: ◯ Extrusive (Volcanic) ◯ Intrusive (Plutonic)

Grain Size: ◯ 10mm or Larger ◯ 1mm to 10mm ◯ Less than 1mm ◯ Non-crystalline

Rock Name: ◯ Obsidian ◯ Pumice ◯ Vesicular Rhyolite ◯ Rhyolite ◯ Granite
◯ Pegmatite ◯ Vesicular Rhyolite ◯ Andesite ◯ Vesicular Andesite
◯ Diorite ◯ Gabbro ◯ Basalt ◯ Basaltic Glass ◯ Peridotite
◯ Dunite ◯ Vesicular Basalt ◯ Vesicular Basaltic Glass

Sedimentary

Procedure:

Decision 1: TEXTURE
- CLASTIC (bits and pieces of other rock)
- CRYSTALLINE (precipitated from sea water)
- BIOCLASTIC (bits & pieces of living organisms)

Decision 2: GRAIN SIZE (gravel, sand, silt or clay)

Decision 2: COMPOSITION (what is it made of?)

ROCK NAME

Texture: ◯ Clastic ◯ Crystalline ◯ Bioclastic

Grain Size: ◯ Gravel ◯ Sand ◯ Silt ◯ Clay

Composition: ◯ Quartz ◯ Feldspar ◯ Clay ◯ Halite ◯ Gypsum
◯ Dolomite ◯ Calcite ◯ Carbon

Rock Name: ◯ Conglomerate ◯ Breccia ◯ Sandstone ◯ Silt Stone
◯ Shale ◯ Rock Salt ◯ Rock Gypsum ◯ Dolostone
◯ Limestone ◯ Bituminous Coal

Metamorphic

Procedure:

Decision 1: TEXTURE
- FOLIATED (minerals start to become aligned, are fully aligned, or are "banded")
- NON-FOLIATED (granular texture, "blurry" form of parent rock)

Decision 2: COMPOSITION (Depends on the "degree" of metamorphism)

Decision 2: COMPOSITION (You can usually still see evidence of the parent material)

ROCK NAME

Texture: ◯ Foliated ◯ Non-Foliated

Grain Size: ◯ Fine ◯ Fine to Medium ◯ Coarse ◯ Fine to Coarse

Composition: ◯ Mica ◯ Quartz ◯ Feldspar ◯ Amphibole
◯ Garnet ◯ Pyroxene ◯ Calcite ◯ Dolomite ◯ Various

Type of Metamorphism: ◯ Regional ◯ Contact

Rock Name: ◯ Slate ◯ Phyllite ◯ Schist ◯ Gneiss
◯ Homfels ◯ Quartzite ◯ Marble ◯ Metaconglomerate

General

Date: _____ GPS Location: _____

Location: ○ Public Land ○ Private Land ○ Pay-to-Dig Site ○ Quarry
○ Roadcut ○ Outcrop ○ Riverbed ○ Creek Bed ○ Beach
○ Mine Tailing ○ Fresh Overturned Soil ○ Other_____

Weather: ○ Sunny & Clear ○ Cloudy/Overcast ○ Windy ○ Rainy / Drizzle
○ Snow ○ Stormy ○ Fog ○ Drought ○ Other_____

Rock Type: ○ Igneous ○ Sedimentary ○ Metamorphic

Equipment ○ Eye Protection ○ Heavy-Duty Gloves ○ Boots / Waterproof
Checklist: ○ First-Aid Kit ○ Hard Hat ○ Rock Hammer / Pick ○ Sieve
(Rockhounding) ○ Colander ○ Small Picks ○ Trowel ○ Small Knife ○ Chisel
○ Small Broom ○ Crack Hammer ○ Pry Bar ○ Sledgehammer
○ Mason's Hammer ○ Shovel ○ Backpack ○ Bucket ○ Map
○ Wrapping Material ○ Small Tubes ○ Boxes / Containers
○ Loupe ○ Magnifying Glass ○ Magnet ○ Compass / GPS

Notes: _____

Mineral Identification

Color: ○ Light ○ Dark Specific Colors: _____

Luster: ○ Metallic ○ Gold ○ Brass   ○ Non-Metallic ○ Adamantine ○ Vitreous
○ Bronze ○ Iron   ○ Resinous ○ Pearly ○ Dull
○ Steel ○ Lead   ○ Greasy ○ Earthy ○ Silky
○ Silver ○ Alum.

Cleavage: ○ 1 Direction ○ 2 Directions at 90° ○ 2 Directions not at 90°
○ 3 Directions at 90° (cubic) ○ 3 Directions not at 90° (rhombohedral)
○ 4 Directions (octahedral) ○ 6 Directions (dodecahedral)

Fracture: ○ Conchoidal (smooth, shell-like, or glass-like breaks) ○ Uneven (irregular, but not conchoidal) ○ Hackly (jagged, as of a metal)
○ Splintery (occurs in aggregates of many slender, brittle crystals) ○ Fibrous (occurs in aggregates of many slender, threadlike crystals)

Crystal ○ Prismatic ○ Acicular ○ Striated ○ Botryoidal ○ Dendritic
Habit: ○ Nodular ○ Banded ○ Other_____

Hardness: ○ 1 Talc ○ 2 Gypsum ○ 2.5 Fingernail ○ 3 Calcite ○ 4 Fluorite
(Mohs Scale) ○ 5 Apatite ○ 5.5 Glass ○ 6 Feldspar ○ 6.5 Steel File
○ 7 Quartz ○ 8 Topaz ○ 9 Corundrum ○ 10 Diamond

Specific ○ Average (like quartz = 2.6 - 2.8)   mass of mineral = weight of mineral in air
Gravity: ○ Heavy (like galena = 7.5)   mass of same volume of water   weight of equal volume of water
○ Light (lighter than quartz = <2.6)

Tenacity: ○ Brittle ○ Ductile ○ Elastic ○ Flexible ○ Friable
○ Malleable ○ Sectile

Diaphaneity: ○ Transparent ○ Translucent ○ Opaque

Notes: _____

Notes

_____
_____
_____
_____
_____
_____
_____
_____
_____
_____

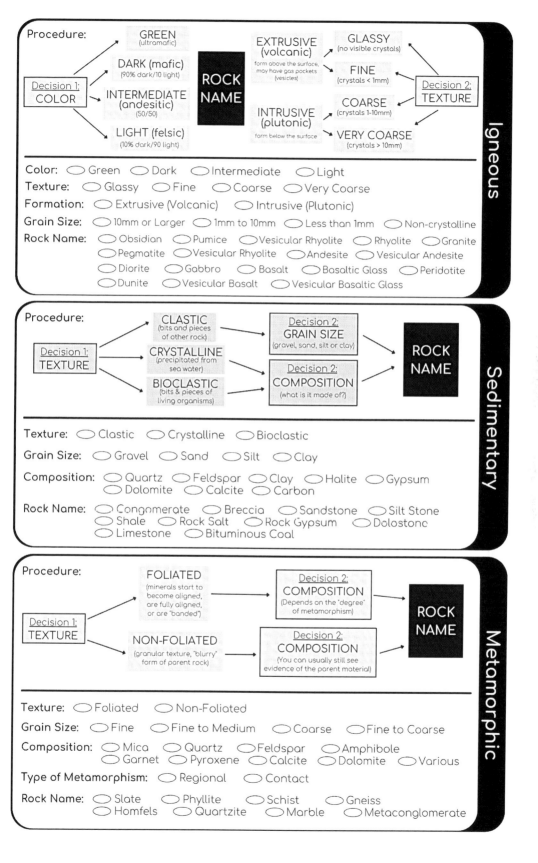

Igneous

Procedure:

Decision 1: COLOR →
- GREEN (ultramafic)
- DARK (mafic) (90% dark/10 light)
- INTERMEDIATE (andesitic) (50/50)
- LIGHT (felsic) (10% dark/90 light)

ROCK NAME

- EXTRUSIVE (volcanic) — form above the surface, may have gas pockets (vesicles)
- INTRUSIVE (plutonic) — form below the surface

- GLASSY (no visible crystals)
- FINE (crystals < 1mm)
- COARSE (crystals 1-10mm)
- VERY COARSE (crystals > 10mm)

Decision 2: TEXTURE

Color: ◯ Green ◯ Dark ◯ Intermediate ◯ Light

Texture: ◯ Glassy ◯ Fine ◯ Coarse ◯ Very Coarse

Formation: ◯ Extrusive (Volcanic) ◯ Intrusive (Plutonic)

Grain Size: ◯ 10mm or Larger ◯ 1mm to 10mm ◯ Less than 1mm ◯ Non-crystalline

Rock Name: ◯ Obsidian ◯ Pumice ◯ Vesicular Rhyolite ◯ Rhyolite ◯ Granite
◯ Pegmatite ◯ Vesicular Rhyolite ◯ Andesite ◯ Vesicular Andesite
◯ Diorite ◯ Gabbro ◯ Basalt ◯ Basaltic Glass ◯ Peridotite
◯ Dunite ◯ Vesicular Basalt ◯ Vesicular Basaltic Glass

Sedimentary

Procedure:

Decision 1: TEXTURE →
- CLASTIC (bits and pieces of other rock)
- CRYSTALLINE (precipitated from sea water)
- BIOCLASTIC (bits & pieces of living organisms)

- Decision 2: GRAIN SIZE (gravel, sand, silt or clay)
- Decision 2: COMPOSITION (what is it made of?)

ROCK NAME

Texture: ◯ Clastic ◯ Crystalline ◯ Bioclastic

Grain Size: ◯ Gravel ◯ Sand ◯ Silt ◯ Clay

Composition: ◯ Quartz ◯ Feldspar ◯ Clay ◯ Halite ◯ Gypsum
◯ Dolomite ◯ Calcite ◯ Carbon

Rock Name: ◯ Conglomerate ◯ Breccia ◯ Sandstone ◯ Silt Stone
◯ Shale ◯ Rock Salt ◯ Rock Gypsum ◯ Dolostone
◯ Limestone ◯ Bituminous Coal

Metamorphic

Procedure:

Decision 1: TEXTURE →
- FOLIATED (minerals start to become aligned, are fully aligned, or are "banded")
- NON-FOLIATED (granular texture, "blurry" form of parent rock)

- Decision 2: COMPOSITION (Depends on the "degree" of metamorphism)
- Decision 2: COMPOSITION (You can usually still see evidence of the parent material)

ROCK NAME

Texture: ◯ Foliated ◯ Non-Foliated

Grain Size: ◯ Fine ◯ Fine to Medium ◯ Coarse ◯ Fine to Coarse

Composition: ◯ Mica ◯ Quartz ◯ Feldspar ◯ Amphibole
◯ Garnet ◯ Pyroxene ◯ Calcite ◯ Dolomite ◯ Various

Type of Metamorphism: ◯ Regional ◯ Contact

Rock Name: ◯ Slate ◯ Phyllite ◯ Schist ◯ Gneiss
◯ Homfels ◯ Quartzite ◯ Marble ◯ Metaconglomerate

General

Date: _____ GPS Location: _____

Location: ⚬ Public Land ⚬ Private Land ⚬ Pay-to-Dig Site ⚬ Quarry
⚬ Roadcut ⚬ Outcrop ⚬ Riverbed ⚬ Creek Bed ⚬ Beach
⚬ Mine Tailing ⚬ Fresh Overturned Soil ⚬ Other_____

Weather: ⚬ Sunny & Clear ⚬ Cloudy/Overcast ⚬ Windy ⚬ Rainy / Drizzle
⚬ Snow ⚬ Stormy ⚬ Fog ⚬ Drought ⚬ Other_____

Rock Type: ⚬ Igneous ⚬ Sedimentary ⚬ Metamorphic

Equipment Checklist: (Rockhounding)
⚬ Eye Protection ⚬ Heavy-Duty Gloves ⚬ Boots / Waterproof
⚬ First-Aid Kit ⚬ Hard Hat ⚬ Rock Hammer / Pick ⚬ Sieve
⚬ Colander ⚬ Small Picks ⚬ Trowel ⚬ Small Knife ⚬ Chisel
⚬ Small Broom ⚬ Crack Hammer ⚬ Pry Bar ⚬ Sledgehammer
⚬ Mason's Hammer ⚬ Shovel ⚬ Backpack ⚬ Bucket ⚬ Map
⚬ Wrapping Material ⚬ Small Tubes ⚬ Boxes / Containers
⚬ Loupe ⚬ Magnifying Glass ⚬ Magnet ⚬ Compass / GPS

Notes: _____

Mineral Identification

Color: ⚬ Light ⚬ Dark Specific Colors: _____

Luster: ⚬ Metallic ⚬ Gold ⚬ Brass   ⚬ Non-Metallic ⚬ Adamantine ⚬ Vitreous
⚬ Bronze ⚬ Iron   ⚬ Resinous ⚬ Pearly ⚬ Dull
⚬ Steel ⚬ Lead   ⚬ Greasy ⚬ Earthy ⚬ Silky
⚬ Silver ⚬ Alum.

Cleavage: ⚬ 1 Direction ⚬ 2 Directions at 90° ⚬ 2 Directions not at 90°
⚬ 3 Directions at 90° (cubic) ⚬ 3 Directions not at 90° (rhombohedral)
⚬ 4 Directions (octahedral) ⚬ 6 Directions (dodecahedral)

Fracture: ⚬ Conchoidal (smooth, shell-like, or glass-like breaks) ⚬ Uneven (irregular, but not conchoidal) ⚬ Hackly (jagged, as of a metal)
⚬ Splintery (occurs in aggregates of many slender, brittle crystals) ⚬ Fibrous (occurs in aggregates of many slender, threadlike crystals)

Crystal Habit: ⚬ Prismatic ⚬ Acicular ⚬ Striated ⚬ Botryoidal ⚬ Dendritic
⚬ Nodular ⚬ Banded ⚬ Other_____

Hardness: (Mohs Scale)
⚬ 1 Talc ⚬ 2 Gypsum ⚬ 2.5 Fingernail ⚬ 3 Calcite ⚬ 4 Fluorite
⚬ 5 Apatite ⚬ 5.5 Glass ⚬ 6 Feldspar ⚬ 6.5 Steel File
⚬ 7 Quartz ⚬ 8 Topaz ⚬ 9 Corundrum ⚬ 10 Diamond

Specific Gravity:
⚬ Average (like quartz = 2.6 - 2.8) $\frac{\text{mass of mineral}}{\text{mass of same volume of water}} = \frac{\text{weight of mineral in air}}{\text{weight of equal volume of water}}$
⚬ Heavy (like galena = 7.5)
⚬ Light (lighter than quartz = <2.6)

Tenacity: ⚬ Brittle ⚬ Ductile ⚬ Elastic ⚬ Flexible ⚬ Friable
⚬ Malleable ⚬ Sectile

Diaphaneity: ⚬ Transparent ⚬ Translucent ⚬ Opaque

Notes: _____

Notes

_____
_____
_____
_____
_____
_____
_____
_____
_____
_____

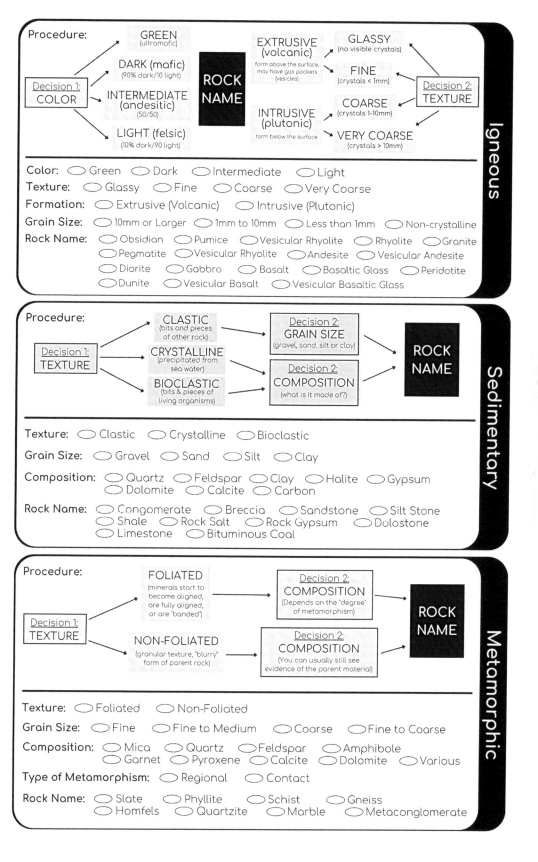

Igneous

Procedure:

Decision 1: COLOR →
- GREEN (ultramafic)
- DARK (mafic) (90% dark/10 light)
- INTERMEDIATE (andesitic) (50/50)
- LIGHT (felsic) (10% dark/90 light)

ROCK NAME

EXTRUSIVE (volcanic) — form above the surface, may have gas pockets (vesicles)

INTRUSIVE (plutonic) — form below the surface

- GLASSY (no visible crystals)
- FINE (crystals < 1mm)
- COARSE (crystals 1-10mm)
- VERY COARSE (crystals > 10mm)

Decision 2: TEXTURE

Color: ◯ Green ◯ Dark ◯ Intermediate ◯ Light

Texture: ◯ Glassy ◯ Fine ◯ Coarse ◯ Very Coarse

Formation: ◯ Extrusive (Volcanic) ◯ Intrusive (Plutonic)

Grain Size: ◯ 10mm or Larger ◯ 1mm to 10mm ◯ Less than 1mm ◯ Non-crystalline

Rock Name: ◯ Obsidian ◯ Pumice ◯ Vesicular Rhyolite ◯ Rhyolite ◯ Granite ◯ Pegmatite ◯ Vesicular Rhyolite ◯ Andesite ◯ Vesicular Andesite ◯ Diorite ◯ Gabbro ◯ Basalt ◯ Basaltic Glass ◯ Peridotite ◯ Dunite ◯ Vesicular Basalt ◯ Vesicular Basaltic Glass

Sedimentary

Procedure:

Decision 1: TEXTURE →
- CLASTIC (bits and pieces of other rock)
- CRYSTALLINE (precipitated from sea water)
- BIOCLASTIC (bits & pieces of living organisms)

Decision 2: GRAIN SIZE (gravel, sand, silt or clay)

Decision 2: COMPOSITION (what is it made of?)

ROCK NAME

Texture: ◯ Clastic ◯ Crystalline ◯ Bioclastic

Grain Size: ◯ Gravel ◯ Sand ◯ Silt ◯ Clay

Composition: ◯ Quartz ◯ Feldspar ◯ Clay ◯ Halite ◯ Gypsum ◯ Dolomite ◯ Calcite ◯ Carbon

Rock Name: ◯ Congomerate ◯ Breccia ◯ Sandstone ◯ Silt Stone ◯ Shale ◯ Rock Salt ◯ Rock Gypsum ◯ Dolostone ◯ Limestone ◯ Bituminous Coal

Metamorphic

Procedure:

Decision 1: TEXTURE →
- FOLIATED (minerals start to become aligned, are fully aligned, or are "banded")
- NON-FOLIATED (granular texture, "blurry" form of parent rock)

Decision 2: COMPOSITION (Depends on the "degree" of metamorphism)

Decision 2: COMPOSITION (You can usually still see evidence of the parent material)

ROCK NAME

Texture: ◯ Foliated ◯ Non-Foliated

Grain Size: ◯ Fine ◯ Fine to Medium ◯ Coarse ◯ Fine to Coarse

Composition: ◯ Mica ◯ Quartz ◯ Feldspar ◯ Amphibole ◯ Garnet ◯ Pyroxene ◯ Calcite ◯ Dolomite ◯ Various

Type of Metamorphism: ◯ Regional ◯ Contact

Rock Name: ◯ Slate ◯ Phyllite ◯ Schist ◯ Gneiss ◯ Homfels ◯ Quartzite ◯ Marble ◯ Metaconglomerate

General

Date: _____ **GPS Location:** _____

Location: ○ Public Land ○ Private Land ○ Pay-to-Dig Site ○ Quarry
○ Roadcut ○ Outcrop ○ Riverbed ○ Creek Bed ○ Beach
○ Mine Tailing ○ Fresh Overturned Soil ○ Other_____

Weather: ○ Sunny & Clear ○ Cloudy/Overcast ○ Windy ○ Rainy / Drizzle
○ Snow ○ Stormy ○ Fog ○ Drought ○ Other_____

Rock Type: ○ Igneous ○ Sedimentary ○ Metamorphic

Equipment Checklist:
(Rockhounding)
○ Eye Protection ○ Heavy-Duty Gloves ○ Boots / Waterproof
○ First-Aid Kit ○ Hard Hat ○ Rock Hammer / Pick ○ Sieve
○ Colander ○ Small Picks ○ Trowel ○ Small Knife ○ Chisel
○ Small Broom ○ Crack Hammer ○ Pry Bar ○ Sledgehammer
○ Mason's Hammer ○ Shovel ○ Backpack ○ Bucket ○ Map
○ Wrapping Material ○ Small Tubes ○ Boxes / Containers
○ Loupe ○ Magnifying Glass ○ Magnet ○ Compass / GPS

Notes: _____

Mineral Identification

Color: ○ Light ○ Dark Specific Colors: _____

Luster: ○ Metallic ○ Gold ○ Brass ○ Non-Metallic ○ Adamantine ○ Vitreous
○ Bronze ○ Iron ○ Resinous ○ Pearly ○ Dull
○ Steel ○ Lead ○ Greasy ○ Earthy ○ Silky
○ Silver ○ Alum.

Cleavage: ○ 1 Direction ○ 2 Directions at 90° ○ 2 Directions not at 90°
○ 3 Directions at 90° (cubic) ○ 3 Directions not at 90° (rhombohedral)
○ 4 Directions (octahedral) ○ 6 Directions (dodecahedral)

Fracture: ○ Conchoidal (smooth, shell-like, or glass-like breaks) ○ Uneven (irregular, but not conchoidal) ○ Hackly (jagged, as of a metal)
○ Splintery (occurs in aggregates of many slender, brittle crystals) ○ Fibrous (occurs in aggregates of many slender, threadlike crystals)

Crystal Habit: ○ Prismatic ○ Acicular ○ Striated ○ Botryoidal ○ Dendritic
○ Nodular ○ Banded ○ Other_____

Hardness:
(Mohs Scale)
○ 1 Talc ○ 2 Gypsum ○ 2.5 Fingernail ○ 3 Calcite ○ 4 Fluorite
○ 5 Apatite ○ 5.5 Glass ○ 6 Feldspar ○ 6.5 Steel File
○ 7 Quartz ○ 8 Topaz ○ 9 Corundrum ○ 10 Diamond

Specific Gravity: ○ Average (like quartz = 2.6 - 2.8) ○ Heavy (like galena = 7.5) ○ Light (lighter than quartz = <2.6)

$$\frac{\text{mass of mineral}}{\text{mass of same volume of water}} = \frac{\text{weight of mineral in air}}{\text{weight of equal volume of water}}$$

Tenacity: ○ Brittle ○ Ductile ○ Elastic ○ Flexible ○ Friable
○ Malleable ○ Sectile

Diaphaneity: ○ Transparent ○ Translucent ○ Opaque

Notes: _____

Notes

_____
_____
_____
_____
_____
_____
_____
_____
_____

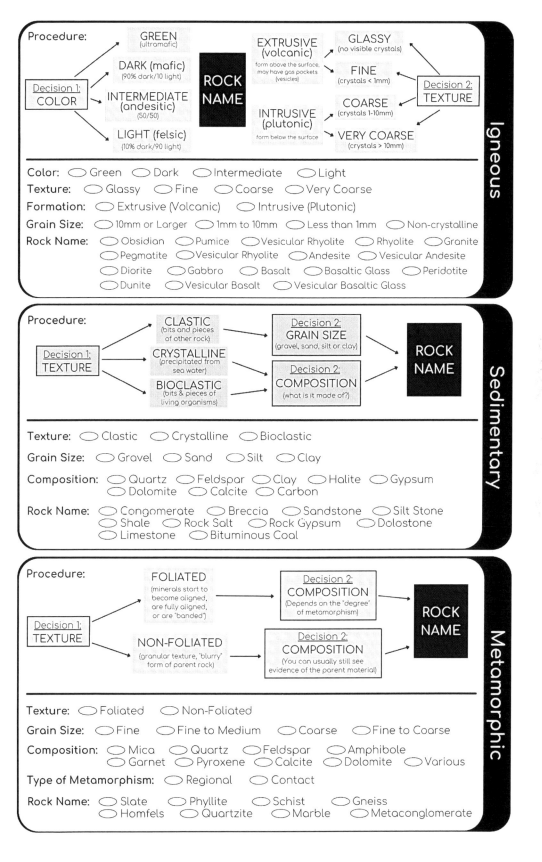

Igneous

Procedure:

Decision 1: COLOR
- GREEN (ultramafic)
- DARK (mafic) (90% dark/10 light)
- INTERMEDIATE (andesitic) (50/50)
- LIGHT (felsic) (10% dark/90 light)

ROCK NAME

EXTRUSIVE (volcanic) — form above the surface, may have gas pockets (vesicles)

INTRUSIVE (plutonic) — form below the surface

Decision 2: TEXTURE
- GLASSY (no visible crystals)
- FINE (crystals < 1mm)
- COARSE (crystals 1-10mm)
- VERY COARSE (crystals > 10mm)

Color: ⬭ Green ⬭ Dark ⬭ Intermediate ⬭ Light

Texture: ⬭ Glassy ⬭ Fine ⬭ Coarse ⬭ Very Coarse

Formation: ⬭ Extrusive (Volcanic) ⬭ Intrusive (Plutonic)

Grain Size: ⬭ 10mm or Larger ⬭ 1mm to 10mm ⬭ Less than 1mm ⬭ Non-crystalline

Rock Name: ⬭ Obsidian ⬭ Pumice ⬭ Vesicular Rhyolite ⬭ Rhyolite ⬭ Granite ⬭ Pegmatite ⬭ Vesicular Rhyolite ⬭ Andesite ⬭ Vesicular Andesite ⬭ Diorite ⬭ Gabbro ⬭ Basalt ⬭ Basaltic Glass ⬭ Peridotite ⬭ Dunite ⬭ Vesicular Basalt ⬭ Vesicular Basaltic Glass

Sedimentary

Procedure:

Decision 1: TEXTURE
- CLASTIC (bits and pieces of other rock)
- CRYSTALLINE (precipitated from sea water)
- BIOCLASTIC (bits & pieces of living organisms)

Decision 2: GRAIN SIZE (gravel, sand, silt or clay)

Decision 2: COMPOSITION (what is it made of?)

ROCK NAME

Texture: ⬭ Clastic ⬭ Crystalline ⬭ Bioclastic

Grain Size: ⬭ Gravel ⬭ Sand ⬭ Silt ⬭ Clay

Composition: ⬭ Quartz ⬭ Feldspar ⬭ Clay ⬭ Halite ⬭ Gypsum ⬭ Dolomite ⬭ Calcite ⬭ Carbon

Rock Name: ⬭ Conglomerate ⬭ Breccia ⬭ Sandstone ⬭ Silt Stone ⬭ Shale ⬭ Rock Salt ⬭ Rock Gypsum ⬭ Dolostone ⬭ Limestone ⬭ Bituminous Coal

Metamorphic

Procedure:

Decision 1: TEXTURE
- FOLIATED (minerals start to become aligned, are fully aligned, or are "banded")
- NON-FOLIATED (granular texture, "blurry" form of parent rock)

Decision 2: COMPOSITION (Depends on the "degree" of metamorphism)

Decision 2: COMPOSITION (You can usually still see evidence of the parent material)

ROCK NAME

Texture: ⬭ Foliated ⬭ Non-Foliated

Grain Size: ⬭ Fine ⬭ Fine to Medium ⬭ Coarse ⬭ Fine to Coarse

Composition: ⬭ Mica ⬭ Quartz ⬭ Feldspar ⬭ Amphibole ⬭ Garnet ⬭ Pyroxene ⬭ Calcite ⬭ Dolomite ⬭ Various

Type of Metamorphism: ⬭ Regional ⬭ Contact

Rock Name: ⬭ Slate ⬭ Phyllite ⬭ Schist ⬭ Gneiss ⬭ Homfels ⬭ Quartzite ⬭ Marble ⬭ Metaconglomerate

General

Date: _____ GPS Location: _____

Location: ○ Public Land ○ Private Land ○ Pay-to-Dig Site ○ Quarry
○ Roadcut ○ Outcrop ○ Riverbed ○ Creek Bed ○ Beach
○ Mine Tailing ○ Fresh Overturned Soil ○ Other_____

Weather: ○ Sunny & Clear ○ Cloudy/Overcast ○ Windy ○ Rainy / Drizzle
○ Snow ○ Stormy ○ Fog ○ Drought ○ Other_____

Rock Type: ○ Igneous ○ Sedimentary ○ Metamorphic

Equipment Checklist:
(Rockhounding)
○ Eye Protection ○ Heavy-Duty Gloves ○ Boots / Waterproof
○ First-Aid Kit ○ Hard Hat ○ Rock Hammer / Pick ○ Sieve
○ Colander ○ Small Picks ○ Trowel ○ Small Knife ○ Chisel
○ Small Broom ○ Crack Hammer ○ Pry Bar ○ Sledgehammer
○ Mason's Hammer ○ Shovel ○ Backpack ○ Bucket ○ Map
○ Wrapping Material ○ Small Tubes ○ Boxes / Containers
○ Loupe ○ Magnifying Glass ○ Magnet ○ Compass / GPS

Notes: _____

Mineral Identification

Color: ○ Light ○ Dark Specific Colors: _____

Luster: ○ Metallic ○ Gold ○ Brass ○ Non-Metallic ○ Adamantine ○ Vitreous
○ Bronze ○ Iron ○ Resinous ○ Pearly ○ Dull
○ Steel ○ Lead ○ Greasy ○ Earthy ○ Silky
○ Silver ○ Alum.

Cleavage: ○ 1 Direction ○ 2 Directions at 90° ○ 2 Directions not at 90°
○ 3 Directions at 90° (cubic) ○ 3 Directions not at 90° (rhombohedral)
○ 4 Directions (octahedral) ○ 6 Directions (dodecahedral)

Fracture: ○ Conchoidal (smooth, shell-like, or glass-like breaks) ○ Uneven (irregular, but not conchoidal) ○ Hackly (jagged, as of a metal)
○ Splintery (occurs in aggregates of many slender, brittle crystals) ○ Fibrous (occurs in aggregates of many slender, threadlike crystals)

Crystal Habit: ○ Prismatic ○ Acicular ○ Striated ○ Botryoidal ○ Dendritic
○ Nodular ○ Banded ○ Other_____

Hardness: (Mohs Scale)
○ 1 Talc ○ 2 Gypsum ○ 2.5 Fingernail ○ 3 Calcite ○ 4 Fluorite
○ 5 Apatite ○ 5.5 Glass ○ 6 Feldspar ○ 6.5 Steel File
○ 7 Quartz ○ 8 Topaz ○ 9 Corundrum ○ 10 Diamond

Specific Gravity:
○ Average (like quartz = 2.6 - 2.8)
○ Heavy (like galena = 7.5)
○ Light (lighter than quartz = <2.6)

$$\frac{\text{mass of mineral}}{\text{mass of same volume of water}} = \frac{\text{weight of mineral in air}}{\text{weight of equal volume of water}}$$

Tenacity: ○ Brittle ○ Ductile ○ Elastic ○ Flexible ○ Friable
○ Malleable ○ Sectile

Diaphaneity: ○ Transparent ○ Translucent ○ Opaque

Notes: _____

Notes

_____
_____
_____
_____
_____
_____
_____
_____
_____

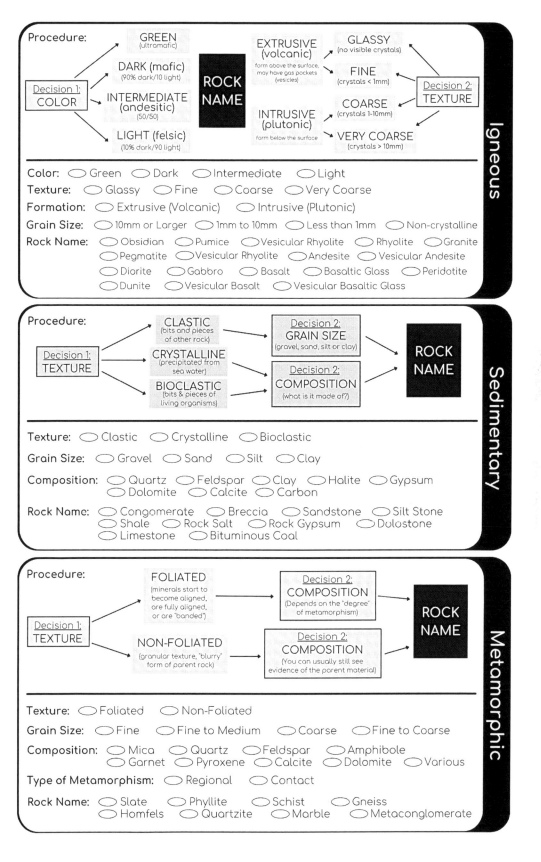

Igneous

Procedure:

Decision 1: COLOR
- GREEN (ultramafic)
- DARK (mafic) (90% dark/10 light)
- INTERMEDIATE (andesitic) (50/50)
- LIGHT (felsic) (10% dark/90 light)

ROCK NAME

- EXTRUSIVE (volcanic) form above the surface, may have gas pockets (vesicles)
- INTRUSIVE (plutonic) form below the surface

Decision 2: TEXTURE
- GLASSY (no visible crystals)
- FINE (crystals < 1mm)
- COARSE (crystals 1-10mm)
- VERY COARSE (crystals > 10mm)

Color: ◯ Green ◯ Dark ◯ Intermediate ◯ Light

Texture: ◯ Glassy ◯ Fine ◯ Coarse ◯ Very Coarse

Formation: ◯ Extrusive (Volcanic) ◯ Intrusive (Plutonic)

Grain Size: ◯ 10mm or Larger ◯ 1mm to 10mm ◯ Less than 1mm ◯ Non-crystalline

Rock Name: ◯ Obsidian ◯ Pumice ◯ Vesicular Rhyolite ◯ Rhyolite ◯ Granite
◯ Pegmatite ◯ Vesicular Rhyolite ◯ Andesite ◯ Vesicular Andesite
◯ Diorite ◯ Gabbro ◯ Basalt ◯ Basaltic Glass ◯ Peridotite
◯ Dunite ◯ Vesicular Basalt ◯ Vesicular Basaltic Glass

Sedimentary

Procedure:

Decision 1: TEXTURE
- CLASTIC (bits and pieces of other rock)
- CRYSTALLINE (precipitated from sea water)
- BIOCLASTIC (bits & pieces of living organisms)

Decision 2: GRAIN SIZE (gravel, sand, silt or clay)

Decision 2: COMPOSITION (what is it made of?)

ROCK NAME

Texture: ◯ Clastic ◯ Crystalline ◯ Bioclastic

Grain Size: ◯ Gravel ◯ Sand ◯ Silt ◯ Clay

Composition: ◯ Quartz ◯ Feldspar ◯ Clay ◯ Halite ◯ Gypsum
◯ Dolomite ◯ Calcite ◯ Carbon

Rock Name: ◯ Conglomerate ◯ Breccia ◯ Sandstone ◯ Silt Stone
◯ Shale ◯ Rock Salt ◯ Rock Gypsum ◯ Dolostone
◯ Limestone ◯ Bituminous Coal

Metamorphic

Procedure:

Decision 1: TEXTURE
- FOLIATED (minerals start to become aligned, are fully aligned, or are "banded")
- NON-FOLIATED (granular texture, "blurry" form of parent rock)

Decision 2: COMPOSITION (Depends on the "degree" of metamorphism)

Decision 2: COMPOSITION (You can usually still see evidence of the parent material)

ROCK NAME

Texture: ◯ Foliated ◯ Non-Foliated

Grain Size: ◯ Fine ◯ Fine to Medium ◯ Coarse ◯ Fine to Coarse

Composition: ◯ Mica ◯ Quartz ◯ Feldspar ◯ Amphibole
◯ Garnet ◯ Pyroxene ◯ Calcite ◯ Dolomite ◯ Various

Type of Metamorphism: ◯ Regional ◯ Contact

Rock Name: ◯ Slate ◯ Phyllite ◯ Schist ◯ Gneiss
◯ Hornfels ◯ Quartzite ◯ Marble ◯ Metaconglomerate

General

Date: _____ GPS Location: _____

Location: ◯ Public Land ◯ Private Land ◯ Pay-to-Dig Site ◯ Quarry
◯ Roadcut ◯ Outcrop ◯ Riverbed ◯ Creek Bed ◯ Beach
◯ Mine Tailing ◯ Fresh Overturned Soil ◯ Other_____

Weather: ◯ Sunny & Clear ◯ Cloudy/Overcast ◯ Windy ◯ Rainy / Drizzle
◯ Snow ◯ Stormy ◯ Fog ◯ Drought ◯ Other_____

Rock Type: ◯ Igneous ◯ Sedimentary ◯ Metamorphic

Equipment Checklist:
(Rockhounding)
◯ Eye Protection ◯ Heavy-Duty Gloves ◯ Boots / Waterproof
◯ First-Aid Kit ◯ Hard Hat ◯ Rock Hammer / Pick ◯ Sieve
◯ Colander ◯ Small Picks ◯ Trowel ◯ Small Knife ◯ Chisel
◯ Small Broom ◯ Crack Hammer ◯ Pry Bar ◯ Sledgehammer
◯ Mason's Hammer ◯ Shovel ◯ Backpack ◯ Bucket ◯ Map
◯ Wrapping Material ◯ Small Tubes ◯ Boxes / Containers
◯ Loupe ◯ Magnifying Glass ◯ Magnet ◯ Compass / GPS

Notes: _____

Mineral Identification

Color: ◯ Light ◯ Dark Specific Colors: _____

Luster: ◯ Metallic ◯ Gold ◯ Brass ◯ Non-Metallic ◯ Adamantine ◯ Vitreous
◯ Bronze ◯ Iron ◯ Resinous ◯ Pearly ◯ Dull
◯ Steel ◯ Lead ◯ Greasy ◯ Earthy ◯ Silky
◯ Silver ◯ Alum.

Cleavage: ◯ 1 Direction ◯ 2 Directions at 90° ◯ 2 Directions not at 90°
◯ 3 Directions at 90° (cubic) ◯ 3 Directions not at 90° (rhombohedral)
◯ 4 Directions (octahedral) ◯ 6 Directions (dodecahedral)

Fracture: ◯ Conchoidal (smooth, shell-like, or glass-like breaks) ◯ Uneven (irregular, but not conchoidal) ◯ Hackly (jagged, as of a metal)
◯ Splintery (occurs in aggregates of many slender, brittle crystals) ◯ Fibrous (occurs in aggregates of many slender, threadlike crystals)

Crystal Habit: ◯ Prismatic ◯ Acicular ◯ Striated ◯ Botryoidal ◯ Dendritic
◯ Nodular ◯ Banded ◯ Other_____

Hardness: (Mohs Scale)
◯ 1 Talc ◯ 2 Gypsum ◯ 2.5 Fingernail ◯ 3 Calcite ◯ 4 Fluorite
◯ 5 Apatite ◯ 5.5 Glass ◯ 6 Feldspar ◯ 6.5 Steel File
◯ 7 Quartz ◯ 8 Topaz ◯ 9 Corundrum ◯ 10 Diamond

Specific Gravity:
◯ Average (like quartz = 2.6 - 2.8)
◯ Heavy (like galena = 7.5)
◯ Light (lighter than quartz = <2.6)

mass of mineral = weight of mineral in air
mass of same volume of water   weight of equal volume of water

Tenacity: ◯ Brittle ◯ Ductile ◯ Elastic ◯ Flexible ◯ Friable
◯ Malleable ◯ Sectile

Diaphaneity: ◯ Transparent ◯ Translucent ◯ Opaque

Notes: _____

Notes

_____
_____
_____
_____
_____
_____
_____
_____
_____
_____

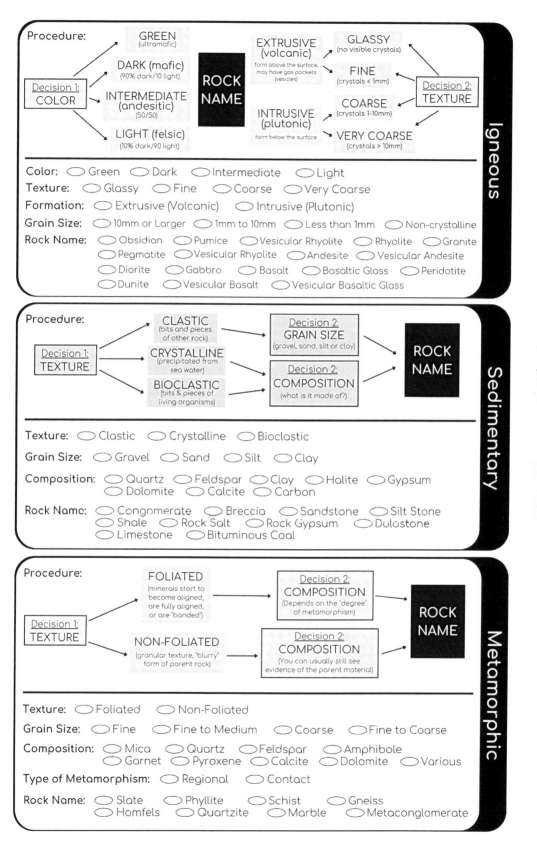

General

Date: _____   GPS Location: _____

Location: ◯ Public Land ◯ Private Land ◯ Pay-to-Dig Site ◯ Quarry
◯ Roadcut ◯ Outcrop ◯ Riverbed ◯ Creek Bed ◯ Beach
◯ Mine Tailing ◯ Fresh Overturned Soil ◯ Other_____

Weather: ◯ Sunny & Clear ◯ Cloudy/Overcast ◯ Windy ◯ Rainy / Drizzle
◯ Snow ◯ Stormy ◯ Fog ◯ Drought ◯ Other_____

Rock Type: ◯ Igneous ◯ Sedimentary ◯ Metamorphic

Equipment Checklist: (Rockhounding)
◯ Eye Protection ◯ Heavy-Duty Gloves ◯ Boots / Waterproof
◯ First-Aid Kit ◯ Hard Hat ◯ Rock Hammer / Pick ◯ Sieve
◯ Colander ◯ Small Picks ◯ Trowel ◯ Small Knife ◯ Chisel
◯ Small Broom ◯ Crack Hammer ◯ Pry Bar ◯ Sledgehammer
◯ Mason's Hammer ◯ Shovel ◯ Backpack ◯ Bucket ◯ Map
◯ Wrapping Material ◯ Small Tubes ◯ Boxes / Containers
◯ Loupe ◯ Magnifying Glass ◯ Magnet ◯ Compass / GPS

Notes: _____

Mineral Identification

Color: ◯ Light ◯ Dark Specific Colors: _____

Luster: ◯ Metallic ◯ Gold ◯ Brass   ◯ Non-Metallic ◯ Adamantine ◯ Vitreous
◯ Bronze ◯ Iron   ◯ Resinous ◯ Pearly ◯ Dull
◯ Steel ◯ Lead   ◯ Greasy ◯ Earthy ◯ Silky
◯ Silver ◯ Alum.

Cleavage: ◯ 1 Direction ◯ 2 Directions at 90° ◯ 2 Directions not at 90°
◯ 3 Directions at 90° (cubic) ◯ 3 Directions not at 90° (rhombohedral)
◯ 4 Directions (octahedral) ◯ 6 Directions (dodecahedral)

Fracture: ◯ Conchoidal (smooth, shell-like, or glass-like breaks) ◯ Uneven (irregular, but not conchoidal) ◯ Hackly (jagged, as of a metal)
◯ Splintery (occurs in aggregates of many slender, brittle crystals) ◯ Fibrous (occurs in aggregates of many slender, threadlike crystals)

Crystal Habit: ◯ Prismatic ◯ Acicular ◯ Striated ◯ Botryoidal ◯ Dendritic
◯ Nodular ◯ Banded ◯ Other_____

Hardness: (Mohs Scale)
◯ 1 Talc ◯ 2 Gypsum ◯ 2.5 Fingernail ◯ 3 Calcite ◯ 4 Fluorite
◯ 5 Apatite ◯ 5.5 Glass ◯ 6 Feldspar ◯ 6.5 Steel File
◯ 7 Quartz ◯ 8 Topaz ◯ 9 Corundrum ◯ 10 Diamond

Specific Gravity:
◯ Average (like quartz = 2.6 - 2.8)
◯ Heavy (like galena = 7.5)
◯ Light (lighter than quartz = <2.6)

$$\frac{\text{mass of mineral}}{\text{mass of same volume of water}} = \frac{\text{weight of mineral in air}}{\text{weight of equal volume of water}}$$

Tenacity: ◯ Brittle ◯ Ductile ◯ Elastic ◯ Flexible ◯ Friable
◯ Malleable ◯ Sectile

Diaphaneity: ◯ Transparent ◯ Translucent ◯ Opaque

Notes:_____

Notes

_____
_____
_____
_____
_____
_____
_____
_____
_____

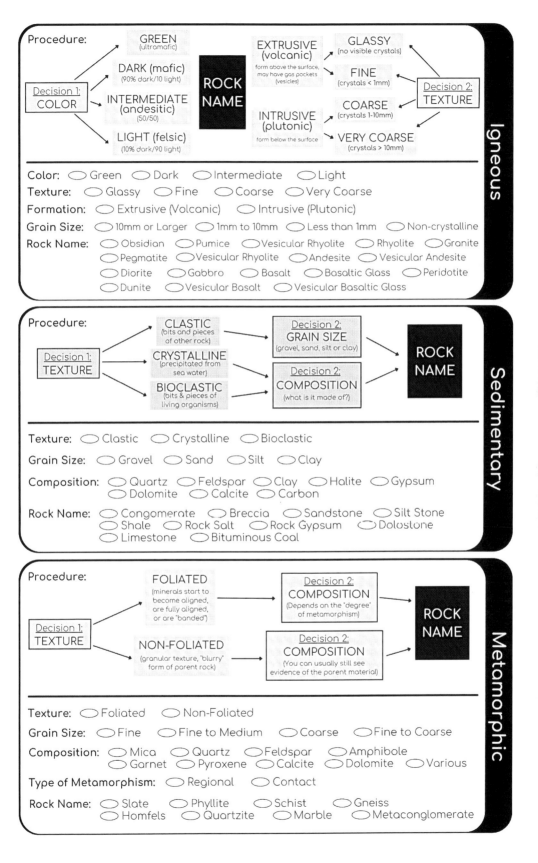

Igneous

Procedure:

Decision 1: COLOR
- GREEN (ultramafic)
- DARK (mafic) (90% dark/10 light)
- INTERMEDIATE (andesitic) (50/50)
- LIGHT (felsic) (10% dark/90 light)

ROCK NAME

- EXTRUSIVE (volcanic) — form above the surface, may have gas pockets (vesicles)
- INTRUSIVE (plutonic) — form below the surface

Decision 2: TEXTURE
- GLASSY (no visible crystals)
- FINE (crystals < 1mm)
- COARSE (crystals 1-10mm)
- VERY COARSE (crystals > 10mm)

Color: ⚬ Green ⚬ Dark ⚬ Intermediate ⚬ Light

Texture: ⚬ Glassy ⚬ Fine ⚬ Coarse ⚬ Very Coarse

Formation: ⚬ Extrusive (Volcanic) ⚬ Intrusive (Plutonic)

Grain Size: ⚬ 10mm or Larger ⚬ 1mm to 10mm ⚬ Less than 1mm ⚬ Non-crystalline

Rock Name: ⚬ Obsidian ⚬ Pumice ⚬ Vesicular Rhyolite ⚬ Rhyolite ⚬ Granite ⚬ Pegmatite ⚬ Vesicular Rhyolite ⚬ Andesite ⚬ Vesicular Andesite ⚬ Diorite ⚬ Gabbro ⚬ Basalt ⚬ Basaltic Glass ⚬ Peridotite ⚬ Dunite ⚬ Vesicular Basalt ⚬ Vesicular Basaltic Glass

Sedimentary

Procedure:

Decision 1: TEXTURE
- CLASTIC (bits and pieces of other rock)
- CRYSTALLINE (precipitated from sea water)
- BIOCLASTIC (bits & pieces of living organisms)

Decision 2: GRAIN SIZE (gravel, sand, silt or clay)

Decision 2: COMPOSITION (what is it made of?)

ROCK NAME

Texture: ⚬ Clastic ⚬ Crystalline ⚬ Bioclastic

Grain Size: ⚬ Gravel ⚬ Sand ⚬ Silt ⚬ Clay

Composition: ⚬ Quartz ⚬ Feldspar ⚬ Clay ⚬ Halite ⚬ Gypsum ⚬ Dolomite ⚬ Calcite ⚬ Carbon

Rock Name: ⚬ Congomerate ⚬ Breccia ⚬ Sandstone ⚬ Silt Stone ⚬ Shale ⚬ Rock Salt ⚬ Rock Gypsum ⚬ Dolostone ⚬ Limestone ⚬ Bituminous Coal

Metamorphic

Procedure:

Decision 1: TEXTURE
- FOLIATED (minerals start to become aligned, are fully aligned, or are "banded")
- NON-FOLIATED (granular texture, "blurry" form of parent rock)

Decision 2: COMPOSITION (Depends on the "degree" of metamorphism)

Decision 2: COMPOSITION (You can usually still see evidence of the parent material)

ROCK NAME

Texture: ⚬ Foliated ⚬ Non-Foliated

Grain Size: ⚬ Fine ⚬ Fine to Medium ⚬ Coarse ⚬ Fine to Coarse

Composition: ⚬ Mica ⚬ Quartz ⚬ Feldspar ⚬ Amphibole ⚬ Garnet ⚬ Pyroxene ⚬ Calcite ⚬ Dolomite ⚬ Various

Type of Metamorphism: ⚬ Regional ⚬ Contact

Rock Name: ⚬ Slate ⚬ Phyllite ⚬ Schist ⚬ Gneiss ⚬ Hornfels ⚬ Quartzite ⚬ Marble ⚬ Metaconglomerate

General

Date: _____ GPS Location: _____

Location: ◯ Public Land ◯ Private Land ◯ Pay-to-Dig Site ◯ Quarry
◯ Roadcut ◯ Outcrop ◯ Riverbed ◯ Creek Bed ◯ Beach
◯ Mine Tailing ◯ Fresh Overturned Soil ◯ Other_____

Weather: ◯ Sunny & Clear ◯ Cloudy/Overcast ◯ Windy ◯ Rainy / Drizzle
◯ Snow ◯ Stormy ◯ Fog ◯ Drought ◯ Other_____

Rock Type: ◯ Igneous ◯ Sedimentary ◯ Metamorphic

Equipment
Checklist:
(Rockhounding)
◯ Eye Protection ◯ Heavy-Duty Gloves ◯ Boots / Waterproof
◯ First-Aid Kit ◯ Hard Hat ◯ Rock Hammer / Pick ◯ Sieve
◯ Colander ◯ Small Picks ◯ Trowel ◯ Small Knife ◯ Chisel
◯ Small Broom ◯ Crack Hammer ◯ Pry Bar ◯ Sledgehammer
◯ Mason's Hammer ◯ Shovel ◯ Backpack ◯ Bucket ◯ Map
◯ Wrapping Material ◯ Small Tubes ◯ Boxes / Containers
◯ Loupe ◯ Magnifying Glass ◯ Magnet ◯ Compass / GPS

Notes: _____

Mineral Identification

Color: ◯ Light ◯ Dark Specific Colors: _____

Luster: ◯ Metallic ◯ Gold ◯ Brass   ◯ Non-Metallic ◯ Adamantine ◯ Vitreous
◯ Bronze ◯ Iron   ◯ Resinous ◯ Pearly ◯ Dull
◯ Steel ◯ Lead   ◯ Greasy ◯ Earthy ◯ Silky
◯ Silver ◯ Alum.

Cleavage: ◯ 1 Direction ◯ 2 Directions at 90° ◯ 2 Directions not at 90°
◯ 3 Directions at 90° (cubic) ◯ 3 Directions not at 90° (rhombohedral)
◯ 4 Directions (octahedral) ◯ 6 Directions (dodecahedral)

Fracture: ◯ Conchoidal (smooth, shell-like, or glass-like breaks) ◯ Uneven (irregular, but not conchoidal) ◯ Hackly (jagged, as of a metal)
◯ Splintery (occurs in aggregates of many slender, brittle crystals) ◯ Fibrous (occurs in aggregates of many slender, threadlike crystals)

Crystal
Habit:
◯ Prismatic ◯ Acicular ◯ Striated ◯ Botryoidal ◯ Dendritic
◯ Nodular ◯ Banded ◯ Other_____

Hardness:
(Mohs Scale)
◯ 1 Talc ◯ 2 Gypsum ◯ 2.5 Fingernail ◯ 3 Calcite ◯ 4 Fluorite
◯ 5 Apatite ◯ 5.5 Glass ◯ 6 Feldspar ◯ 6.5 Steel File
◯ 7 Quartz ◯ 8 Topaz ◯ 9 Corundrum ◯ 10 Diamond

Specific
Gravity:
◯ Average (like quartz = 2.6 - 2.8) $\dfrac{\text{mass of mineral}}{\text{mass of same volume of water}} = \dfrac{\text{weight of mineral in air}}{\text{weight of equal volume of water}}$
◯ Heavy (like galena = 7.5)
◯ Light (lighter than quartz = <2.6)

Tenacity: ◯ Brittle ◯ Ductile ◯ Elastic ◯ Flexible ◯ Friable
◯ Malleable ◯ Sectile

Diaphaneity: ◯ Transparent ◯ Translucent ◯ Opaque

Notes: _____

Notes

_____
_____
_____
_____
_____
_____
_____
_____
_____
_____

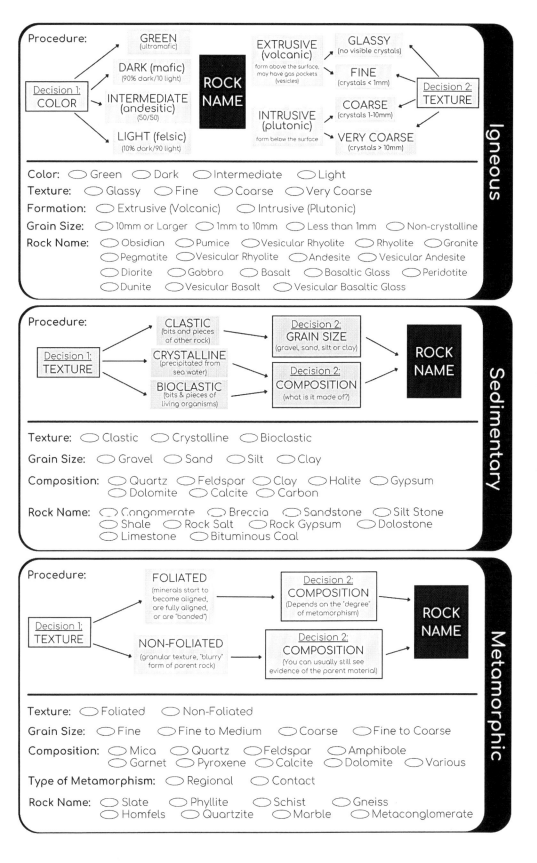

General

Date: _____   GPS Location: _____

Location: ◯ Public Land   ◯ Private Land   ◯ Pay-to-Dig Site   ◯ Quarry
◯ Roadcut   ◯ Outcrop   ◯ Riverbed   ◯ Creek Bed   ◯ Beach
◯ Mine Tailing   ◯ Fresh Overturned Soil   ◯ Other_____

Weather: ◯ Sunny & Clear   ◯ Cloudy/Overcast   ◯ Windy   ◯ Rainy / Drizzle
◯ Snow   ◯ Stormy   ◯ Fog   ◯ Drought   ◯ Other_____

Rock Type: ◯ Igneous   ◯ Sedimentary   ◯ Metamorphic

Equipment   ◯ Eye Protection   ◯ Heavy-Duty Gloves   ◯ Boots / Waterproof
Checklist: ◯ First-Aid Kit   ◯ Hard Hat   ◯ Rock Hammer / Pick   ◯ Sieve
(Rockhounding)   ◯ Colander   ◯ Small Picks   ◯ Trowel   ◯ Small Knife   ◯ Chisel
◯ Small Broom   ◯ Crack Hammer   ◯ Pry Bar   ◯ Sledgehammer
◯ Mason's Hammer   ◯ Shovel   ◯ Backpack   ◯ Bucket   ◯ Map
◯ Wrapping Material   ◯ Small Tubes   ◯ Boxes / Containers
◯ Loupe   ◯ Magnifying Glass   ◯ Magnet   ◯ Compass / GPS

Notes: _____

Mineral Identification

Color: ◯ Light   ◯ Dark   Specific Colors: _____

Luster: ◯ Metallic   ◯ Gold   ◯ Brass   ◯ Non-Metallic   ◯ Adamantine   ◯ Vitreous
◯ Bronze   ◯ Iron   ◯ Resinous   ◯ Pearly   ◯ Dull
◯ Steel   ◯ Lead   ◯ Greasy   ◯ Earthy   ◯ Silky
◯ Silver   ◯ Alum.

Cleavage: ◯ 1 Direction   ◯ 2 Directions at 90°   ◯ 2 Directions not at 90°
◯ 3 Directions at 90° (cubic)   ◯ 3 Directions not at 90° (rhombohedral)
◯ 4 Directions (octahedral)   ◯ 6 Directions (dodecahedral)

Fracture: ◯ Conchoidal (smooth, shell-like, or glass-like breaks)   ◯ Uneven (irregular, but not conchoidal)   ◯ Hackly (jagged, as of a metal)
◯ Splintery (occurs in aggregates of many slender, brittle crystals)   ◯ Fibrous (occurs in aggregates of many slender, threadlike crystals)

Crystal   ◯ Prismatic   ◯ Acicular   ◯ Striated   ◯ Botryoidal   ◯ Dendritic
Habit: ◯ Nodular   ◯ Banded   ◯ Other_____

Hardness: ◯ 1 Talc   ◯ 2 Gypsum   ◯ 2.5 Fingernail   ◯ 3 Calcite   ◯ 4 Fluorite
(Mohs Scale)   ◯ 5 Apatite   ◯ 5.5 Glass   ◯ 6 Feldspar   ◯ 6.5 Steel File
◯ 7 Quartz   ◯ 8 Topaz   ◯ 9 Corundrum   ◯ 10 Diamond

Specific   ◯ Average (like quartz = 2.6 - 2.8)
Gravity: ◯ Heavy (like galena = 7.5) $$\frac{\text{mass of mineral}}{\text{mass of same volume of water}} = \frac{\text{weight of mineral in air}}{\text{weight of equal volume of water}}$$
◯ Light (lighter than quartz = <2.6)

Tenacity: ◯ Brittle   ◯ Ductile   ◯ Elastic   ◯ Flexible   ◯ Friable
◯ Malleable   ◯ Sectile

Diaphaneity: ◯ Transparent   ◯ Translucent   ◯ Opaque

Notes:_____

Notes

_____
_____
_____
_____
_____
_____
_____
_____
_____

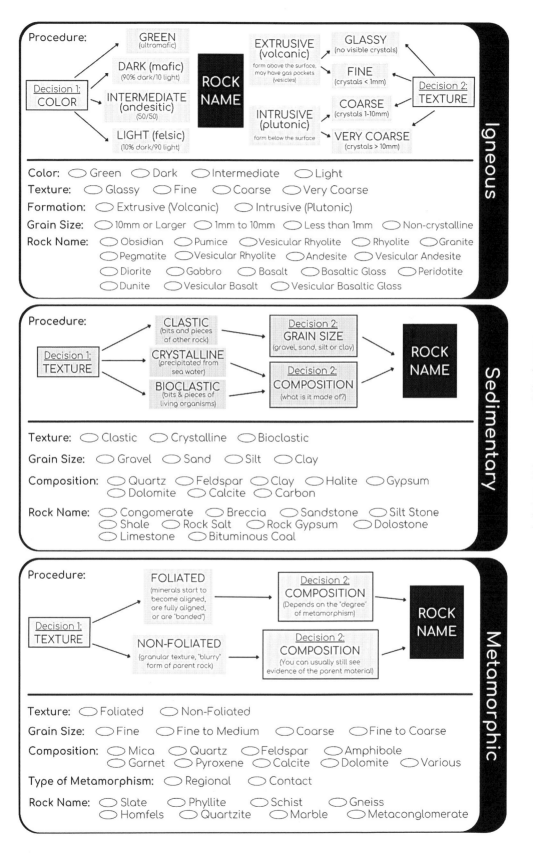

Igneous

Procedure:

Decision 1: COLOR
- GREEN (ultramafic)
- DARK (mafic) (90% dark/10 light)
- INTERMEDIATE (andesitic) (50/50)
- LIGHT (felsic) (10% dark/90 light)

ROCK NAME

EXTRUSIVE (volcanic) — form above the surface, may have gas pockets (vesicles)

INTRUSIVE (plutonic) — form below the surface

Decision 2: TEXTURE
- GLASSY (no visible crystals)
- FINE (crystals < 1mm)
- COARSE (crystals 1-10mm)
- VERY COARSE (crystals > 10mm)

Color: ◯ Green ◯ Dark ◯ Intermediate ◯ Light

Texture: ◯ Glassy ◯ Fine ◯ Coarse ◯ Very Coarse

Formation: ◯ Extrusive (Volcanic) ◯ Intrusive (Plutonic)

Grain Size: ◯ 10mm or Larger ◯ 1mm to 10mm ◯ Less than 1mm ◯ Non-crystalline

Rock Name: ◯ Obsidian ◯ Pumice ◯ Vesicular Rhyolite ◯ Rhyolite ◯ Granite
◯ Pegmatite ◯ Vesicular Rhyolite ◯ Andesite ◯ Vesicular Andesite
◯ Diorite ◯ Gabbro ◯ Basalt ◯ Basaltic Glass ◯ Peridotite
◯ Dunite ◯ Vesicular Basalt ◯ Vesicular Basaltic Glass

Sedimentary

Procedure:

Decision 1: TEXTURE
- CLASTIC (bits and pieces of other rock)
- CRYSTALLINE (precipitated from sea water)
- BIOCLASTIC (bits & pieces of living organisms)

Decision 2: GRAIN SIZE (gravel, sand, silt or clay)

Decision 2: COMPOSITION (what is it made of?)

ROCK NAME

Texture: ◯ Clastic ◯ Crystalline ◯ Bioclastic

Grain Size: ◯ Gravel ◯ Sand ◯ Silt ◯ Clay

Composition: ◯ Quartz ◯ Feldspar ◯ Clay ◯ Halite ◯ Gypsum
◯ Dolomite ◯ Calcite ◯ Carbon

Rock Name: ◯ Congomerate ◯ Breccia ◯ Sandstone ◯ Silt Stone
◯ Shale ◯ Rock Salt ◯ Rock Gypsum ◯ Dolostone
◯ Limestone ◯ Bituminous Coal

Metamorphic

Procedure:

Decision 1: TEXTURE
- FOLIATED (minerals start to become aligned, are fully aligned, or are "banded")
- NON-FOLIATED (granular texture, "blurry" form of parent rock)

Decision 2: COMPOSITION (Depends on the "degree" of metamorphism)

Decision 2: COMPOSITION (You can usually still see evidence of the parent material)

ROCK NAME

Texture: ◯ Foliated ◯ Non-Foliated

Grain Size: ◯ Fine ◯ Fine to Medium ◯ Coarse ◯ Fine to Coarse

Composition: ◯ Mica ◯ Quartz ◯ Feldspar ◯ Amphibole
◯ Garnet ◯ Pyroxene ◯ Calcite ◯ Dolomite ◯ Various

Type of Metamorphism: ◯ Regional ◯ Contact

Rock Name: ◯ Slate ◯ Phyllite ◯ Schist ◯ Gneiss
◯ Homfels ◯ Quartzite ◯ Marble ◯ Metaconglomerate

General

Date: _____   GPS Location: _____

Location: ○ Public Land   ○ Private Land   ○ Pay-to-Dig Site   ○ Quarry
○ Roadcut   ○ Outcrop   ○ Riverbed   ○ Creek Bed   ○ Beach
○ Mine Tailing   ○ Fresh Overturned Soil   ○ Other_____

Weather: ○ Sunny & Clear   ○ Cloudy/Overcast   ○ Windy   ○ Rainy / Drizzle
○ Snow   ○ Stormy   ○ Fog   ○ Drought   ○ Other_____

Rock Type: ○ Igneous   ○ Sedimentary   ○ Metamorphic

Equipment Checklist:
(Rockhounding)
○ Eye Protection   ○ Heavy-Duty Gloves   ○ Boots / Waterproof
○ First-Aid Kit   ○ Hard Hat   ○ Rock Hammer / Pick   ○ Sieve
○ Colander   ○ Small Picks   ○ Trowel   ○ Small Knife   ○ Chisel
○ Small Broom   ○ Crack Hammer   ○ Pry Bar   ○ Sledgehammer
○ Mason's Hammer   ○ Shovel   ○ Backpack   ○ Bucket   ○ Map
○ Wrapping Material   ○ Small Tubes   ○ Boxes / Containers
○ Loupe   ○ Magnifying Glass   ○ Magnet   ○ Compass / GPS

Notes: _____

Mineral Identification

Color: ○ Light   ○ Dark   Specific Colors: _____

Luster: ○ Metallic   ○ Gold ○ Brass   ○ Non-Metallic ○ Adamantine ○ Vitreous
                ○ Bronze ○ Iron   ○ Resinous ○ Pearly ○ Dull
                ○ Steel ○ Lead   ○ Greasy ○ Earthy ○ Silky
                ○ Silver ○ Alum.

Cleavage: ○ 1 Direction   ○ 2 Directions at 90°   ○ 2 Directions not at 90°
○ 3 Directions at 90° (cubic)   ○ 3 Directions not at 90° (rhombohedral)
○ 4 Directions (octahedral)   ○ 6 Directions (dodecahedral)

Fracture: ○ Conchoidal (smooth, shell-like, or glass-like breaks)   ○ Uneven (irregular, but not conchoidal)   ○ Hackly (jagged, as of a metal)
○ Splintery (occurs in aggregates of many slender, brittle crystals)   ○ Fibrous (occurs in aggregates of many slender, threadlike crystals)

Crystal Habit: ○ Prismatic   ○ Acicular   ○ Striated   ○ Botryoidal   ○ Dendritic
○ Nodular   ○ Banded   ○ Other_____

Hardness: (Mohs Scale)
○ 1 Talc   ○ 2 Gypsum   ○ 2.5 Fingernail   ○ 3 Calcite   ○ 4 Fluorite
○ 5 Apatite   ○ 5.5 Glass   ○ 6 Feldspar   ○ 6.5 Steel File
○ 7 Quartz   ○ 8 Topaz   ○ 9 Corundrum   ○ 10 Diamond

Specific Gravity:
○ Average (like quartz = 2.6 - 2.8) $\frac{mass\ of\ mineral}{mass\ of\ same\ volume\ of\ water} = \frac{weight\ of\ mineral\ in\ air}{weight\ of\ equal\ volume\ of\ water}$
○ Heavy (like galena = 7.5)
○ Light (lighter than quartz = <2.6)

Tenacity: ○ Brittle   ○ Ductile   ○ Elastic   ○ Flexible   ○ Friable
○ Malleable   ○ Sectile

Diaphaneity: ○ Transparent   ○ Translucent   ○ Opaque

Notes: _____

Notes

_____
_____
_____
_____
_____
_____
_____
_____
_____

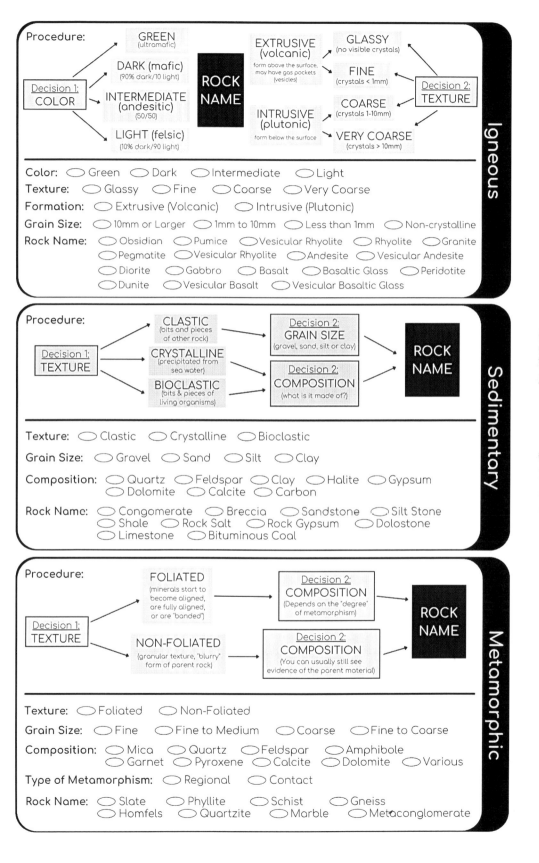

Igneous

Procedure:

Decision 1: COLOR
- GREEN (ultramafic)
- DARK (mafic) (90% dark/10 light)
- INTERMEDIATE (andesitic) (50/50)
- LIGHT (felsic) (10% dark/90 light)

ROCK NAME

EXTRUSIVE (volcanic) — form above the surface, may have gas pockets (vesicles)
INTRUSIVE (plutonic) — form below the surface

Decision 2: TEXTURE
- GLASSY (no visible crystals)
- FINE (crystals < 1mm)
- COARSE (crystals 1-10mm)
- VERY COARSE (crystals > 10mm)

Color: ◯ Green ◯ Dark ◯ Intermediate ◯ Light

Texture: ◯ Glassy ◯ Fine ◯ Coarse ◯ Very Coarse

Formation: ◯ Extrusive (Volcanic) ◯ Intrusive (Plutonic)

Grain Size: ◯ 10mm or Larger ◯ 1mm to 10mm ◯ Less than 1mm ◯ Non-crystalline

Rock Name: ◯ Obsidian ◯ Pumice ◯ Vesicular Rhyolite ◯ Rhyolite ◯ Granite ◯ Pegmatite ◯ Vesicular Rhyolite ◯ Andesite ◯ Vesicular Andesite ◯ Diorite ◯ Gabbro ◯ Basalt ◯ Basaltic Glass ◯ Peridotite ◯ Dunite ◯ Vesicular Basalt ◯ Vesicular Basaltic Glass

Sedimentary

Procedure:

Decision 1: TEXTURE
- CLASTIC (bits and pieces of other rock)
- CRYSTALLINE (precipitated from sea water)
- BIOCLASTIC (bits & pieces of living organisms)

Decision 2: GRAIN SIZE (gravel, sand, silt or clay)
Decision 2: COMPOSITION (what is it made of?)

ROCK NAME

Texture: ◯ Clastic ◯ Crystalline ◯ Bioclastic

Grain Size: ◯ Gravel ◯ Sand ◯ Silt ◯ Clay

Composition: ◯ Quartz ◯ Feldspar ◯ Clay ◯ Halite ◯ Gypsum ◯ Dolomite ◯ Calcite ◯ Carbon

Rock Name: ◯ Congomerate ◯ Breccia ◯ Sandstone ◯ Silt Stone ◯ Shale ◯ Rock Salt ◯ Rock Gypsum ◯ Dolostone ◯ Limestone ◯ Bituminous Coal

Metamorphic

Procedure:

Decision 1: TEXTURE
- FOLIATED (minerals start to become aligned, are fully aligned, or are "banded")
- NON-FOLIATED (granular texture, "blurry" form of parent rock)

Decision 2: COMPOSITION (Depends on the "degree" of metamorphism)
Decision 2: COMPOSITION (You can usually still see evidence of the parent material)

ROCK NAME

Texture: ◯ Foliated ◯ Non-Foliated

Grain Size: ◯ Fine ◯ Fine to Medium ◯ Coarse ◯ Fine to Coarse

Composition: ◯ Mica ◯ Quartz ◯ Feldspar ◯ Amphibole ◯ Garnet ◯ Pyroxene ◯ Calcite ◯ Dolomite ◯ Various

Type of Metamorphism: ◯ Regional ◯ Contact

Rock Name: ◯ Slate ◯ Phyllite ◯ Schist ◯ Gneiss ◯ Hornfels ◯ Quartzite ◯ Marble ◯ Metaconglomerate

Date: _____ GPS Location: _____

Location: ◯ Public Land ◯ Private Land ◯ Pay-to-Dig Site ◯ Quarry
◯ Roadcut ◯ Outcrop ◯ Riverbed ◯ Creek Bed ◯ Beach
◯ Mine Tailing ◯ Fresh Overturned Soil ◯ Other_____

Weather: ◯ Sunny & Clear ◯ Cloudy/Overcast ◯ Windy ◯ Rainy / Drizzle
◯ Snow ◯ Stormy ◯ Fog ◯ Drought ◯ Other_____

Rock Type: ◯ Igneous ◯ Sedimentary ◯ Metamorphic

Equipment Checklist:
(Rockhounding)
◯ Eye Protection ◯ Heavy-Duty Gloves ◯ Boots / Waterproof
◯ First-Aid Kit ◯ Hard Hat ◯ Rock Hammer / Pick ◯ Sieve
◯ Colander ◯ Small Picks ◯ Trowel ◯ Small Knife ◯ Chisel
◯ Small Broom ◯ Crack Hammer ◯ Pry Bar ◯ Sledgehammer
◯ Mason's Hammer ◯ Shovel ◯ Backpack ◯ Bucket ◯ Map
◯ Wrapping Material ◯ Small Tubes ◯ Boxes / Containers
◯ Loupe ◯ Magnifying Glass ◯ Magnet ◯ Compass / GPS

Notes: _____

Color: ◯ Light ◯ Dark Specific Colors: _____

Luster: ◯ Metallic ◯ Gold ◯ Brass   ◯ Non-Metallic ◯ Adamantine ◯ Vitreous
◯ Bronze ◯ Iron   ◯ Resinous ◯ Pearly ◯ Dull
◯ Steel ◯ Lead   ◯ Greasy ◯ Earthy ◯ Silky
◯ Silver ◯ Alum.

Cleavage: ◯ 1 Direction ◯ 2 Directions at 90° ◯ 2 Directions not at 90°
◯ 3 Directions at 90° (cubic) ◯ 3 Directions not at 90° (rhombohedral)
◯ 4 Directions (octahedral) ◯ 6 Directions (dodecahedral)

Fracture: ◯ Conchoidal (smooth, shell-like, or glass-like breaks) ◯ Uneven (irregular, but not conchoidal) ◯ Hackly (jagged, as of a metal)
◯ Splintery (occurs in aggregates of many slender, brittle crystals) ◯ Fibrous (occurs in aggregates of many slender, threadlike crystals)

Crystal Habit: ◯ Prismatic ◯ Acicular ◯ Striated ◯ Botryoidal ◯ Dendritic
◯ Nodular ◯ Banded ◯ Other_____

Hardness: (Mohs Scale)
◯ 1 Talc ◯ 2 Gypsum ◯ 2.5 Fingernail ◯ 3 Calcite ◯ 4 Fluorite
◯ 5 Apatite ◯ 5.5 Glass ◯ 6 Feldspar ◯ 6.5 Steel File
◯ 7 Quartz ◯ 8 Topaz ◯ 9 Corundrum ◯ 10 Diamond

Specific Gravity:
◯ Average (like quartz = 2.6 - 2.8) $\frac{\text{mass of mineral}}{\text{mass of same volume of water}} = \frac{\text{weight of mineral in air}}{\text{weight of equal volume of water}}$
◯ Heavy (like galena = 7.5)
◯ Light (lighter than quartz = <2.6)

Tenacity: ◯ Brittle ◯ Ductile ◯ Elastic ◯ Flexible ◯ Friable
◯ Malleable ◯ Sectile

Diaphaneity: ◯ Transparent ◯ Translucent ◯ Opaque

Notes:_____

_____
_____
_____
_____
_____
_____
_____
_____
_____

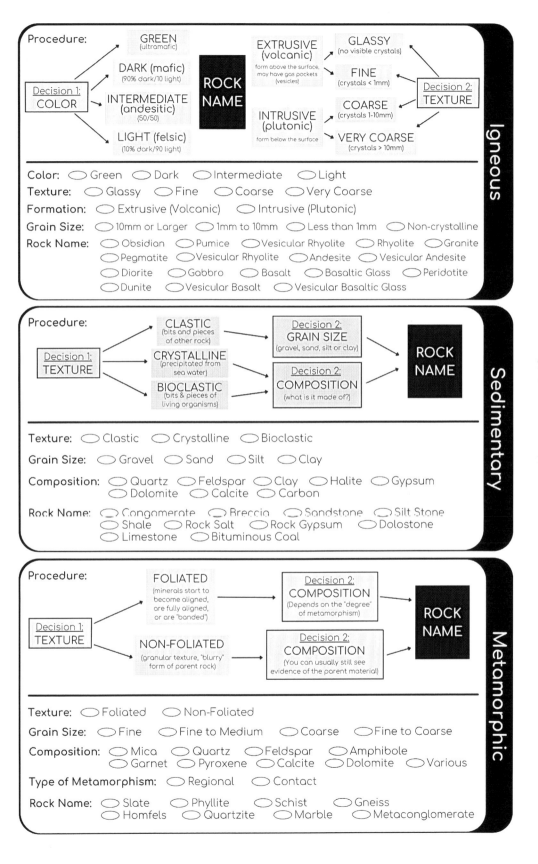

Igneous

Procedure:

Decision 1: COLOR
- GREEN (ultramafic)
- DARK (mafic) (90% dark/10 light)
- INTERMEDIATE (andesitic) (50/50)
- LIGHT (felsic) (10% dark/90 light)

ROCK NAME

EXTRUSIVE (volcanic) — form above the surface, may have gas pockets (vesicles)
INTRUSIVE (plutonic) — form below the surface

Decision 2: TEXTURE
- GLASSY (no visible crystals)
- FINE (crystals < 1mm)
- COARSE (crystals 1-10mm)
- VERY COARSE (crystals > 10mm)

Color: ◯ Green ◯ Dark ◯ Intermediate ◯ Light

Texture: ◯ Glassy ◯ Fine ◯ Coarse ◯ Very Coarse

Formation: ◯ Extrusive (Volcanic) ◯ Intrusive (Plutonic)

Grain Size: ◯ 10mm or Larger ◯ 1mm to 10mm ◯ Less than 1mm ◯ Non-crystalline

Rock Name: ◯ Obsidian ◯ Pumice ◯ Vesicular Rhyolite ◯ Rhyolite ◯ Granite ◯ Pegmatite ◯ Vesicular Rhyolite ◯ Andesite ◯ Vesicular Andesite ◯ Diorite ◯ Gabbro ◯ Basalt ◯ Basaltic Glass ◯ Peridotite ◯ Dunite ◯ Vesicular Basalt ◯ Vesicular Basaltic Glass

Sedimentary

Procedure:

Decision 1: TEXTURE
- CLASTIC (bits and pieces of other rock)
- CRYSTALLINE (precipitated from sea water)
- BIOCLASTIC (bits & pieces of living organisms)

Decision 2: GRAIN SIZE (gravel, sand, silt or clay)
Decision 2: COMPOSITION (what is it made of?)

ROCK NAME

Texture: ◯ Clastic ◯ Crystalline ◯ Bioclastic

Grain Size: ◯ Gravel ◯ Sand ◯ Silt ◯ Clay

Composition: ◯ Quartz ◯ Feldspar ◯ Clay ◯ Halite ◯ Gypsum ◯ Dolomite ◯ Calcite ◯ Carbon

Rock Name: ◯ Conglomerate ◯ Breccia ◯ Sandstone ◯ Silt Stone ◯ Shale ◯ Rock Salt ◯ Rock Gypsum ◯ Dolostone ◯ Limestone ◯ Bituminous Coal

Metamorphic

Procedure:

Decision 1: TEXTURE
- FOLIATED (minerals start to become aligned, are fully aligned, or are "banded")
- NON-FOLIATED (granular texture, "blurry" form of parent rock)

Decision 2: COMPOSITION (Depends on the "degree" of metamorphism)
Decision 2: COMPOSITION (You can usually still see evidence of the parent material)

ROCK NAME

Texture: ◯ Foliated ◯ Non-Foliated

Grain Size: ◯ Fine ◯ Fine to Medium ◯ Coarse ◯ Fine to Coarse

Composition: ◯ Mica ◯ Quartz ◯ Feldspar ◯ Amphibole ◯ Garnet ◯ Pyroxene ◯ Calcite ◯ Dolomite ◯ Various

Type of Metamorphism: ◯ Regional ◯ Contact

Rock Name: ◯ Slate ◯ Phyllite ◯ Schist ◯ Gneiss ◯ Hornfels ◯ Quartzite ◯ Marble ◯ Metaconglomerate

General

Date: _____ GPS Location: _____

Location: ⭘ Public Land ⭘ Private Land ⭘ Pay-to-Dig Site ⭘ Quarry
⭘ Roadcut ⭘ Outcrop ⭘ Riverbed ⭘ Creek Bed ⭘ Beach
⭘ Mine Tailing ⭘ Fresh Overturned Soil ⭘ Other_____

Weather: ⭘ Sunny & Clear ⭘ Cloudy/Overcast ⭘ Windy ⭘ Rainy / Drizzle
⭘ Snow ⭘ Stormy ⭘ Fog ⭘ Drought ⭘ Other_____

Rock Type: ⭘ Igneous ⭘ Sedimentary ⭘ Metamorphic

Equipment Checklist: (Rockhounding)
⭘ Eye Protection ⭘ Heavy-Duty Gloves ⭘ Boots / Waterproof
⭘ First-Aid Kit ⭘ Hard Hat ⭘ Rock Hammer / Pick ⭘ Sieve
⭘ Colander ⭘ Small Picks ⭘ Trowel ⭘ Small Knife ⭘ Chisel
⭘ Small Broom ⭘ Crack Hammer ⭘ Pry Bar ⭘ Sledgehammer
⭘ Mason's Hammer ⭘ Shovel ⭘ Backpack ⭘ Bucket ⭘ Map
⭘ Wrapping Material ⭘ Small Tubes ⭘ Boxes / Containers
⭘ Loupe ⭘ Magnifying Glass ⭘ Magnet ⭘ Compass / GPS

Notes: _____

Mineral Identification

Color: ⭘ Light ⭘ Dark Specific Colors: _____

Luster: ⭘ Metallic ⭘ Gold ⭘ Brass ⭘ Non-Metallic ⭘ Adamantine ⭘ Vitreous
⭘ Bronze ⭘ Iron ⭘ Resinous ⭘ Pearly ⭘ Dull
⭘ Steel ⭘ Lead ⭘ Greasy ⭘ Earthy ⭘ Silky
⭘ Silver ⭘ Alum.

Cleavage: ⭘ 1 Direction ⭘ 2 Directions at 90° ⭘ 2 Directions not at 90°
⭘ 3 Directions at 90° (cubic) ⭘ 3 Directions not at 90° (rhombohedral)
⭘ 4 Directions (octahedral) ⭘ 6 Directions (dodecahedral)

Fracture: ⭘ Conchoidal (smooth, shell-like, or glass-like breaks) ⭘ Uneven (irregular, but not conchoidal) ⭘ Hackly (jagged, as of a metal)
⭘ Splintery (occurs in aggregates of many slender, brittle crystals) ⭘ Fibrous (occurs in aggregates of many slender, threadlike crystals)

Crystal Habit: ⭘ Prismatic ⭘ Acicular ⭘ Striated ⭘ Botryoidal ⭘ Dendritic
⭘ Nodular ⭘ Banded ⭘ Other_____

Hardness: (Mohs Scale)
⭘ 1 Talc ⭘ 2 Gypsum ⭘ 2.5 Fingernail ⭘ 3 Calcite ⭘ 4 Fluorite
⭘ 5 Apatite ⭘ 5.5 Glass ⭘ 6 Feldspar ⭘ 6.5 Steel File
⭘ 7 Quartz ⭘ 8 Topaz ⭘ 9 Corundrum ⭘ 10 Diamond

Specific Gravity:
⭘ Average (like quartz = 2.6 - 2.8)
⭘ Heavy (like galena = 7.5)
⭘ Light (lighter than quartz = <2.6)

$$\frac{\text{mass of mineral}}{\text{mass of same volume of water}} = \frac{\text{weight of mineral in air}}{\text{weight of equal volume of water}}$$

Tenacity: ⭘ Brittle ⭘ Ductile ⭘ Elastic ⭘ Flexible ⭘ Friable
⭘ Malleable ⭘ Sectile

Diaphaneity: ⭘ Transparent ⭘ Translucent ⭘ Opaque

Notes: _____

Notes

_____
_____
_____
_____
_____
_____
_____
_____
_____
_____

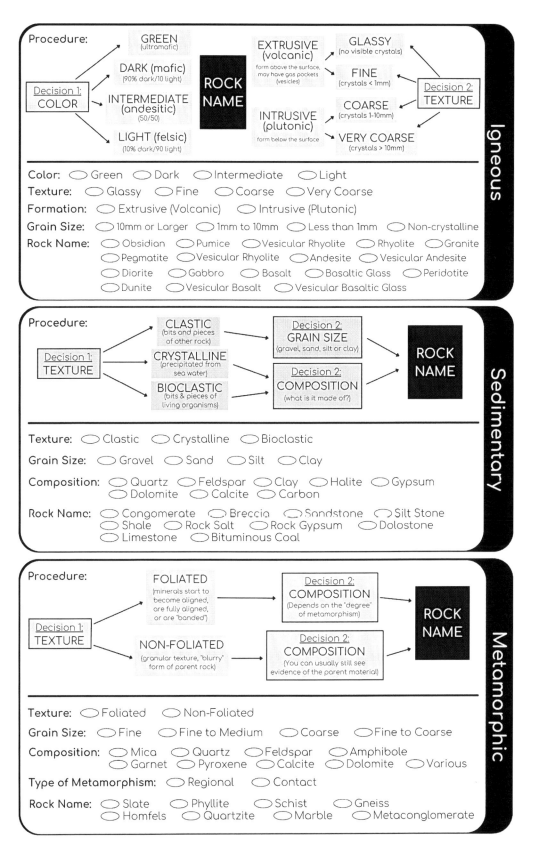

Igneous

Procedure:

Decision 1: COLOR
- GREEN (ultramafic)
- DARK (mafic) (90% dark/10 light)
- INTERMEDIATE (andesitic) (50/50)
- LIGHT (felsic) (10% dark/90 light)

ROCK NAME

EXTRUSIVE (volcanic) — form above the surface, may have gas pockets (vesicles)
- GLASSY (no visible crystals)
- FINE (crystals < 1mm)

INTRUSIVE (plutonic) — form below the surface
- COARSE (crystals 1-10mm)
- VERY COARSE (crystals > 10mm)

Decision 2: TEXTURE

Color: ◯ Green ◯ Dark ◯ Intermediate ◯ Light

Texture: ◯ Glassy ◯ Fine ◯ Coarse ◯ Very Coarse

Formation: ◯ Extrusive (Volcanic) ◯ Intrusive (Plutonic)

Grain Size: ◯ 10mm or Larger ◯ 1mm to 10mm ◯ Less than 1mm ◯ Non-crystalline

Rock Name: ◯ Obsidian ◯ Pumice ◯ Vesicular Rhyolite ◯ Rhyolite ◯ Granite
◯ Pegmatite ◯ Vesicular Rhyolite ◯ Andesite ◯ Vesicular Andesite
◯ Diorite ◯ Gabbro ◯ Basalt ◯ Basaltic Glass ◯ Peridotite
◯ Dunite ◯ Vesicular Basalt ◯ Vesicular Basaltic Glass

Sedimentary

Procedure:

Decision 1: TEXTURE
- CLASTIC (bits and pieces of other rock)
- CRYSTALLINE (precipitated from sea water)
- BIOCLASTIC (bits & pieces of living organisms)

Decision 2: GRAIN SIZE (gravel, sand, silt or clay)

Decision 2: COMPOSITION (what is it made of?)

ROCK NAME

Texture: ◯ Clastic ◯ Crystalline ◯ Bioclastic

Grain Size: ◯ Gravel ◯ Sand ◯ Silt ◯ Clay

Composition: ◯ Quartz ◯ Feldspar ◯ Clay ◯ Halite ◯ Gypsum
◯ Dolomite ◯ Calcite ◯ Carbon

Rock Name: ◯ Congomerate ◯ Breccia ◯ Sandstone ◯ Silt Stone
◯ Shale ◯ Rock Salt ◯ Rock Gypsum ◯ Dolostone
◯ Limestone ◯ Bituminous Coal

Metamorphic

Procedure:

Decision 1: TEXTURE
- FOLIATED (minerals start to become aligned, are fully aligned, or are "banded")
- NON-FOLIATED (granular texture, "blurry" form of parent rock)

Decision 2: COMPOSITION (Depends on the "degree" of metamorphism)

Decision 2: COMPOSITION (You can usually still see evidence of the parent material)

ROCK NAME

Texture: ◯ Foliated ◯ Non-Foliated

Grain Size: ◯ Fine ◯ Fine to Medium ◯ Coarse ◯ Fine to Coarse

Composition: ◯ Mica ◯ Quartz ◯ Feldspar ◯ Amphibole
◯ Garnet ◯ Pyroxene ◯ Calcite ◯ Dolomite ◯ Various

Type of Metamorphism: ◯ Regional ◯ Contact

Rock Name: ◯ Slate ◯ Phyllite ◯ Schist ◯ Gneiss
◯ Homfels ◯ Quartzite ◯ Marble ◯ Metaconglomerate

General

Date: _____   GPS Location: _____

Location: ○ Public Land   ○ Private Land   ○ Pay-to-Dig Site   ○ Quarry
○ Roadcut   ○ Outcrop   ○ Riverbed   ○ Creek Bed   ○ Beach
○ Mine Tailing   ○ Fresh Overturned Soil   ○ Other_____

Weather: ○ Sunny & Clear   ○ Cloudy/Overcast   ○ Windy   ○ Rainy / Drizzle
○ Snow   ○ Stormy   ○ Fog   ○ Drought   ○ Other_____

Rock Type: ○ Igneous   ○ Sedimentary   ○ Metamorphic

Equipment   ○ Eye Protection   ○ Heavy-Duty Gloves   ○ Boots / Waterproof
Checklist: ○ First-Aid Kit   ○ Hard Hat   ○ Rock Hammer / Pick   ○ Sieve
(Rockhounding)   ○ Colander   ○ Small Picks   ○ Trowel   ○ Small Knife   ○ Chisel
○ Small Broom   ○ Crack Hammer   ○ Pry Bar   ○ Sledgehammer
○ Mason's Hammer   ○ Shovel   ○ Backpack   ○ Bucket   ○ Map
○ Wrapping Material   ○ Small Tubes   ○ Boxes / Containers
○ Loupe   ○ Magnifying Glass   ○ Magnet   ○ Compass / GPS

Notes: _____

Mineral Identification

Color: ○ Light   ○ Dark   Specific Colors: _____

Luster: ○ Metallic   ○ Gold   ○ Brass   ○ Non-Metallic ○ Adamantine ○ Vitreous
○ Bronze ○ Iron   ○ Resinous ○ Pearly ○ Dull
○ Steel ○ Lead   ○ Greasy ○ Earthy ○ Silky
○ Silver ○ Alum.

Cleavage: ○ 1 Direction   ○ 2 Directions at 90°   ○ 2 Directions not at 90°
○ 3 Directions at 90° (cubic)   ○ 3 Directions not at 90° (rhombohedral)
○ 4 Directions (octahedral)   ○ 6 Directions (dodecahedral)

Fracture: ○ Conchoidal (smooth, shell-like, or glass-like breaks)   ○ Uneven (irregular, but not conchoidal)   ○ Hackly (jagged, as of a metal)
○ Splintery (occurs in aggregates of many slender, brittle crystals)   ○ Fibrous (occurs in aggregates of many slender, threadlike crystals)

Crystal   ○ Prismatic   ○ Acicular   ○ Striated   ○ Botryoidal   ○ Dendritic
Habit: ○ Nodular   ○ Banded   ○ Other_____

Hardness: ○ 1 Talc   ○ 2 Gypsum   ○ 2.5 Fingernail   ○ 3 Calcite   ○ 4 Fluorite
(Mohs Scale)   ○ 5 Apatite   ○ 5.5 Glass   ○ 6 Feldspar   ○ 6.5 Steel File
○ 7 Quartz   ○ 8 Topaz   ○ 9 Corundrum   ○ 10 Diamond

Specific   ○ Average (like quartz = 2.6 - 2.8)   mass of mineral _____ = weight of mineral in air
Gravity: ○ Heavy (like galena = 7.5)   mass of same volume of water   weight of equal volume of water
○ Light (lighter than quartz = <2.6)

Tenacity: ○ Brittle   ○ Ductile   ○ Elastic   ○ Flexible   ○ Friable
○ Malleable   ○ Sectile

Diaphaneity: ○ Transparent   ○ Translucent   ○ Opaque

Notes:_____

Notes

_____
_____
_____
_____
_____
_____
_____
_____
_____

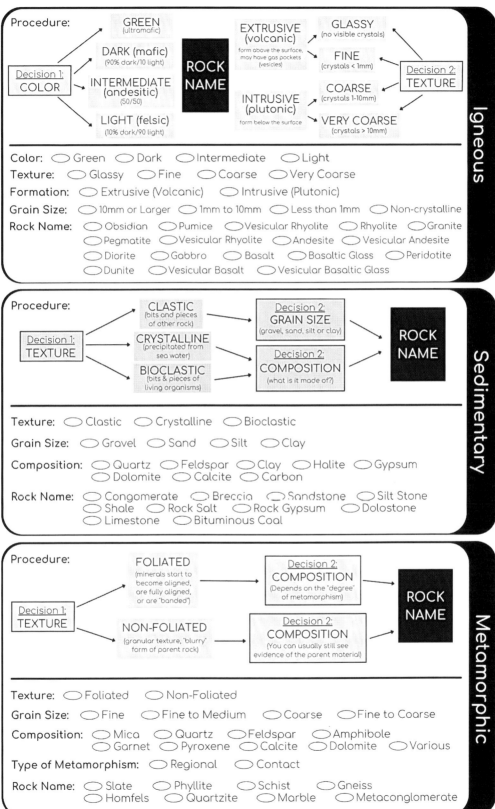

Igneous

Procedure:

Decision 1: COLOR
- GREEN (ultramafic)
- DARK (mafic) (90% dark/10 light)
- INTERMEDIATE (andesitic) (50/50)
- LIGHT (felsic) (10% dark/90 light)

ROCK NAME

- EXTRUSIVE (volcanic) — form above the surface, may have gas pockets (vesicles)
- INTRUSIVE (plutonic) — form below the surface

Decision 2: TEXTURE
- GLASSY (no visible crystals)
- FINE (crystals < 1mm)
- COARSE (crystals 1-10mm)
- VERY COARSE (crystals > 10mm)

Color: ◯ Green ◯ Dark ◯ Intermediate ◯ Light

Texture: ◯ Glassy ◯ Fine ◯ Coarse ◯ Very Coarse

Formation: ◯ Extrusive (Volcanic) ◯ Intrusive (Plutonic)

Grain Size: ◯ 10mm or Larger ◯ 1mm to 10mm ◯ Less than 1mm ◯ Non-crystalline

Rock Name: ◯ Obsidian ◯ Pumice ◯ Vesicular Rhyolite ◯ Rhyolite ◯ Granite ◯ Pegmatite ◯ Vesicular Rhyolite ◯ Andesite ◯ Vesicular Andesite ◯ Diorite ◯ Gabbro ◯ Basalt ◯ Basaltic Glass ◯ Peridotite ◯ Dunite ◯ Vesicular Basalt ◯ Vesicular Basaltic Glass

Sedimentary

Procedure:

Decision 1: TEXTURE
- CLASTIC (bits and pieces of other rock)
- CRYSTALLINE (precipitated from sea water)
- BIOCLASTIC (bits & pieces of living organisms)

Decision 2: GRAIN SIZE (gravel, sand, silt or clay)

Decision 2: COMPOSITION (what is it made of?)

ROCK NAME

Texture: ◯ Clastic ◯ Crystalline ◯ Bioclastic

Grain Size: ◯ Gravel ◯ Sand ◯ Silt ◯ Clay

Composition: ◯ Quartz ◯ Feldspar ◯ Clay ◯ Halite ◯ Gypsum ◯ Dolomite ◯ Calcite ◯ Carbon

Rock Name: ◯ Conglomerate ◯ Breccia ◯ Sandstone ◯ Silt Stone ◯ Shale ◯ Rock Salt ◯ Rock Gypsum ◯ Dolostone ◯ Limestone ◯ Bituminous Coal

Metamorphic

Procedure:

Decision 1: TEXTURE
- FOLIATED (minerals start to become aligned, are fully aligned, or are "banded")
- NON-FOLIATED (granular texture, "blurry" form of parent rock)

Decision 2: COMPOSITION (Depends on the "degree" of metamorphism)

Decision 2: COMPOSITION (You can usually still see evidence of the parent material)

ROCK NAME

Texture: ◯ Foliated ◯ Non-Foliated

Grain Size: ◯ Fine ◯ Fine to Medium ◯ Coarse ◯ Fine to Coarse

Composition: ◯ Mica ◯ Quartz ◯ Feldspar ◯ Amphibole ◯ Garnet ◯ Pyroxene ◯ Calcite ◯ Dolomite ◯ Various

Type of Metamorphism: ◯ Regional ◯ Contact

Rock Name: ◯ Slate ◯ Phyllite ◯ Schist ◯ Gneiss ◯ Hornfels ◯ Quartzite ◯ Marble ◯ Metaconglomerate

General

Date: _____ GPS Location: _____

Location: ○ Public Land ○ Private Land ○ Pay-to-Dig Site ○ Quarry
○ Roadcut ○ Outcrop ○ Riverbed ○ Creek Bed ○ Beach
○ Mine Tailing ○ Fresh Overturned Soil ○ Other_____

Weather: ○ Sunny & Clear ○ Cloudy/Overcast ○ Windy ○ Rainy / Drizzle
○ Snow ○ Stormy ○ Fog ○ Drought ○ Other_____

Rock Type: ○ Igneous ○ Sedimentary ○ Metamorphic

Equipment Checklist:
(Rockhounding)
○ Eye Protection ○ Heavy-Duty Gloves ○ Boots / Waterproof
○ First-Aid Kit ○ Hard Hat ○ Rock Hammer / Pick ○ Sieve
○ Colander ○ Small Picks ○ Trowel ○ Small Knife ○ Chisel
○ Small Broom ○ Crack Hammer ○ Pry Bar ○ Sledgehammer
○ Mason's Hammer ○ Shovel ○ Backpack ○ Bucket ○ Map
○ Wrapping Material ○ Small Tubes ○ Boxes / Containers
○ Loupe ○ Magnifying Glass ○ Magnet ○ Compass / GPS

Notes: _____

Mineral Identification

Color: ○ Light ○ Dark Specific Colors: _____

Luster: ○ Metallic ○ Gold ○ Brass ○ Non-Metallic ○ Adamantine ○ Vitreous
  ○ Bronze ○ Iron   ○ Resinous ○ Pearly ○ Dull
  ○ Steel ○ Lead   ○ Greasy ○ Earthy ○ Silky
  ○ Silver ○ Alum.

Cleavage: ○ 1 Direction ○ 2 Directions at 90° ○ 2 Directions not at 90°
○ 3 Directions at 90° (cubic) ○ 3 Directions not at 90° (rhombohedral)
○ 4 Directions (octahedral) ○ 6 Directions (dodecahedral)

Fracture: ○ Conchoidal (smooth, shell-like, or glass-like breaks) ○ Uneven (irregular, but not conchoidal) ○ Hackly (jagged, as of a metal)
○ Splintery (occurs in aggregates of many slender, brittle crystals) ○ Fibrous (occurs in aggregates of many slender, threadlike crystals)

Crystal Habit: ○ Prismatic ○ Acicular ○ Striated ○ Botryoidal ○ Dendritic
○ Nodular ○ Banded ○ Other_____

Hardness: (Mohs Scale)
○ 1 Talc ○ 2 Gypsum ○ 2.5 Fingernail ○ 3 Calcite ○ 4 Fluorite
○ 5 Apatite ○ 5.5 Glass ○ 6 Feldspar ○ 6.5 Steel File
○ 7 Quartz ○ 8 Topaz ○ 9 Corundrum ○ 10 Diamond

Specific Gravity:
○ Average (like quartz = 2.6 - 2.8)
○ Heavy (like galena = 7.5)
○ Light (lighter than quartz = <2.6)

$$\frac{\text{mass of mineral}}{\text{mass of same volume of water}} = \frac{\text{weight of mineral in air}}{\text{weight of equal volume of water}}$$

Tenacity: ○ Brittle ○ Ductile ○ Elastic ○ Flexible ○ Friable
○ Malleable ○ Sectile

Diaphaneity: ○ Transparent ○ Translucent ○ Opaque

Notes: _____

Notes

_____
_____
_____
_____
_____
_____
_____
_____
_____
_____

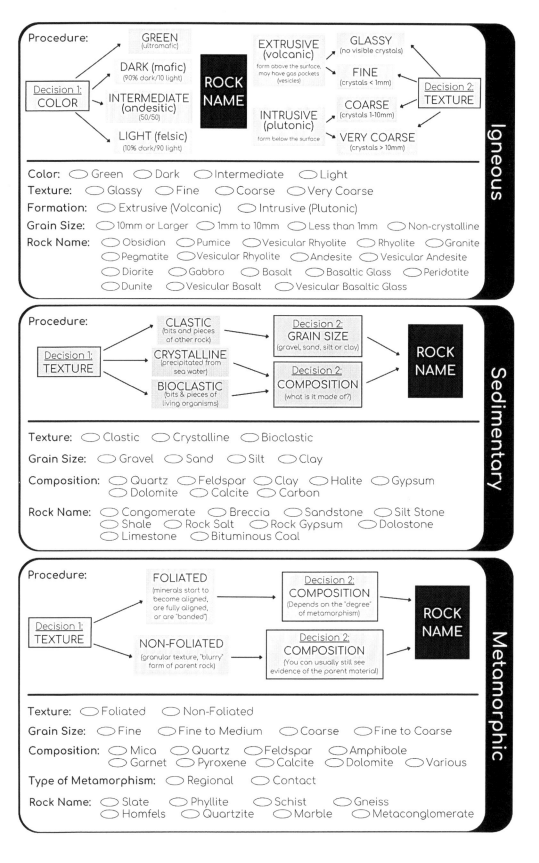

Igneous

Procedure:

Decision 1: COLOR →
- GREEN (ultramafic)
- DARK (mafic) (90% dark/10 light)
- INTERMEDIATE (andesitic) (50/50)
- LIGHT (felsic) (10% dark/90 light)

ROCK NAME

EXTRUSIVE (volcanic) — form above the surface, may have gas pockets (vesicles)
INTRUSIVE (plutonic) — form below the surface

- GLASSY (no visible crystals)
- FINE (crystals < 1mm)
- COARSE (crystals 1-10mm)
- VERY COARSE (crystals > 10mm)

Decision 2: TEXTURE

Color: ◯ Green ◯ Dark ◯ Intermediate ◯ Light

Texture: ◯ Glassy ◯ Fine ◯ Coarse ◯ Very Coarse

Formation: ◯ Extrusive (Volcanic) ◯ Intrusive (Plutonic)

Grain Size: ◯ 10mm or Larger ◯ 1mm to 10mm ◯ Less than 1mm ◯ Non-crystalline

Rock Name: ◯ Obsidian ◯ Pumice ◯ Vesicular Rhyolite ◯ Rhyolite ◯ Granite
◯ Pegmatite ◯ Vesicular Rhyolite ◯ Andesite ◯ Vesicular Andesite
◯ Diorite ◯ Gabbro ◯ Basalt ◯ Basaltic Glass ◯ Peridotite
◯ Dunite ◯ Vesicular Basalt ◯ Vesicular Basaltic Glass

Sedimentary

Procedure:

Decision 1: TEXTURE →
- CLASTIC (bits and pieces of other rock)
- CRYSTALLINE (precipitated from sea water)
- BIOCLASTIC (bits & pieces of living organisms)

Decision 2: GRAIN SIZE (gravel, sand, silt or clay)
Decision 2: COMPOSITION (what is it made of?)

ROCK NAME

Texture: ◯ Clastic ◯ Crystalline ◯ Bioclastic

Grain Size: ◯ Gravel ◯ Sand ◯ Silt ◯ Clay

Composition: ◯ Quartz ◯ Feldspar ◯ Clay ◯ Halite ◯ Gypsum
◯ Dolomite ◯ Calcite ◯ Carbon

Rock Name: ◯ Congomerate ◯ Breccia ◯ Sandstone ◯ Silt Stone
◯ Shale ◯ Rock Salt ◯ Rock Gypsum ◯ Dolostone
◯ Limestone ◯ Bituminous Coal

Metamorphic

Procedure:

Decision 1: TEXTURE →
- FOLIATED (minerals start to become aligned, are fully aligned, or are "banded")
- NON-FOLIATED (granular texture, "blurry" form of parent rock)

Decision 2: COMPOSITION (Depends on the "degree" of metamorphism)
Decision 2: COMPOSITION (You can usually still see evidence of the parent material)

ROCK NAME

Texture: ◯ Foliated ◯ Non-Foliated

Grain Size: ◯ Fine ◯ Fine to Medium ◯ Coarse ◯ Fine to Coarse

Composition: ◯ Mica ◯ Quartz ◯ Feldspar ◯ Amphibole
◯ Garnet ◯ Pyroxene ◯ Calcite ◯ Dolomite ◯ Various

Type of Metamorphism: ◯ Regional ◯ Contact

Rock Name: ◯ Slate ◯ Phyllite ◯ Schist ◯ Gneiss
◯ Homfels ◯ Quartzite ◯ Marble ◯ Metaconglomerate

Made in the USA
Las Vegas, NV
25 September 2023

78112525R00066